Invitation and Belonging in a Christian Ashram

Also Available from Bloomsbury:

Beyond Religion in India and Pakistan: Gender and Caste, Borders and Boundaries
Virinder S. Kalra and Navtej K. Purewal

*Christianity and Belonging in Shimla, North India:
Sacred Entanglements of a Himalayan Landscape*
Jonathan Miles-Watson

Material Devotion in a South Indian Poetic World
Leah Elizabeth Comeau

Invitation and Belonging in a Christian Ashram

Building Interreligious Community in Northern India

Nadya Pohran

BLOOMSBURY ACADEMIC
LONDON • NEW YORK • OXFORD • NEW DELHI • SYDNEY

BLOOMSBURY ACADEMIC
Bloomsbury Publishing Plc
50 Bedford Square, London, WC1B 3DP, UK
1385 Broadway, New York, NY 10018, USA
29 Earlsfort Terrace, Dublin 2, Ireland

BLOOMSBURY, BLOOMSBURY ACADEMIC and the Diana logo are trademarks of Bloomsbury Publishing Plc

First published in Great Britain 2022
This paperback edition published 2024

Copyright © Nadya Pohran, 2022, 2024

Nadya Pohran has asserted her right under the Copyright, Designs and Patents Act, 1988, to be identified as Author of this work.

For legal purposes the Acknowledgements on pp. vi–viii constitute an extension of this copyright page.

Cover design: Tjasa Krivec
Cover image © Nadya Pohran

All rights reserved. No part of this publication may be reproduced or transmitted in any form or by any means, electronic or mechanical, including photocopying, recording, or any information storage or retrieval system, without prior permission in writing from the publishers.

Bloomsbury Publishing Plc does not have any control over, or responsibility for, any third-party websites referred to or in this book. All internet addresses given in this book were correct at the time of going to press. The author and publisher regret any inconvenience caused if addresses have changed or sites have ceased to exist, but can accept no responsibility for any such changes.

A catalogue record for this book is available from the British Library.

A catalog record for this book is available from the Library of Congress.

ISBN: HB: 978-1-3502-3816-9
PB: 978-1-3502-3821-3
ePDF: 978-1-3502-3818-3
eBook: 978-1-3502-3819-0

Typeset by Newgen KnowledgeWorks Pvt. Ltd., Chennai, India

To find out more about our authors and books visit www.bloomsbury.com and sign up for our newsletters.

Contents

Acknowledgements	vi
A note on translation and transliteration	ix
A note on pseudonyms and titles	x
Introduction	1
1 An introduction to belief-inclusive research	19
2 Foreignness or Indianness? Indigenizations and representations of Christianity in India	37
3 The origins of Sat Tal Christian Ashram and E. Stanley Jones's 'Ashram Ideals'	65
4 The School of Evangelism and its challenge to the ideal of 'truly Christian and truly Indian'	97
5 The negotiations of belonging: Relational dynamics of World Amrita and Sat Tal Christian Ashram	129
Conclusion	163
Appendix 1: Key Hindi terms and their English translations	171
Appendix 2: Social mapping	172
Notes	175
Bibliography	193
Index	207

Acknowledgements

This book draws upon my research at the University of Cambridge, where I was fortunate to have received significant financial support from the Social Sciences and Humanities Research Council (SSHRC) and the Cambridge International Trust. Throughout the course of my doctoral degree, additional financial grants were also provided by the Teape Trust, the Spalding Trust, Hughes Hall College, the Faculty of Divinity, and the Wenner-Gren Anthropological Foundation. Their financial support allowed me to spend four years in Cambridge pursuing in-depth academic contemplation and inquiry alongside some of the most inspirational and erudite individuals I have ever come across, and also enabled me to take multiple trips to India so to live alongside some of the most thought-provoking, hospitable and compassionate people.

And, for the roughly one-year period of transforming my PhD research into a book, I offer my sincere gratitude to my family and friends who helped me live a remarkably frugal life during the writing-up process, and who also encouraged me by impressing upon me that the entire ordeal was worthwhile. I resided in three different countries – including eighteen homes, two ashrams, a yoga school and one tent – during the period in which this book took shape, and thus experienced first-hand an ongoing sense of 'invitation' – if not also 'belonging'. Thanks to all who welcomed me!

An earlier version of Chapter 1 was accepted for publication by *Current Anthropology* on 8 August 2020. An earlier, condensed version of Chapter 2 was published by Nidan in 2019 and has been reprinted with permission from Editor-in-Chief Professor Pratap Kumar. An earlier version of Chapter 5 was published in the edited volume *Hindu-Christian Dual Belonging* edited by Daniel Soars and Nadya Pohran and published by Routledge Press – the volume was still in print while this present manuscript was being completed, and it is published with permission from Routledge Press.

I am deeply grateful for the influential guidance and the invaluable feedback that I have received from Dr Ankur Barua. Even after we parted ways as official supervisor and student, Dr Barua has continued to patiently offer me academic, philosophical and spiritual insights. While I have sometimes felt strained from my attempts to produce coherent and clever work, Ankur's pedagogical stance has always been more of a warm *invitation* – to read this, to reflect on that, to go on a long walk while rethinking such and such, and so on. Among many other teaching points, he has invited me to embrace pluralities; to specify particularities; to deconstruct binaries; and to welcome in paradoxes. Spurred on by his thirst for – and delight in – knowledge, I have, in turn, learned at a deeper depth and wider breadth than I could ever have anticipated. Thank you for your wise *upaya*.

I also give my sincere gratitude to the colleagues and anonymous reviewers of various chapters of this book; they provided insightful and valuable feedback which undoubtedly improved the work itself, and they also offered some very welcome encouragement when I began to inevitably wonder about the reach of the content.

Several friends in India (including those made at STA during the research process itself) helped me feel at home while doing fieldwork in a foreign country and, at times, in a foreign tongue. There are too many to thank by name, but I would specifically like to thank both Esther Ghosh and Indira Auntie for on-the-fly translation during my earliest months at STA, as well as Rukhsar Shaikh for her ongoing assistance in transcription and translation. These three women helped me gain a far more nuanced understanding of my Hindi exchanges than I would have been able to make sense of on my own.

Additionally, there are a few friends whom I would like to personally thank for our (seemingly) endless conversations about life, religion and even some of the specific arguments contained in this book: thanks to Barney Aspray, Kaitlin Carlson, Emily Kempson, Nika Kuchuk, Nick Lackenby, Julian Perlmutter and Daniel Soars for your insights, inspirations and steadfast support.

My parents and siblings – as well as my friends who feel just as close as family – have been wonderfully supportive throughout my life, and their love throughout this particular period of my life has been just as constant, unrelenting and life-giving. But my Babcia has always been a particularly noteworthy role model of what it can look like to be loving and welcoming in the midst of hardship, difficulties and differences – and so it seems only fitting that a work devoted to exploring the motivations (and challenges!) of belonging would gesture specifically back to her. A gracious, graceful and soft-spoken yet stubborn matriarch, my Babcia has cheered me on and cheered me up when I have felt physically or existentially tired; she has also encouraged me to strive to do my best, to prioritize my own mental and physical well-being, to be open to difference, and to act with kindness and generosity towards others. I am forever grateful to her for her love, and I would have loved to have been able to celebrate the publication of this book with her. *Istniejemy na tyle, na ile kochamy.*

Finally, I cannot hold back from offering my whole-hearted appreciation to the many people in India who have helped me in my fieldwork processes, and more specifically to the individuals at Sat Tal Christian ashram and the individuals of World Amrita who welcomed me into their lives, conversations and homes – thank you for letting me hear, see and partake in (some of) your stories. In the early days of STA, E. Stanley Jones initiated a rather lovely tradition at the Winter Ashram programme: at the beginning of the week, everyone would share their expectations and desires with the group; at the end, everyone would share some personal highlights of the previous week. This latter time of sharing is aptly called 'Over-Flowing Heart'. My research journey has been entirely different from what I expected, but my own heart is bursting with gratitude for the many ways I was invited in.

A note on translation and transliteration

Whenever the original wording seemed to contain nuances that could not be adequately expressed in translation, I have provided the original Hindi alongside my translation – either in-text for short phrases or specific words, or in the footnotes for longer sections. In order to allow for fluid reading for an English-language audience, I have not used the Devanagari script; further, when transliterating Hindi words into Roman script, I have avoided diacritical marks entirely and rendered all words to a purposely simple phonetic spelling. In such cases, the long vowel (e.g. usually rendered '*ā*' in the case of आ) is here represented by 'aa', and so forth. There is one exception to this: I use a macron in Chapter 2 (Section 2.2.2) in my discussion of the words *maari* and *maāri*, simply to highlight the fact that (at least to an ear accustomed to the nuances of Indian-language pronunciations) they are indeed two distinct words.

I have provided a list of key Hindi terms along with their translations in Appendix 1.

A note on pseudonyms and titles

I have used pseudonyms for every individual mentioned in this book other than E. Stanley Jones and his family members. While this practice may confuse readers who wish to understand (or, even more, are already familiar with) the social history of Sat Tal ashram, I have done so out of a desire to protect the identities of those involved.

Apart from the pseudonyms themselves, I refer to individuals by the titles that I addressed them with while living at STA. Generally, my choice to use an honorific ('Auntie', 'Acharya', 'Mr' etc.) was in keeping with what I generally do in other social situations in India: when an individual is noticeably older than me, I refer to them as 'Uncle' or 'Auntie' unless they explicitly tell me otherwise. Thus, I refer to 'Auntie Eleanor', 'Uncle William', 'Acharya G.', 'Mr D.' and so forth. But Kabir and Dorothy (both of whom vehemently rejected my use of 'Uncle'/'Mr' or 'Auntie'/'Ms') are referred to by their first names even though they are older than me. Individuals who were closer to my age (or younger than me) such as Suhasini, Vihaan and others, are referred to on a first-name basis.

I have provided a social map of all of the individuals and their affiliations in Appendix 2.

Introduction

When my friends and family members hear that I conduct research about concepts such as *invitation, interreligious relations* and *belonging*, they often respond to my cursory summary of my research questions with their own queries. 'So what's the solution?', they ask – sometimes warily, sometimes eagerly. 'What works and what doesn't?' and 'Have you found an answer for what people should do in order to get along with one another?' While, admittedly, the task-oriented and solution-driven side of me delights in such inquiries, this book does not seek to provide straightforward solutions and well-crafted answers. What I offer, instead, is a detailed, nuanced and contextualized exploration of the ways that these philosophical questions regarding interpersonal relations, communitarian dynamics and existential belonging have played out in several on-the-ground scenarios within my ethnographic fieldsite – across various sociopolitical contexts – since it was established in 1930. In the midst of exploring the ways that *invitation and belonging* play out on the ground, I offer up-close examinations of some of the tensions, ambiguities, struggles, negotiations and resolutions of my fieldsite – microprocesses which are woven together and, acting like a thread, which subsequently stitch together our broader story of *invitation and belonging*. Like any storyteller worth their salt, I often unravel this thread in my work – not with the aim to rip apart the seams of the story but to instead highlight the ways that the processes of *invitation and belonging* are, in turn, composed of multiple microprocesses which merit our attention and understanding. In describing the multiple layers, expressions and processes of *invitation and belonging*, I offer new and nuanced understandings of the concepts of otherness, spiritual and interpersonal belonging, and belief/doubt.

Put alternately, in this book I explore the various facets and phases of both *inviting* others and *belonging* alongside others in spiritual contexts. I have found that neither process is neat, tidy, straightforward or simple. However, rather than this discovery resulting in us throwing up our proverbial hands in exhaustion, I believe that ethnographically exploring the messiness, nuances and complexities of invitation and belonging can shed light on the reality that these human processes should not be left unattended, assuming that they will come into fruition of their own accord. Indeed, both *invitation* and *belonging* merit our time, energy and intention: like gardeners who want to create a space for growth and beauty, we can tend and attend to ourselves, and the communities we are a part of, in efforts to cultivate more habitable and flourishing environments. And it might be worth explicitly noting that gardens, if you permit me to continue the metaphor, are not identical across time and space. Some are wild while others are scrupulously clean; some are variegated while others are monochrome; some plants are sun-drenched while others prosper in shade; and so forth. These vast differences of the possible specifics – in literal gardens as well as in the communities we are born into, transplant ourselves into, or otherwise find ourselves growing alongside and within – do not eradicate the fact that they become the best possible versions of themselves when they are cultivated with intention. All this to say, I am not advocating for a singular spiritual community archetype in which belonging can occur. Nonetheless, if we want to *invite* or *belong* in a way that allows for flourishing, we ought to foster an environment where it is possible.

Thus, I explore these processes ethnographically. I first learned of my ethnographic fieldsite, Sat Tal Christian ashram (henceforth STA) via a recommendation from a colleague, when I asked in a group email thread in the Hindu-Christian studies listserv if anyone knew of a place in India where I could explore some of the possible ways that Christianity is being shaped by devotional Hinduism. At that time, I was deeply and personally intrigued by how devotion to Jesus might look outside of the conservative Protestant milieus I had grown accustomed to in Canada. My intrigue had been nourished: in the years leading up to my PhD, I had spent some time in India with Yeshu bhaktas (devotees of Jesus) and then, recalling that my Yeshu bhakta friends had often spoken of the musical elements of their devotion, in the first year of my PhD, I regularly retrieved stacks of books from different libraries in order to read devotional *bhajans* (hymns). I poured over the *bhajans* themselves – first gravitating towards ones written by renowned Indian figures like Mirabai, Tulsidas and Kabir, and then also reading contemporary *bhajans* by individuals like Chris Hale of Aradhana.[1] Captivated, I began attending classical Indian musical classes in Cambridge and even tried my hand at learning to play the sarod. These musical immersions were not only, no doubt, because I felt drawn to the soulful beauty of Indian classical music in its own right but also because I wanted to intentionally cultivate the kind of research participation that Linda Hess described in her study of Ramlila performances. Speaking of the embodied aspect of the performance, Hess told her reader: 'You can't understand what that means by reading this essay. But you can get a hint, and you can appreciate the importance of putting your body into research.'[2] All this to say: when a colleague told me about STA, and when I then came across terms like 'Yeshu bhakti' in STA's internal literature, I began to imaginatively envision how conducting fieldwork at such a place could open expansive doors through which to explore my inquiries about the relational dynamics between devotional Hinduism and Christianity. And, typical to my 'all-in' approach in most matters of my life, I consequently began to make inquiries about how and where I could acquire a sarod (which apparently was best acquired through custom craftsmanship) so that I could 'put my body into' the research process. All too romantically, I imagined myself strumming away on my sarod, playing *ragas* (a melodic framework within Indian musical theory) while sitting cross-legged amongst a group of devoted bhaktas.

As it turned out, however, STA was not the hub for Yeshu bhakti that I had imagined it would be. As I explore in more detail in Chapter 4, there was certainly ample devotion as well as plenty of music at STA, but the kind of dynamic interplay (or what we might simply call 'play', invoking the Hindu concept of *lila*) between Hinduism and Christianity that occurred at STA was of a rather different ilk than what I had envisioned. Once I finally arrived at STA, I began to hear about, witness and participate in a rather different type of interreligious play: one that, in due time, caused me to realize that the relational and religious dynamics that occurred at STA were strikingly resonant with emergent scholarly discussions pertaining to multiple religious belonging.

The scholarly exploration of multiple religious belonging was gaining more traction during the course of my ethnographic fieldwork,[3] but it was already on my radar as a phenomenon due to some early discussions about it that had occurred within the Theology Without Walls group in the 2015 conference of the American Academy of Religion. While I am not aware of any individual at STA, present or past, who would describe STA's mission or vision as having anything to do with 'multiple religious belonging', there seem to me to be a great deal of resonances. STA was established by the American Methodist missionary E. Stanley Jones (1884–1973) in 1930 in northern India. Using motifs of what was later to be termed 'inculturation', Jones envisioned STA as a place that was both 'truly Christian and truly Indian', and he actively sought to impart a

Christ-centred spirituality that would not be bound to Westernized institutional Christianity. As I explore in more detail in Chapter 3, when Jones said 'truly *Indian*' he meant (perhaps uncritically) 'truly *Hindu*' or, more specifically, 'truly *Advaitic*'. And, thus, by striving to create a place where *both* were welcome, he unknowingly began to tread in the waters of multiple (or, at least, dual) belonging. Jones furthermore desired STA to be a place where people from all religious backgrounds (or, as he carefully specified, even from 'no religion') could participate together in a spiritual community which would, he articulated, act as a miniature Kingdom of God. Christian movements in India which have sought to do this type of 'inculturation' have received copious scrutiny from certain spheres of Hinduism – mostly, though not exclusively, from individuals within right-winged Hindu nationalist movements.[4] I explore this scrutiny and criticism in more detail in Chapters 2 and 3, but it is nonetheless worthwhile noting that STA was envisioned as being a place where people from a multitude of religious backgrounds were invited to come together in spiritual community.

Based on a close reading of Jones's published writings, archival work and several months of ethnographic fieldwork in India, I present a social history of STA while engaging with philosophical questions such as: 'What are the motivations and challenges of being part of a community in which people believe and act in ways that are different from you?' 'What does it look like to invite (religious, social, doctrinal) others into one's midst?' and 'How does one navigate the existential challenges and the interpersonal processes of belonging to a community that is notably different from oneself?'

This social history can be understood in several different ways. The first step is to demonstrate the several ways in which STA is a site of *transitional and developmental sociality*: we see that identities such as 'Christian' and 'Indian' are formed, contested and occasionally reworked on the ground through complex, ever-developing processes. Indeed, STA – and all of the individuals past and present who comprise its sociality – is not only the product of Jones's own transitions regarding his views of Christ and Christianity (theological transitions which, as we shall explore, were themselves the result of social interactions that Jones had with other individuals, mostly in India), but STA has itself undergone several distinct transitions over the decades following its establishment – each of these transitions have transformed the social systems and social interactions that occur at STA. As we shall see in Chapter 3, Jones's own understanding of what is signified by 'Christian' underwent multiple shifts throughout his career as a missionary which impacted the ways that he sought to fashion STA as an environment that would be 'truly Christian and truly Indian'. Further, as we shall see in Chapters 4 and 5, STA itself, more broadly, experienced several shifts in the decades after Jones's death in 1973, due to its development of the School of Evangelism (henceforth SoE) and its relational negotiations with a group which I call World Amrita (henceforth WA). Clearly, STA does not work with a static, monolithic understanding of communal and personal identities such as 'Indian' and 'Christian', and throughout this book we shall see some of the various ways that STA's social systems are fluid, processive and changing.

A second lens through which we will explore STA's social history is by focusing on its *embodied sociality*. As we shall see, STA is overflowing with embodied gestures and corporeal practices which are used for communication between its social members. Through considering the diverse embodied interactions that occur at STA – such as the three-fingered 'Jesus is Lord' gesture that individuals use to greet each other, the *shramdaan* (work period), the eating of vegetarian food or physical postures of meditation – all of which we will explore in more detail in subsequent chapters – we see that these somatic practices play crucial roles in establishing and communicating an individual's identity place within STA's social settings. Furthermore, as we shall see in Chapter 3, in the earliest years of STA, certain embodied gestures – including some of those mentioned above – played a key role in forming STA as a sociocultural environment which could effectively invite the Other into its midst. Yet, as time went on and as the social demographics of STA underwent significant changes, some of these embodied dimensions of life at STA were cast aside as spiritually irrelevant or unimportant; as we shall see in Chapter 4, individuals' participation (or lack thereof) in some of these corporeal practices can be explored to better understand the ways that people at STA conceptualize – and actively perform – their identities as Christians and Indians in the present day. Chapter 5 illustrates how some of the decisions surrounding these present-day relational dynamics are shaped by active contestations over the corporeal practices of individuals and groups who visit STA. Voicing their hesitation and concerns about WA's presence, some members of STA ask questions such as the following: 'In what style do they worship?', 'Which meditative postures do they use?' and so on. Many such social interactions, and the decisions surrounding them, are indelibly linked to embodied sociality.

As we consider the *transitional* and *embodied* elements of the sociality of STA, we should also keep in mind that STA, as an active site of social history, should be understood *synergistically*. To be certain, the multitude of mundane interactions which occur at STA – that is, as processes embedded in various sociohistorical and ideological backdrops – is greater than the sum of its parts. We need to understand the parts not just as parts, but as puzzle-piece components of a complex whole. And yet, to understand the whole, we must often narrow in on the parts. For STA, this means we must proverbially excavate the sedimented layers of the complex past and present sociopolitical and historical contexts of STA – the presence of colonial powers and the acts of anticolonial resistance, the self-organization of right-wing Hindu sociopolitical movements, the representations and practices of Christian evangelists, the increasing self-assertion and vocalizations of Dalits and other oppressed milieus, and so forth. As we do this, we can gain a more nuanced and deepened understanding of present-day life at STA.

Taking into account this degree and depth of contextualization, STA becomes something like – to borrow a rich metaphor from Hindu contexts – the mouth of the infant Krishna: though small enough to be viewed at a single glance, it simultaneously contains and encapsulates the entire universe. STA, then, can be understood as a *microcosm* through which we can gain insights about certain *macro* philosophical questions relating to self-and-other dynamics which undergird this work.[5] That is to say, through deeply studying the social microhistory of STA *synergistically* along with all its conceptual intricacies and sociopolitical specificities, we can make use of STA as a particular, nuanced vantage point from which we can consider broader discussions about the contested processes of inviting religious Others into our midst.

0.1 Summary of chapters

In order to make sense of STA as a microcosm, we must first familiarize ourselves with its frames of social reference. Accordingly, Chapters 1 and 2 offer crucial contexts to situate and understand Chapters 3, 4 and 5. Because the qualitative data on which Chapters 3–5 are founded was, of course, filtered through the wondrously and wonderfully subjective processes involved in ethnographic fieldwork, I first outline the methodological and theoretical contexts within which I operated. Most crucially, I argue that the qualitative data which my informants at STA shared with me was granted because of the ways I consciously positioned myself as both an academic researcher and a spiritual seeker while conducting my fieldwork. Thus, Chapter 1 interrogates the ethnographic practice of 'methodological bracketing' and consequently offers Belief-Inclusive Research (henceforth 'BIR') as a potentially fruitful research stance for anthropologists and social scientists who work in and within religious (especially Protestant

Christian) contexts. BIR is, in effect, an intentional decision not only to be self-reflexive, but also to *include* one's religious beliefs (along with one's doubts) throughout the processes of fieldwork. I suggest that my intentional adoption of BIR is linked to the particular types and depths of qualitative data that my informants shared with me. The chapter, which was first published as an article, stands on its own as a contribution to the theory surrounding researcher participation and the dynamic and dialogical meeting-up of researcher and informant. While it may appear non-essential to an ethnographic study focused on Christian ashrams in the north of India, it contextualizes the methodological and theoretical approach which enabled me to access the subsequent data that this book explores. I suspect that individuals unaffected by or disinterested in the methodological and theoretical debates concerning how to position oneself as an anthropologist working within Protestant Christian contexts could skim the chapter and skip directly to Chapter 2.

Chapter 2 sketches some rather different contexts that link more thematically to the topics explored in subsequent chapters: it outlines some sociopolitical histories in Indic contexts during Portuguese and British periods of colonial rule (roughly 1498–1947) so as to situate Jones's vision of 'inculturated Christianity' against the backdrop of 'foreign Christianity'. Due to the ways that some individuals who were associated with European colonial powers consistently sought to remove any traces of Hinduism from Indian Christian communities, and instead strove to impart their respective own Eurocentric practices of Christianity to the Indians whom they encountered, Christianity had gained a reputation within broader Indian public spheres of being a religion exclusively of foreigners. It was against this notion of 'foreignness' that Jones, along with some other Christians – both foreign missionaries and Indian Christians alike – consciously began to enact and encourage forms of Christianity which were not 'foreign' but which rather actively embraced and incorporated Indian cultural idioms. Importantly, Chapter 2 also outlines some movements of inculturation which predate Jones's establishment of STA. Going beyond a historical summary of Hindu-Christian relations in India, this chapter's exploration of select movements of inculturation lays the groundwork for understanding Jones's own approach to inculturation in the 1930s.

With these wider sociohistorical contexts in mind, Chapters 3–5 focus specifically on the fieldsite of STA itself, both chronologically and thematically. Chapter 3 focuses primarily on Jones's original visions and aims for STA to be a place of open dialogue and spiritual exploration for all individuals, while still being both 'truly Christian and truly Indian'. Jones penned his

'Ashram Ideals' in 1930, and some of the sentiments from it have been carved, quite literally, into stone: a few large marble plaques which hang outside the main building of STA proclaim that 'Jesus Christ is the Guru of the ashram but men [*sic*] of all faiths and of no faith are welcome to share this kingdom of God fellowship'. Another plaque reads, 'All who sincerely desire to find God are welcome'. Chapter 3 also provides biographical material about Jones, including some of the key influences which inspired him to establish STA and, more broadly, it highlights some of the theological convictions which shaped Jones's missionary efforts. Chapters 4 and 5 then present two distinctive variations on how Jones's foundational visions have been variously received, rejected or reworked at STA. Chapter 4 explores some crucial disjunctures that materialized at STA during the 1990s through the formation of the SoE in 1991, when the ashram began to position itself as a training school for evangelists, aspiring theologians and any other individuals who were new to – or interested in – the basic tenets of Christian doctrine. STA now experienced a marked increase in attendance of individuals from low-caste Hindu backgrounds. This demographic presented a sharp contrast to the educated, high-caste Brahmins whom Jones had envisioned as coming to participate in interreligious dialogue sessions and spiritual community at STA; Chapter 4 thus highlights some vital differences in spiritual orientation between Jones's Brahmin Hindus and the low-caste students of the SoE, as well as some differences between SoE students and teachers. Chapter 5 explores some of the relational dynamics between STA and WA, an interreligious meditation group which first came to STA in 2003 and is the only non-Christian group who attends the ashram on an annual basis.[6] These relational dynamics prompt us to explore the various practical challenges faced by both parties, as STA seeks to open up their institutional spaces to WA, and as WA navigates the processes of belonging there. I consider WA's presence through the lens of recent scholarship on the burgeoning phenomenon of multiple religious belonging, and I reflect on WA's somewhat agonistic relationship with STA in the light of Jones's desire for all individuals to be welcomed at STA, regardless of their faith affiliations. Crucially, using the WA-STA dynamic as a case study, Chapter 5 argues that some fundamental assumptions within much of the current scholarship on multiple religious belonging need to be reconsidered and given further nuance in the light of the ground realities of navigating belonging in such contexts.

We will encounter a number of people throughout this book – some of whom work in STA in some capacity, others who are long-term ashramites of STA and attend its Winter and Summer programmes, and yet others who come to STA for different purposes. To enable the reader to keep track of them, I have provided a social map in Appendix 2 which may prove useful throughout Chapters 3 to 5.

I do not cover all the decades which have unfolded at STA since its establishment in 1930. There are a couple of pragmatic reasons for this: first, I could not possibly do justice to a period of ninety years within the methodological confines of a single book; and, second, even if I had enough space to engage with that vast scope of micro-history, the available data on STA between 1940 and 1990 is scarce, and to attempt to document these decades would be stretching the limits of credible research.[7] Consequently, I concentrate on three distinct yet overlapping time periods of STA: pre-Independence (pre-1947), 1991–present and 2003–present, which are taken up in Chapters 3, 4 and 5, respectively. My punctuation of the timeline with these specific markers is therefore a heuristic device, which allows me to concentrate on and discuss certain distinctive shifts of focus which have occurred at STA. As with any effort to categorize living streams of historical processes, my delineation of the timeline is somewhat inadequate, because such clear delineations almost always make temporal periods seem more clean-cut than they are in real life. This messiness of everyday sociality is why I have insisted on working with three temporal periods which, though distinct, all come forward into the present day. To be clear: although Chapter 3 focuses on Jones's original visions for STA, Chapter 4 focuses on the SoE and Chapter 5 sketches the relational dynamics between WA and STA, each of these transitions remain operative in the present day. Importantly, in attempting to understand life at STA in the 1930s and the 1990s, I draw upon not only oral histories and interviews but also participant observation that I conducted during my ethnographic fieldwork (2016–18). In other words, I sometimes draw upon STA's Winter Programme 2016, or the SoE 2016 programme, in an attempt to imaginatively envision what the respective programmes would have been like in the 1930s and 1990s. Thus, my temporal model relies crucially on a conception of time as fluid, albeit punctuated by specific disjunctures: as I understand and interpret STA's social history, earlier features of STA are not entirely lost when new features are introduced. Rather than replacing earlier aspects of ashram life, new aspects are densely layered on to the previously existing ones – not unlike the impasto technique in oil painting, in which thick layers of paint are added on top of what is already on the canvas; often, glimpses of an earlier layer come through the top layer while, conversely, the added layer becomes fundamentally changed due to the persistence of what came before it. And, as I have already stated and shall reiterate, the establishment of STA itself must, in turn, be understood synergistically within the contexts of its sociopolitical histories (see Figure 0.1).

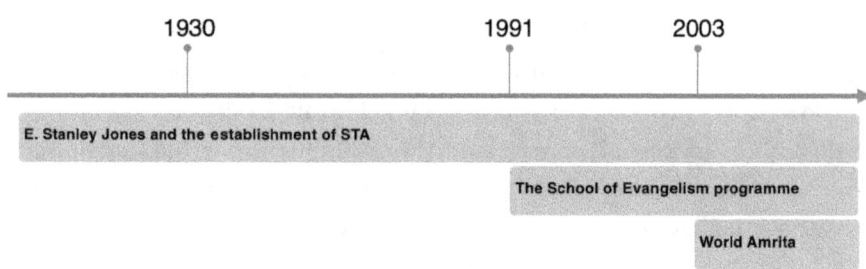

Figure 0.1 Temporal model of STA.

0.2 Contextualizing 'inviting the Other' in existing academic literature

It is also helpful to contextualize this project within some broader scholarly fields of study that it draws from and contributes to. As an ethnographically informed social history of a Christian ashram in northern India, this work contributes new ethnographic material and sociohistorical data to the field of Indian Christianity by shedding light on a fieldsite which is relatively unaddressed in the existing scholarship. Some scholarly works have indeed been written about Jones and his approach to evangelism in a general sense, but they do not consistently situate his evangelical approach in the historical contexts which preceded it nor do they extensively draw upon ethnographic fieldwork at STA itself – both of which are carefully contextualized throughout this book. Based on the most recent national census (2011), Christians constitute less than 3 per cent of India's population.[8] Given this demographic, and keeping in mind the rich diversity of religious traditions throughout India's many cultures, it is not altogether surprising that relatively little scholarship has focused on Indian Christianity. Some of this scholarship is discussed in Chapter 2 and the reader may note there that the relatively small canon of scholarship on Indian Christianity seems to focus predominantly on one or more of three subfields: Syrian Christianity, Advaita-inflected Christianity and Dalit Christianity. This book engages with these in Chapters 2, 3 and 4, respectively and thus acts as a sort of conceptual bridge between the studies of these diverse expressions of Indian Christianity.

It seems particularly fitting to consider this work – focused on one specific Christian ashram – in the context of existing studies of the various Christian ashrams and other attempts at inculturation in present-day India. Falling under the umbrella of this scholarship, the works of Kerry San Chirico, Darren Todd Duerksen and Israel Selvanayagam are especially worth mentioning.[9]

Their erudite studies of what we can broadly understand as expressions of inculturation in present-day India have been illuminating and helpful for me as I conceptualized and conducted my own research. And yet, as I note in more detail in Chapter 4, Christian ashrams are, for the most part, suffering from a declining attendance in Indian spaces,[10] and several once-vibrant Christian ashrams have either closed down completely or instigated significant changes in the content and purpose of their institutional presences. In the light of what seems to be a general decline of scholarly and spiritual interest in Christian ashrams, we might ask the question (as some of my colleagues have, rather pointedly, done throughout the course of this research): 'Why study a phenomenon that is already on the decline?' That is, why look at Christian ashrams, and why not, instead, focus one's efforts at understanding a different facet of Indian Christianity – one which is gaining momentum and rapidly growing in numbers? To this legitimate query, I respectfully point out, first, that a declining phenomenon mandates urgent study if we wish to better understand it before it either becomes transformed beyond recognition or dies out completely. And, second, one needs only to open an introductory history textbook to highlight the multiple ways that understanding the past can help us to navigate the present. That being said, STA, despite its at-times shaky financial situations, does not seem to be under any immediate threat of becoming an outdated relic: as a multifaceted and multi-operational institution, it is still alive and well. But, undeniably and unsurprisingly, it too has undergone significant transformations since its establishment in 1930, and our close-up examinations of some of these transformative processes will help us map out STA as a social site which is shaped by dynamic processes of self-other entanglements.

We could also consider the question, 'Why now?' That is, out of the inexhaustible topics that could be pursued in the present academic settings, why *now* pose questions of interreligious relations and existential belonging? As suggested by its title, this book is undeniably concerned with the motifs of invitation and otherness. But we can alternately articulate this thematic focus by invoking the terminologies of borders and boundaries. Late-modern, twentieth-twentieth-first-century societies are rife with examples of the age-old human preoccupation with borders and boundaries: current global news routinely documents the various proclamations of building walls, raising the drawbridge, strengthening borders, reinforcing the bonds of 'us' against 'them' and delineating boundaries. And the central motif of understanding the Self in relationship to one's own Otherness has had significant philosophical attention devoted to it.[11] With this zeitgeist in mind, I believe that the present constitutes a crucial moment to look closely at a particular fieldsite whose inhabitants, as we shall see, are preoccupied with these very questions of the bonds of the community, the boundaries of the Self and the borders of the Other.

0.3 Blurring boundaries and borders

We can, I propose, simultaneously consider these themes of Otherness, bonds, boundaries, borders and belonging with reference not just – as we shall see in the social history of STA – to societies and individuals but also to scholarly disciplines. Throughout this book, I am not only drawing upon overlapping fields of scholarship – Hindu-Christian studies, anthropology of Christianity, Indian Christianity, interreligious relations, multiple religious belonging and the like – but I am also intentionally inhabiting an 'in-between' space when it comes to the academic disciplines of cultural anthropology and philosophical theology. From early on in my research, I seemed to be configuring an eclectic mix of the two disciplines; I felt 'interstitial' (from the Latin *interstitium* – meaning 'to stand between') in the sense that I occupied the liminal spaces between anthropology and theology. To borrow from *Merriam Webster's Dictionary* definition of 'interstitial', I felt that I was 'situated within but not restricted to or characteristic of' both disciplines.

On one side, my methodological approach was vitally informed by the influences of cultural anthropology – indeed, of the two disciplines, it is cultural anthropology, not theology, within which I have been formally trained and with which I am more familiar. Among cultural anthropologists, the ethnographic tools of interviews, participant observation and researcher participation are usually used in order to understand the nuances of the beliefs and the practices of a particular community – tools which I, of course, used throughout my fieldwork. (I provide more details about my methodology below.) Anthropologists use these fine-grained tools to gain an empathetic understanding of a community's practices and motivations. Through employing other conceptual tools such as cultural relativity, the anthropologist brings these insights back into everyday contexts which their readers can understand or relate to, thus transforming 'the strange' into 'the familiar'.[12] It is due to my training in social scientific methodologies, and my academic mentorship by anthropologists, that I remain more aligned with the discipline of cultural anthropology than with theology.

But, still, I also found myself intrigued by, and drawn to, theology during the PhD research on which this book is based. My interest in theology was especially keen when I transitioned from a Religious Studies faculty in Canada to the University of Cambridge's Faculty of Divinity where theology – especially Christian theology – has historically been the normative discipline. Despite consistently correcting the colleagues who lumped me with the 'other' theologians in my midst (*'I'm not a theologian!'*), I frequently found myself wanting, in fact, to write about theological questions and ideas. And the more I reflected on works which I found to be interesting and inspiring in the manner of engaging with questions of God, community, meaning, truth, love and so on, the more I was struck by the reality that the vast majority of these authors were theologians and philosophers – that is, they were not anthropologists. Perhaps, I realized one afternoon with genuine shock (and some disciplinary concern!) that I might be a sort of theologian after all.

In essence, my dilemma in articulating, and inhabiting, my intended methodological and theoretical framework was this: if I wished to do 'pure' cultural anthropology, why was I yet so preoccupied ('haunted' might be a more truthful confession) by theological and philosophical questions rather than remaining focused more exclusively on the standard topics that so many other anthropologists would expect me to explore, given the location of my fieldsite – 'orthodox' anthropological topics like caste, kinship, postcolonial theory, marriage, clothing, gender, power dynamics, appropriation and the like? On the other hand, if my main end goal was theological inquiry, and if I thus only wanted my fieldwork to serve as a discussion board for the broader theological questions which had already planted themselves in my mind, could I not eliminate the middleman of fieldwork entirely? After grappling with this dilemma for months, the conviction grew in me that ethnographic fieldwork for me was not strictly about acquiring knowledge and understanding about why people are the way they are and why they believe what they believe, and subsequently noting the intricacies and interwovenness of their social, political and family dynamics (and the like) – though it was all of that too. Rather, from my interstitial locations, it was *also* about engaging deeply in conversations and being regularly confronted with real-life scenarios which could rigorously challenge some of my pre-existing assumptions about the very theological and philosophical themes that I sought to understand better. Undeniably, I fall short of some of the expectations that people would rightly have of me if I were a bona-fide theologian – I refrain from explicitly speaking of 'truth' or what is 'noble' or 'right', at least in the ways that theologians often do. Nonetheless, by exploring these topics in their own right, it is equally undeniable that I do not fall neatly into the disciplinary category of cultural anthropology.

Upon reading this book, cultural anthropologists may therefore note the various ways that my research project does *not* comply with some of the standards and expectations of the discipline. Theologians may be equally quick to point out that I am not firmly planted within any one theological tradition, and thus I do not seem to be a strong or suitable candidate to occupy a doctrinal space clearly designated for confessional theologians. I would agree with both these objections. However, I contend that I am particularly well placed to occupy the interstitial spaces between anthropology and theology and, as Chapter 1 shall argue more extensively, I believe that anthropologists can learn from theologians – especially from the discipline of (Protestant) Christian theology and its preoccupation with religious belief. I am deeply intrigued and inspired by some of the pioneering conversations of scholars like Joel Robbins, Fenella Cannell, Natalie Wigg Stevenson and others who are beginning to contemplate and explore the reciprocal benefits that can come into fruition if the disciplines of anthropology and theology consciously co-inhabit their overlapping spheres and learn from one another.[13] This book is, however, not primarily a theoretical argument for this methodological and disciplinary interstitiality – though I do engage with such arguments in Chapter 1 – but it is an extended example of how such interstitial locations can generate scholarship by interweaving ethnographic observation with theological reflection.

0.4 Three dialogical encounters

Before one can begin to *invite*, one must first *encounter* the Other. Several dialogical encounters have occurred leading up to the creation of this book. Three encounters are especially worth noting.

0.4.1 The fieldwork encounter: Methodological tools used during fieldwork

First, as the researcher, I encountered first-hand the ethnographic material which has informed my thoughts for this book whilst conducting my fieldwork. While I was living in India between August 2016 and May 2017, I spent several months at STA; during the months of this period that I was not at STA, I lived in Delhi, Mumbai and surrounding areas (including a short trip to the villages near Faridpur with one of STA's former managers), which facilitated my ongoing interactions with a number of key informants who are themselves long-time ashramites of STA but who spend the greater part of the year living in their respective cities. I also returned to STA in April 2018 for five weeks, most of which was spent attending WA retreats and conversing with WA participants after the retreats were finished. During these cumulative eleven months of fieldwork, I conducted participant observation, with several unstructured and semi-structured interviews, as well as a few group interviews. I audio recorded these conversations whenever possible, and I transcribed each of the recordings word for word before employing a thematic analysis of the material; my thematic coding of this ethnographic data provided the lenses of focus that appear in subsequent chapters. I also used questionnaires and surveys with several past and present leaders (Acharyas) of the ashram, as well as with the students who participated in the SoE programme in September 2016. The survey I conducted amongst SoE participants gathered sixteen responses (55 per cent of the group) and I audio recorded, transcribed and performed a line-by-line discourse analysis on twenty-two personal testimonies and twenty semi-structured interviews. A number of other semi-structured interviews took place which I did not audio record, and for these I instead relied on my memory (I almost always slipped away to write down notes immediately following such a conversation). Sometimes, I jotted down notes during the conversations themselves and later expanded on them in further detail when I typed up my field notes at night. I also recorded, transcribed and translated several of the *bhajans* and other devotional songs sung at the STA – some of which we shall discuss in Chapter 4. In addition to these more-sophisticated modes of data collection, I also meditated, ate, worked, sang, swam, hiked, ran away from poisonous snakes and skipped out on the odd devotional class together with my informants. This 'deep hanging out'[14] allowed for a great number of informal conversations, which also gave me insights and provided me with basic information about individuals' backgrounds and motives for coming to STA.

As Chapter 1 will highlight in more detail in my discussion of BIR, I was intentionally open with my informants about my own religious beliefs and doubts; this existential transparency, I contend, vitally affected the qualitative data I was able to access. Most people at STA knew, for example, that I had grown up in a Protestant Christian family in Canada and was thus relatively familiar with Christian scriptures and (Protestant) doctrinal teachings. They also knew that I had personal leanings towards certain Buddhist and Hindu philosophies, and thus I had hesitated when asked if I was a *Christian*; my informants also knew there were certain spiritual practices (including, e.g. the invitation to deliver a sermon at one of STA's Sunday services) that my own world view did not allow me to participate in. I entered into friendly terms with most of the people I met at STA, and, indeed, some became my good friends – we exchanged stories about our respective families; we spoke of our beliefs, fears, dreams; I was unhesitatingly and unconditionally cared for when I fell ill and when I required medical care; we made plans to stay in touch after my fieldwork ended, and so forth. Despite our friendships, I often held on to philosophical and doctrinal convictions that were rather different from those of my informants, and on more than one occasion our discussions quickly revealed our difference of opinions – sometimes, these differences were illuminating pathways for me to gain deeper understandings of my informants' beliefs and practices, while at other times, the differences – I can only assume – prohibited me from truly understanding their viewpoints. All of these intricacies surrounding the nature of fieldwork and access to qualitative data will be taken up in more detail in Chapter 1.

0.4.2 The writing-up encounter: Selecting ethnographic data

The second encounter is one I experienced when beginning to sift through my ethnographic data and to give structural shape to the book that you now hold in your hands. Anyone who has embarked on ethnographic fieldwork is aware of the sheer overabundance of data with which one returns from the field. It is impossible to write about all the phenomena that I observed, or all the topics that came up in an interview setting. Ethnographers have to trust that, as we selectively sift through our data by using the various systematic tools of our craft, we are doing our utmost to *re*present our fieldsites in ways that do not obscure or twist the experiences of our informants. In effect, we generally hope that our sketches are sound, faithful and coherent, and are not overly shaped by our unique preconceptions – I have done my best in this regard. Still, as I shall return to it in Chapter 1 in greater detail, there is no 'view from nowhere'[15] and I have undoubtedly picked up on certain ethnographic moments from my nowhere which were of particular interest to me on account of my own spiritual and social preoccupations, and these prejudgements have guided and lured me to explore certain questions over others. While remaining critically aware of my own existential leanings, I have done my best to *re*present STA, and its past and present realities in ways that, I think, accurately illustrate its dynamic past and present lifeworlds. Indeed, I hope that my informants, even if they do not agree with all of my conclusions or topics of discussion, will agree that I have represented their lives and their ashram in good faith.

0.4.3 The writer-reader encounter

A third dialogical encounter for any writer occurs once the written product is finished and shelved within a library for potential readers. This is the hermeneutic encounter of a 'fusion of horizons' between the written work and the reader's own interpretive frameworks.[16] Some qualitative researchers succeed in writing thoughtful, gripping ethnographies which draw the reader into the multifaceted universes that their ethnographic writing creatively opens up, but even the most compelling written work can only stay alive through a reader's projective readings and simultaneous (re)interpretations. By continuing to read – and gradually inhabiting – this text, you, the reader, are entering into a third type of dialogical exchange with me, the writer: one between *my* words and *your* thoughts.[17] (I wonder what thoughts you are constructing even now as you read these words – Am I being too informal in my writing? Too personal? Too naive? Have I disrespected the seemingly sacred genre of the academic monograph? Is eschewing the scholarly norm permissible? Desirable?) I am under no delusions about the limited outreach of the proverbial ivory tower: my final contribution of this particular research – this text, formed dialogically – will not live on unless it is engaged with by readers like yourself. (I wonder, again, in which ways you will engage with it – Will it spark a discussion at a dinner table? Might these descriptions of different ways of being, thinking and doing pique your curiosity? Will you seek out a place where you can learn more about the spiritual beliefs and practices you have glimpsed through this text? Will my words prompt you to see anything or anyone in a new light? Does anything within us actually change on account of reading others' stories?) It may sound presumptuous to hope for such an existential impact with mere words, but it is the hope that you *will* engage in some way that has inspired me to write. And, having placed all these contexts, caveats and clauses before you, I invite you to read on.

1

An introduction to belief-inclusive research

1.1 Introduction

There was a knock on my door and, surprised, I answered it and found Suhasini standing on my balcony. 'Why aren't you at the class?' I asked her in Hindi. She simply shrugged, unapologetic for her truancy. '*You* aren't there either. I find it so boring … don't tell the Acharya, but I am so bored by it. I don't understand it. Why must they teach us so many boring things?' Suhasini paused before continuing, staring at me: 'I want *you* to teach me instead. You can teach me, can't you? I am not going to keep going to that class when you can just teach me what you know.'

'But Suhasini', I objected, 'you are here to take the classes of the ashram, aren't you? And there are teachers here to teach you! What do you want me to teach you? I am not a pastor, Suhasini. In fact, I am a student! I am also here to learn!'

'But you must know so much about Jesus. Have you read very much of the Bible?'

> 'Yes, I have read the Bible'. I answered, suddenly becoming aware that Suhasini was not the first at STA to have asked me this question.
>
> 'The whole thing?' she asked as she held up her Bible and flipped through its pages.
>
> 'Yes, Suhasini, I have read the whole thing.'
>
> 'How many times? Once or more than once?'
>
> 'I have read the whole thing at least once and then I have read several parts of it many, many times.'

'The whole thing! The whole thing!' Suhasini repeated my words, as if emphatically pronouncing the words would help her to process my feat. 'So … so, Nadya, you must know the Bible very well. …Then you can teach it to me!!' she exclaimed, seeming both ecstatic and relieved by her new-found solution for continuing to skip the 'boring' classes while still learning the information she had come to STA to learn.

I tried to explain to Suhasini that I did not believe exactly the same things as the pastors at her home in Varanasi, or even the teachers at this ashram, but that, if she really wanted, I could tell her some of the stories about Jesus in the Bible. And, of course, I told her, we could talk about any questions she might have – but maybe she would prefer to pose her questions to the Acharya. This, Suhasini agreed, seemed like a good arrangement – but she was not about to let me get off that easy with my casual profession of disbelief.

'But Nadya, now I know that you've read so much of the Bible, so now I know you must know so much about Jesus. So, tell me, why don't you sing any Jesus songs when you sing? All your songs are devotional songs (*bhakti bhajans*), yes, but they're not Jesus songs! If you've read the Bible you must know Jesus. And if you know Jesus you must want to sing Jesus songs!!' Suhasini expressed, flabbergasted.

'Well, I used to sing Jesus songs, Suhasini. And I still know very many – I can even teach them to you if you'd like. We can translate them into Hindi during one of our English lessons! But I don't sing Jesus songs anymore, because now I'm confused about what I believe.'

'Well, if you have confusion, you should speak with Acharya G. Ask him your questions! And pray to God the Father (*Pita Parmeshwar*), He will answer you … the Bible says!'

* * *

This chapter goes beyond the brief methodological details mentioned in the introduction: it is an outline of how I approached my ethnographic fieldwork at STA and why I chose to approach it in that way; I also explore some of the repercussions of this methodological posture insofar as my project is situated alongside other ethnographic research projects within the anthropology of religion. I introduce the concept 'belief-inclusive research' (henceforth 'BIR') to refer to the ways that I intentionally and regularly included my own (religious) beliefs, and also doubts, into the conversations that I had with my informants; and I offer BIR as a distinctive theoretical and methodological posture for ethnographers who work in and with religious contexts.[1]

I chose to utilize BIR, as the second half of this chapter will discuss in greater detail, for three reasons. First, I desired to be as existentially transparent as possible in my interactions at my fieldsite – that is, I wanted to relate to my informants both as friends and as spiritual co-seekers at STA, while being aware, of course, that my role as a researcher crucially affected some of our interpersonal and social dynamics. Second, closely linked to the first reason, I felt that the particular environment of STA as a place that is, in its own words, open to people of 'the *Christian* faith, a *different* faith, or even *no* faith [emphasis added]'[2] made it an appropriate site to explore and articulate the spectrum of my own beliefs and doubts. I might otherwise, as I have indeed done in other ethnographic settings, have exercised greater restraint about voicing my inner doubts. Third, I had an initial sense that my intentional openness about my own beliefs and doubts would give me a certain degree of access to some types of qualitative data that I otherwise might not have been able to access.

Elsewhere, I have articulated in some detail the extent to which social scientific researchers, including anthropologists who work in religious contexts, have been expected to 'bracket out' their own spiritual beliefs and doubts during their fieldwork. Influenced by theoretical frameworks articulated by Martin Heidegger, Edmund Husserl, Peter Berger and Clifford Geertz, present-day religious studies scholarship has a disciplinary unease with researchers sharing their own metaphysical views during their research.[3] Yet, I have found that my intentional decision to candidly voice my beliefs and doubts in various conversations with my informants – that is, to conduct BIR – has played a vital role in my ethnographic research. Thus, I contend, BIR has the potential to crucially widen an anthropologist's access to ethnographic data – perhaps, as I shall return to below, specifically in certain research contexts where belief is deemed by informants to be a uniquely indispensable aspect of life.

1.1.1 BIR can provide unique access to ethnographic data

I am not the first to advocate for the inclusion of a researcher's beliefs and doubts in the context of ethnographic fieldwork nor am I the first to claim that this inclusion would be of benefit to the discipline of anthropology; similar arguments have been offered by Brian Howell,[4] Eloise Meneses et al.,[5] Meneses[6] and Naomi Haynes,[7] to give some recent examples. Where my argument differs from these other defences is in my justification: while others have focused on important elements such as the potential for a deepened interpretation through drawing upon one's own religious experiences, I instead focus on the researcher's ability to access ethnographic data.

I have compiled several instances which demonstrate that the informants' assessments of a researcher's beliefs and world views can inform and shape the data that is shared in an interview setting, as well as critically influence whether the researcher is invited by their informants to observe certain social phenomena. Since interviews and participant observation are two crucial pillars of qualitative research, a researcher's access to these modes of data collection are of the utmost importance, and any limitations are worth noting and addressing. I argue that there are certain circumstances in which some degree of shared belief should exist (or, rather, a degree which the informants think exists – a subtle yet important nuance that I shall return to momentarily) between the researcher and informants in order to gain a certain type of data-access in interviews and participant observation. This space of *shared belief* between researcher and informant can either take the form of mutually held doctrinal convictions in which researchers and informants possess resonating understandings of what is metaphysically true – such as 'Christ resurrected on the third day' or, pertinent to the ethnographic encounters I explore below, 'Jesus can heal the body through prayer.' Such iterations of doctrinal belief are likely what comes to mind most readily when individuals consider the concept of *shared belief*. Alternately, shared belief can sometimes take the form of an existential openness to the category of belief itself. That is to say, the very willingness of a researcher to voice their own beliefs and doubts, and thus participate in a shared quest for metaphysical truth, can convey the sense that such quests are not simply topics of social scientific inquiry but are themselves of vital existential importance and, consequently, what we can call *a wider shared belief* between informant and researcher can be forged even when the specific believed-in doctrines substantially differ. In other words, by speaking about our own beliefs and doubts, we signal that we care about metaphysical truth claims. (I will return to this below. Still, BIR itself is not as problem-free as one might hope – thus, I shall also expand upon the messiness of BIR, which necessitates the forthcoming caveats: I argue that, *sometimes*, *some* anthropologists should intentionally bring *some* of their own beliefs and doubts into the forefront of their ethnographic research, thereby *sometimes* increasing their access to ethnographic data with *some of* their informants.

Before proceeding, it is important to quickly clarify a few points – I offer lengthier explanations elsewhere. First, the phrase the 'researcher's belief' is used as a shorthand expression to refer to the somewhat unpredictable manner that informants can interpret and make sense of the researcher's beliefs. A researcher's own ideas about themselves (e.g. including any religious identities that they hold or not) might be notably different from their informants' understandings of the same. The 'researcher's belief' is dialogically formed during fieldwork encounters, and is multiply resituated. Second, the concept of 'belief' draws upon specifically Protestant Christian understandings of belief, in which belief is deemed especially important.[8] There are, of course, alternate viewpoints of belief[9] which place natural limitations on the scope of my own exploration, but I nonetheless feel that it is an interesting and helpful starting point – it is a specific enough context which, as Meneses suggests in her commentary on the way that anthropology-theology conversations tend to emerge from specifically Christian contexts, can be an 'appropriate' way to 'generate an interesting conversation'.[10] Third, I am not advocating that BIR be applied across the board in all research contexts; to suggest a cognitively superior or ideal theoretical framework in which to conduct ethnographic research would fly in the face of ethnographic data, which undeniably shows that different research postures helpfully enable different types of access to different sorts of ethnographic data. I value these differences. Given that no human being – and, therefore, no anthropologist – occupies the Archimedean point of an impartial spectator (and this includes those embedded in secular world views),[11] a greater degree of 'attachment' to one perspective or person is usually concurrent with a greater degree of 'detachment' from another perspective or person. One lesson I take from this multidimensionality of human interactive spaces is that each anthropologist's unique status has the potential to give them access to distinct elements and different degrees of ethnographic data; yet, in gaining access to some of these elements, we lose sight of others. BIR, then, can be one of many possible approaches; I hope its value will be clearly shown.

1.2 Methodological bracketing: Noting some limitations

Elsewhere, I have traced the relationship between methodological bracketing and the current-day practice of anthropologists who refrain from speaking of their own metaphysical views while conducting their fieldwork. Anthropologists are taught that they must 'neither affirm nor deny the existence of the gods' lest they confuse their methodological and theoretical frameworks with those of the theologians.[12] Peter Berger referred to this disciplinary refusal to explore questions of metaphysical truth as an 'intrinsic limitation' of the social scientific discipline and, importantly, he felt no need to overcome it. Rather than think of Berger's 'limitation' as negative, we might instead consider it as the boundary line or wall that exists at a swimming pool: the boundary line is what allows the pool to fill up with water and, thus, to be useful and enjoyed. Berger's 'limitation' was viewed as a necessary component of the discipline in order to be able to explore aspects which are social and empirical – rather than metaphysical. Thus, it is not surprising that social scientists – even, or rather *especially* those within the anthropology of religion (a scholarly circle where, as Jon Bialecki comments tongue-in-cheek, the optimistic and the innocent 'might expect [talk of God] the most'[13]) often do not speak of God at all. And if anthropologists do not *speak* of God, then they surely do not make metaphysical truth claims regarding God! This is not altogether surprising. But, since Berger, many anthropologists have regarded other limitations as clear indications that a certain measure of theoretical reformation of the discipline of anthropology is needed. There are two limitations that I have found to be communicated – either directly or indirectly – by several scholars who are broadly situated in the field of the social scientific study of religion, and which are sometimes also conveyed by scholars in the hard sciences. First, we see the limitation that total objectivity is conceptually impossible even with systematic attempts at bracketing.[14] Second, we note the limitation that bracketing is, in any case, deeply hegemonic because it reinforces a power dynamic which privileges the researcher's world views and interpretive frameworks over those of their informants. In short, when researchers deem that any question of metaphysical truth can be neatly extracted from other anthropological considerations, we implicitly favour our interpretive framework over those of our informants – many of whom would never accept such a division.[15]

1.2.1 Methodological bracketing limits access to ethnographic data

I propose that we should add another limitation to our list. Specifically, my ethnographic research has highlighted some ways that intentionally bracketing out our own views of metaphysical truth during our research, in fact, limits our access to ethnographic data. Simply put, I wonder: Are we approaching our research in a way that invites our informants to speak truthfully, and, without glossing over their spiritual viewpoints, openly speak with us in an interview setting? Further, are we approaching our research in ways where our informants would be comfortable enough to invite *us* to observe, or to even participate alongside, certain events? Or does the absence of conversations concerning our own metaphysical beliefs and quests – and, indeed, even our very disciplinary tendency towards secularist explanations and an *absence* of 'talk about God'[16] – limit our access to ethnographic data, thereby resulting in incomplete – if not inaccurate – explanations of the very emic views which we are striving to understand? In other words, do ethnographers experience any belief-related limitations in their attempts to collect ethnographic data?

Throughout the fieldwork I conducted at a Christian ashram for my PhD, I consciously chose to honestly incorporate my beliefs and doubts about Protestant Christian doctrines into the conversations that I had with my informants. To be sure, I did not always share the same beliefs as my informants but nor did I strive for a Geertzian form of neutrality. My willingness to speak openly about my own beliefs and doubts to my informants indicated a more general willingness and eagerness to understand, in turn, their own beliefs and doubts. As they saw it, I was evidently interested in, and committed to, discussing metaphysical truth and this conveyed a form of interest in, and commitment to, the category of belief itself.

1.2.2 Information volunteered by informants (interviews)

First, let us consider some ways in which a researcher's beliefs can shape the information volunteered by informants in interview settings. I have myself experienced moments with my informants – and also noted other anthropologists' experiences – in which a perceived absence of shared belief between researcher and informant can sometimes inhibit informants from sharing freely with anthropologists. We can see this conscious inhibition by informants playing out in Blanes's succinct documentation of his experience of admitting to one of his informants – an elder in the gypsy Pentecostal group that Blanes was studying – that Blanes was, in fact, an atheist. During their initial conversation, the elder asked Blanes which church he belonged to. Blanes, recalling the incident, reports, 'When I answered that I wasn't a believer, he bluntly turned his back on me and spoke no more.'[17]

Let us consider, in more detail, a case from the fieldwork of Marie-Françoise Guédon as she documented it in 1994. Guédon notes that, during her ethnographic research among the Dene in Northern Canada, she was 'tested by [her] instructors [informants who occupied a place of leadership in the community] before they gave an answer' to her questions concerning shamanic medicine.[18] She goes on to explain that her informants initially provided her with explanations of the same type and depth that they would usually provide to a young child; it was only upon Guédon sharing her own experiences with them (such as her dreams that resulted in her informants attributing to her the status of a spiritual healer) that individuals began to inform her more thoroughly about their own spiritual beliefs. As one of her informants said, '[there is no point in talking about certain things] to a white man, even an anthropologist, unless you knew he was going to understand'.[19] This insightful, succinct and also poignant comment raises important questions about what it means to 'understand' our informants and our research topics more broadly. Guédon's informants wanted her to not only understand – and, indeed, *believe* – their own world view in a conceptual or intellectual manner, but they also wanted her to vitally 'understand' in a more personal, somatic and experiential way. Crucially, it was her informants' view that Guédon had arrived at her *own experiential understanding*, and also that she *shared some of their beliefs* or was at least *open to exploring the possibility* that her informants' configuring of Guédon as a healer might indeed be metaphysically truthful, that led them, in turn, to relay their own beliefs and experiences more directly and thoroughly to her. Importantly, we can note that a sincere openness to belief itself was of crucial importance to these informants in order to speak authentically in an interview.

1.2.3 Observations accessed by researchers (participant observation)

There are also instances in the ethnographic literature where a researcher's belief has affected the types of data they are able to access via participant observation. Anthropologist Jacob Loewen (1974) documents an account of working alongside a certain Christian missionary, David, in Panama. Despite their eagerness to be involved, David and Loewen were excluded from the community's healing rituals due to – somewhat ironically – what the community described as the missionaries' 'lack of faith'. The community interpreted certain biblical passages on healing (provided by the Christian missionaries themselves) to mean that authentic faith was required for healing results. But because Loewen and David were seen as favouring biomedical views of healing over the concept of faith-based prayer healing, the Christian community intentionally excluded them from the community's prayer time. Loewen recalls the leading men of the church apologetically pulling him aside and saying, 'I am sorry, but [the healing] doesn't work when you and David are in the circle. You and David don't really believe.'[20] How might Loewen's ethnographic fieldwork have been altered had he been able to observe the healing rituals, an evidently important aspect of the community's practice? And, more generically, what types and depths of participant observation are ethnographers consistently prevented from accessing due to the ways in which they are perceived by their informants as lacking in genuine belief?

I also encountered some belief-related limitations during my ethnographic work on spiritual healing in Charismatic Protestant communities in Canada.

The following vignette demonstrates that my informants' willingness to allow me to conduct participant observation depended heavily on their certification of my own belief: in the Charismatic-inflected view of my informants, the universe is understood as being in a constant state of a spiritual battle where Christian soldiers are easily wounded. The entire cosmos is conceptualized as teeming with legions of evil spirits that – if given the opportunity – will distract, disrupt, torment or, possibly, violently possess an individual. Evil spirits are equipped with particular specializations and abilities, and they are named after their sinister predilections: 'Lust', 'Trauma', 'Death' and so on. Accordingly, many of my informants described themselves as 'soldiers' who are constantly on the spiritual battlefield where one's thoughts, actions, and even one's involuntary experiences, can 'create an opening' for an evil spirit to wreak havoc in that individual's life. Charismatics thus see themselves not only as potential targets but also as key players in this cosmic battle.

Four months into my ethnographic research, the topic of whether I could attend a 'personal ministry appointment', that is, an individual prayer healing session, as a participant observer came up in casual conversation. Maureen, the woman who would receive the prayer healing session, was someone with whom I had formed a friendship, and it seemed to me that attending her session would be permissible on account of our mutual acquaintance. But this possibility of my attending as simply an allegedly *neutral* observer was met with hesitation by the 'Lead' (the primary of the two Healers in any individual healing session). The Lead's hesitations were due to her uncertainty about my own world view and personal practices. Was I engaged in any sort of activity – deliberately or accidentally, known or unknown – that might 'give territory' to an evil spirit? If and when any spirits were cast out of Maureen, would they simply enter me instead? Further, had I undergone the necessary rituals that would eradicate any existing evil spirits from me, or might I in fact invite, or even actively bring in, evil spirits into the prayer healing session by my very presence? And, even if I were willing to go through the cleansing rituals, would such rituals be effective on me without a proper and personal foundation of genuine faith that is thought to be necessary in order for the rituals to be efficacious? Even more generally, the spiritual healing community wanted assurance that the research process was 'more than an academic exercise' for me. Indeed, many individuals were hesitant to share any of their more meaningful spiritual healing experiences – even in casual conversational settings – unless they were assured that I would find the process of learning from them enriching, or at least challenging, on a personal and spiritual level.[21]

Any careful skirting around the question of metaphysical truth was simply dissatisfactory to my informants.

In my attempt to establish credibility and trust with my informants, I had already followed the advice that I received in the earliest stage of my research from an influential member of this Christian community: before beginning any formal interviews or participant observation sessions, I first attended a group spiritual healing retreat where I had my own 'personal ministry appointment' with a Lead and a Second Healer. They had walked me through various reflections upon my life experiences and family lineages, and then prompted me to speak out certain prayers loudly in order to 'break ungodly soul ties' that might be wreaking havoc in me. The specificities of this process were outside my own spiritual practices and beliefs, but I participated in all of it as best as I could – and my informants, including Maureen and the Healers who would be facilitating Maureen's personal ministry appointment, knew that I had undergone my own personal ministry appointment. I am not sure what else I could have done in order to become someone whom my informants would view as trustworthy, and whom they might be freely willing to invite as an observer of their practices. Yet, I was aware that it was my belief – or, in this particular case, my assumed lack of belief in the structures of their cosmological universe and their teachings of spiritual redemption – which continued to concern them. Looking back, it probably did not help matters that I tried to enact a sort of curious-but-overall-indifferent *neutrality* in those conversations. They wanted more than a mere inclination or willingness to go through the motions of participation. They wanted me to *know* not just in the sense of accumulating bits of information or even acquiring knowledge (in the sense of the French *savoir* or the German *wissen*) but also to *intimately know* (*connaître* in French or *kennen* in German) my own healing. They wanted me to, deeply and truly, *believe*.

In the end, mainly due to the plea of Maureen who felt that my ability to observe the event would be of crucial importance to my developing an understanding of the community's spiritual healing practices, I was invited to attend the session. Observing the healing session first-hand turned out to be extraordinarily helpful to my understanding of the community's healing practices; it provided me with a much more nuanced grasp of the practices involved with healing, and also with some context for many of my later interviews. As far as I am concerned, the invitation to observe a personal healing was crucial in increasing my understanding of the phenomena. But the two Healers later commented on my attendance at Maureen's ministry session, and reflected regretfully that it was a mistake to have allowed me to attend at all. They speculated that my presence had changed the atmosphere substantially and was likely to be the reason that the healing had not been as efficacious as had been hoped for. To illustrate, the Lead gave me an example: 'You know when we had Maureen lay down in the coffin and we called her up from the dead?'[22] She didn't take it seriously. She caught your eye, smiled, and went along as if it were all a hoke [melodramatic] ritual. Because probably somewhere she knew that you weren't taking it seriously, either.'

The controversies and the negotiations which unravelled due to my desire to attend Maureen's personal ministry session, and other similar moments, were the first experiences which forced me to grapple with the question of my own belief as a researcher. Specifically, these experiences made me consider how my informants' perception of my belief shaped the ethnographic data they allowed me to access: I began to wonder what else I might have missed out on observing due to the ways they perceived my belief. While I never contemplated strategically changing the specifics of my (religious) beliefs and doubts for the purpose of gaining better ethnographic access, I could not escape the conviction that my own belief – or rather, the lack of shared belief in the specific doctrinal points that my informants deeply valued – was a barrier to my research.

But, interestingly and crucially, this reflection did not then lead me to conclude that I must share my informants' specific doctrinal beliefs in order to gain access. (I return to this.) My reflections instead led me to ask more generally: 'What posture must anthropologists actively cultivate in order to demonstrate that they are willing to "take seriously" the beliefs of their informants?'[23] Motivated by this experience at the healing session, I began to understand that a researcher's belief and the broader questions of truth claims cannot be neatly quarantined from anthropological reflection and practice. Indeed, the anthropologist's assessment of what is *really* happening out there matters vitally for the anthropologist's craft, because it crucially affects, and even shapes, the data that we seek to, and are able to, access – both in interviews and in participant observation settings. To be sure, it is our informants who, to some extent, decide what we are able to have access to; yet, at the same time, our conscious refusal to speak candidly about our own (religious) beliefs and doubts can all too readily communicate that we simply do not care about the pursuit of metaphysical truth itself. Indeed, through refraining from speaking of our beliefs and doubts, researchers are being abruptly denied access to the very phenomena we wish to observe and understand. Conducting BIR, at least in *some* instances, could solve this dilemma.

1.3 Attaining a 'wider' shared belief despite doctrinal differences

I want to be clear that, when I say an anthropologist can use BIR as a way of attaining a *shared* belief with their informants, I am not suggesting that conducting BIR entails possessing and professing the specific doctrinal beliefs (e.g. that bodily healing can result from prayer and/or certain rituals) of our informants. Indeed, there are and will always be a number of researchers who cannot be 'believers' – at least not in the fully committed ways our informants might desire us to be. Some anthropologists even work with informants who hold beliefs that are distinctly unpalatable to the researcher: speaking candidly of his view of his informants, Leo Coleman confesses, 'In short, I didn't like some of the people I had to participate with as I observed them, and I didn't like their politics.'[24] Other anthropologists, while having no specific moral or ethical disagreements with the beliefs held by their informants, simply cannot adopt those particular beliefs as their own. My own ethnographic encounters are a testament of this: in addition to being an inadequate believer insofar as my fieldwork with Maureen and other Charismatic healers was concerned, I also experienced a sheer inability to be, in their eyes, a satisfactory believer during my fieldwork at STA. I can recall one poignant moment when Shreya, a young and fervent ashramite whose Protestant beliefs were inflected with Charismatic Christianity, asked me to join a small group who would pray with her, requesting Jesus to powerfully intervene in a difficult family situation and heal her uncle's illness. 'The Bible says', Shreya told me with faith-filled conviction, 'that if we believe, then Jesus will heal'. I had come to like Shreya very much during the weeks we spent together at the ashram, and I would have loved to tell her: '*Absolutely* I will pray to Jesus with the others!' But my (religious) belief (or, rather, my doubt) did not permit me to sincerely say such a thing about intercessory prayer – or, at least, my (Protestant-shaped) conscience did not allow me to falsely profess to her. Sometimes, some beliefs are simply not attainable. Keeping what we might call the *intrinsic limitations* of belief-formation in mind, at this point, we might ask: What are the implications of BIR for an anthropologist who is, unbudgingly unable to embrace their informants' deeply held religious beliefs?

In addition to the reality, discussed above, that all anthropologists access unique data based on our unique vantage points,[25] there are further pragmatic reasons why it would be problematic to argue that BIR must entail holding the same doctrinal beliefs as our informants. What about the social reality that a 'community' of informants is not entirely homogenous in their beliefs, so that an ethnographer simply cannot experience shared doctrinal beliefs with every individual alongside whom they are conducting research? Which beliefs are then to be given precedence and deemed to be the *most* important ones to share in order to gain access to the ethnographic data which, I have argued, hinges around a perceived shared belief between researcher and informant? Doctrinal beliefs? Or beliefs about justice, politics, social systems, environmental crises, gender roles and gender fluidity, science and the laws of nature, education? One must also consider whether a researcher could be justified in simply pretending to believe so as to potentially gain more access and greater insight into the phenomenon. That is to say, to what extent, if at all, are mere professions of belief ethically permissible? If, as Joel Robbins has suggested, anthropologists are becoming 'more and more interested in rendering frank judgments'[26] and are increasingly seeking to offer the world 'hope for real change',[27] are there certain phenomena which would ethically justify false professions of belief – assuming that such a profession might, in turn, lead the anthropologist to gain a better understanding of the phenomena they studied? And what of the reality that, recalling our subtle yet important nuance articulated towards the beginning of this chapter, no matter what the precise details are of a researcher's own beliefs, the informants will inevitably form their own conclusions about the researcher's beliefs which may or may not align with the ways that the researcher understands their own beliefs?

These questions, centred around the notion of sharing doctrinal beliefs, are interesting in their own regard, and they will require further exploration when we reach a point of developing a model for precisely how BIR might fit into anthropology's conceptual spaces. But these questions also compel me to consider something that I first hinted at in the introductory pages of this chapter and which I again gestured to in this section's opening paragraph. Namely, is there a way to attain a shared belief that does not necessitate sharing the particular doctrinal beliefs of others? Throughout this chapter I have mentioned some of the ways that I divulged my (religious) beliefs, as well as my doubts, to my informants at the Christian ashram. I did not strive to convince them that we possessed identical doctrinal beliefs – though sometimes we did seem to mutually hold certain beliefs such as the benefit of reading the Bible. And this very willingness to divulge my beliefs and doubts seemed to convey and confirm to my informants that I deeply valued the category of belief, and the pursuit of metaphysical truth, itself. In this sense, although our doctrinal beliefs differed, we indeed attained what we could here call a *wider* shared belief – by which I mean a belief that does not hinge upon believing the same specific doctrines.

The ongoing conversations between anthropology (of Christianity) and (Christian) theology are insightful in both grounding and deepening what I mean by *wider* shared belief – I especially find some of the thoughts on what anthropology can 'take', that is, to learn and to adopt/adapt, from theology to be very helpful.[28] In this vein of anthropologists learning from theologians, we can consider one particularly helpful and thought-provoking idea proposed by the Christian theologian Christopher Morse. Morse offers a helpful launching pad for our present consideration of a *wider* shared belief that is not limited to doctrinal specifics. Christian theology itself is wrought with what Morse calls 'faithful disbelief'.[29] Amongst a community of Christians, there is a shared understanding of what one should *not* believe; these shared *disbeliefs* can sometimes be a more-than-adequate doctrinal basis for solidarity. That is to say: Morse highlights that it is through faithfully disbelieving what is *not* of God that Christian groups can be formed and sustained.

I want to take Morse's insight and apply it more generally. From Morse, we learn that it is not *only* through mutually inhabiting specific doctrinal beliefs that individuals can form a sense of institutional cohesion. Crucially, there is something beyond specific doctrinal beliefs which can bind individuals together and cause them to feel trust and ease. Applying this insight from Christian theology to the context of BIR, I want to suggest that it is not *just* doctrinal beliefs themselves which necessarily establish a rapport between researcher and informant and thus allow the researcher to access certain types of ethnographic data. Perhaps, more simply, it could be the shared belief that the quest for belief – and the pursuit of metaphysical truth – matters at all. That is to say, even though I am an anthropologist who does not hold the same set of doctrinal beliefs and the same types of doubts as (some of) my Protestant Christian informants, it is nonetheless precisely my theological preoccupation with belief, and my unrelenting Protestantism-shaped emphasis on the soteriological importance of belief, which might be enough to establish a sufficient measure of cognitive-affective solidarity with, and, consequently, gain the trust of, my Christian informants.[30] Put alternately: my meta-belief *that belief matters* may be significant enough so as to suffice – at least as a starting point – for gaining access to the types of ethnographic data that I have been concerned with herein. Although I may have disagreed with some of the specifics, I resoundingly agreed that beliefs, and the very category of belief, should not be trivialized.

With this understanding of the possibility of attaining a *wider* shared belief, we can begin to understand that BIR does not necessitate that an anthropologist shares the specific doctrinal details of their informants' beliefs. And so, while my original questions on this broad topic emerged from my failure to share the specific doctrinal beliefs (in my case, regarding Charismatic prayer healing) of my informants, the process of reflecting on this barrier has led me to suspect that it is, in fact, this form of a *wider* shared belief that is within our control. Indeed, anthropologists can attain a form of shared belief with our informants through our own willingness to divulge our own religious beliefs and doubts. As we speak honestly about our own beliefs and doubts, we signal that we genuinely care about metaphysical truth. We can recall, from my ethnographic encounter in my 2014–15 fieldwork, that the Lead Healer of the Charismatic Christian group I worked with thought that I was not 'taking seriously' the doctrinal beliefs that she and Maureen held onto about healing and prayer. Perhaps, had I been willing to intentionally voice the spectrum of my own beliefs and doubts, they might have seen that I indeed did take their experiences seriously. Through my willingness to speak honestly rather than try to act neutrally, she might have even seen that we indeed shared the importance of seeking, sifting through and proclaiming truth(s). Applying Morses's insights, I think there is reason to think that this type of *wider* shared belief might, in turn, be enough to overcome the existing barriers that have been preventing our informants from sharing truthfully in interview settings and/or in inviting us to observe or even participate in certain phenomena.

1.4 Conclusion

We have seen that the habitual placing aside of the question of metaphysical truths can limit our access to ethnographic data. Thus, I contend that we need more conceptual space in anthropology for ethnographers to adopt, cultivate and sustain a stance of BIR when conducting their fieldwork and writing up their ethnography. The content of this chapter has demonstrated that the need for this sort of conceptual space is vital; we need a methodological posture like BIR to be not only tolerated but also actively encouraged so that individuals within the wider anthropological community can confidently choose to approach their research in a way that discusses metaphysical truths without worrying that they are betraying the normatively secular foundations of their discipline or worrying that they will be 'dismissed by colleagues as one who has foolishly gone native'.[31]

I hope that this chapter, and its articulation of some of the more utilitarian reasons behind adopting BIR, can lay the groundwork for encouraging myself and other scholars to creatively and laboriously imagine, design and enact some type of belief-inclusive research in the midst of our research . Embracing such a posture will involve significant rethinking of the ways that we advise young anthropologists to approach their fieldwork – but the potential fruits of this change are well worth the inevitable toils involved.

In the edited volume *Reinventing Anthropology*, Bob Scholte argues that 'intellectual paradigms, including anthropological traditions, are culturally mediated, that is they are contextually situated and relative ... if anthropological activity is culturally mediated, it is in turn subject to ethnographic description and ethnological analysis'.[32] While Scholte is not advocating for a form of meta-ethnography (whereby, e.g. an anthropologist conducts an ethnographic study amongst anthropologists who themselves are conducting ethnographic studies), he draws our attention to the often-overlooked reality that anthropologists are themselves part of a wider cultural community whose actions and beliefs are influenced by their surrounding environments. If, in simple terms, we can describe cultural anthropology as a discipline which concludes that 'research participant X acts in a particular way largely due to the cultural influences of Y and Z', then we must be willing to envision the very discipline of cultural anthropology in a similar fashion. That is, 'anthropologist X acts in a particular manner largely due to the cultural influences of Y and Z'. The anthropologist's beliefs and actions, *qua* anthropologist, have not been formed in a cultural vacuum; we can – and, as erudite scholars, we *should* – interrogate these very beliefs and practices related to the ways we approach our research. The ways that anthropologists approach their craft are the result of a series of numerous interactions, teaching moments, textbook instructions and even anecdotes shared amongst anthropologist peers on the way to (and at) the local pub. Some of these influences are fairly explicit – such as the moments of formal mentorship and instruction which anthropologists undergo – while others can be more implicit – such as reading ethnographies and subtly absorbing the methodological tendencies embodied and portrayed within them, or noting a striking absence of conversations relating to the researcher's beliefs and doubts. Not all of these influences need to be uncritically and unwaveringly adhered to. This chapter has looked at the disciplinary influences that have shaped the adoption by some anthropologists of methodological bracketing as their normative research posture and, subsequently, has argued that anthropology as a discipline needs to make space for researchers to include their own (religious) beliefs and doubts in the fieldwork process. By our willingness to speak with vulnerability and honesty about our own beliefs and doubts, thus signalling our commitment to the pursuit of metaphysical truth, we have the potential to attain a *wider* shared belief with our informants. Consequently, we have the potential to broaden our access to ethnographic data. And *that*, after all, is what we cultural anthropologists are after.

2

Foreignness or Indianness? Indigenizations and representations of Christianity in India

2.1 Introduction

As will become clear in Chapter 3, Jones's visions for STA, although unique in their own respect, must also be understood in the contexts of the multiple and diverse interactions that Christianity has had with various people in specific locations of the Indian subcontinent over the last two millennia. To be sure, Jones's visions did not exist in a cultural or missiological vacuum; they were profoundly shaped by the long and somewhat complicated relationships that some Indians had developed with Christianity since 52 CE, when the apostle Thomas is said to have visited India, resulting in the formation of the Nasrani communities (more commonly referred to as the Syrian Christians or St Thomas Christians) in Kerala. Centuries later, various foreign powers brought with them their Christian beliefs and practices which had been shaped by European cultures – the Portuguese introduced Roman Catholicism when they arrived on the western coast in 1498, and the British subsequently introduced forms of Protestant and Anglican Christianities during the periods of the Company Rule (1757–1858) and the Crown Rule (1858–1947). Additionally, spurred on largely by the nineteenth-century development of cultural formations called the 'Bengal renaissance', and also resonating with the indigenization practices of much earlier figures such as the Roman Catholic missionary Roberto de Nobili (1577–1656), both Indian Christians and European missionaries actively practised and sometimes publicly advocated what would today be broadly referred to as styles of 'inculturated' Christianity. It is worth making explicit that the word 'inculturation' itself was not commonly used until the 1960s – approximately three decades after Jones had established STA – and so in this discussion I am retroactively applying the term to individuals and leaders of religious movements who would not have described themselves as consciously enacting 'inculturation'. However, I use it – sometimes interchangeably with 'indigenized' or 'Indianized' – as a short-hand expression for the actions and attitudes relating to these earlier attempts to interweave Christianity into Indic milieus through the use of cultural idioms and ritual practices that were common in various Indian contexts. The term that Jones himself eventually used for this process, as we shall see in Chapter 3, is 'naturalization'.[1] I do not know the extent of Jones's own awareness of the details of the diverse, and at times problematic, interactions between Christianity and Indian cultures; nonetheless, the aspects that I will outline of the historical interactions that Christianity has had with Indian cultures are highly significant, because, I argue, it is these details which influenced and shaped (even if only at a level of unconscious response) several of Jones's decisions with regards to the conceptualization and formation of STA. Consequently, to set the stage for Chapter 3, which explores Jones's founding visions for the ashram, the present chapter explores some of the historical trajectories of the presence of Christianity in India, and also contextualizes some of the key associations that the Indian public at large had developed about Christianity as a result of these historical interactions. In these trajectories, we can see several missionaries' attempts to bring Christian messages into Indian cultures; these approaches are important so as to be able to understand the unique, as well as the shared, aspects of Jones's own missiological approach.

More specifically, Section 2.2 summarizes some of the key interactions that two European powers – Portugal and Britain – have had with Syrian Christian communities, and then articulates the ways in which these interactions have broadly led to the perception of Christianity as a religion of foreigners. I first provide an introduction to the sociohistorical locations of Syrian Christian communities, and subsequently examine some of the ways that both the Portuguese and the British tried to apply corrective measures to Syrian Christian beliefs and practices. I also examine some of the policies and attitudes that these colonists adopted with regards to Hindu socioreligious institutions and practices. Though STA has next to no structural links with Syrian Christianity (I am only aware of a few photos and archival materials I came across, both at STA and at the E. Stanley Jones archives in Kentucky, which suggested that Jones had at least some social interactions with leaders of Syrian Christian churches), Syrian Christian communities are relevant for our consideration because they epitomize an early expression of indigenized Christianity. Indigenized Christianity, understood in its most broad terms, is precisely what Jones sought to offer through the creation of STA. Through examining the ways that the European colonial powers of Portugal and Britain interacted with

Syrian Christian communities, I demonstrate that the contested engagements surrounding Indian Christianity have an established long-standing history of being driven by European missionaries who, while interacting with certain Indianized expressions of Christianity, diagnosed these configurations as inauthentic, defective or just plainly erroneous, and consequently attempted to repair, reform and realign them with what the Europeans regarded as doctrinally orthodox. Through this study of some of the attitudes and actions of missionaries from both Portugal and Britain, we can see that these colonial powers implicitly – and sometimes explicitly – associated their own Christian beliefs and practices with the normative systems of European cultures. This section is not meant to be an exhaustive historical survey of the relationships between Christianity and Indians in the early precolonial centuries – though through it, I seek to provide adequate contexts which will help us to understand these interactions especially in the last three hundred years or so leading up to, and also shaping, the sociocultural contexts in which Jones would attempt his own styles of inculturation. Thus, it seeks to demonstrate that foreign missionaries in Indian contexts have often rejected and/or attempted to *normalize* the religious practices not only of non-Christians but also, crucially, of local Christians. I demonstrate that these frequent and calculated historical efforts to correct local expressions of Christianity feed into the public opinion within India, especially over the last two hundred years or so, that Christianity is a religion imported by foreigners; consequently, according to this view, Christianity ought to be associated not with an Indian identity but with a Western or European identity. As we shall see, these concepts are of the utmost relevance to STA.

Next, Section 2.3 focuses on some specific examples of Christian inculturation in India which predate the establishment of STA in 1930. I highlight certain aspects of indigenization attempted by several key individuals who are consistently referenced by scholars as having practised a form of Christianity that was understood by their Indian contemporaries themselves not as 'foreign' but as authentically 'Indian'. Some of the individuals whom I explore were foreign missionaries who intentionally sought to practise, and thereby inspire, a Christian lifestyle which did not stand out disjunctively from, but could rather seem to blend into, their local Indian cultural milieus. Other individuals whom I look at in this regard are Indians – many of whom were born into upper-caste Hindu families – who, upon learning more about Christianity, began to actively incorporate some Christian beliefs and practices into their Hindu world views, thereby blurring the lines of what some European missionaries had formerly conceptualized as a rigid dichotomy whereby one was *either*

Hindu *or* Christian. Their lifestyles and writings paved the way for broadening Christianity beyond its specifically Western expressions and, through concretely embodying and living out a Christianity that was steeped in Indian cultural idioms, they consequently challenged the notion that Christianity was to be exclusively associated with foreign cultures. But this establishment of an *Indianized* or *inculturated* Christianity was also, as I shall show towards the end of this chapter, heavily inflected by the sociocultural and political discourses of the early twentieth century that articulated, from some majoritarian Hindu nationalist perspectives, precisely what an Indian identity should look like and, accordingly, also the shape that an *Indianized* Christianity would have to take. Consequently, I argue that the types of inculturated Christianity that emerged in the early twentieth century were deeply influenced by the emerging notion that being Indian was to be associated not only with being Hindu but also with being a proponent of particular strands of Hinduism that contained specifically Brahmanical and Advaita Vedantic undertones. While Jones was inarguably interested in promoting Christianity, not Hinduism, it seems that he believed that Christianity would be successfully embraced if it became accented with, or decorated by, carefully selected strokes of Hinduism. In (unconsciously) embracing this specific expression of Hinduism as *the* way to be Indian, Jones himself, in his attempts to 'naturalize' Christianity, often ignored the diverse forms of Indianness that were being played out outside such Hindu contexts. The need to understand the diversity and multiplicity of Indianness, rather than adopting a monolithic understanding of Indian as Hindu, will be a key part of our discussions in Chapters 3 and 4.

There are two further sociopolitical realities which are so significant that it would be negligent on my part to leave them totally unaddressed in this discussion. I do not engage in detail with these because, for the most part, they post-date the establishment of STA while I am concerned primarily with the sociocultural and political influences leading up to Jones's founding of STA in 1930. However, they are important developments to keep in mind when exploring the questions of foreignness and inculturation, and they merit some discussion. First, the various practices of inculturation raised suspicions among some Vedantically oriented Hindu intellectuals, who accused Christian missionaries of being deceitful swindlers who were nefariously using the idioms of inculturation to harvest souls for Christ through conversions. We see such suspicions and accusations expressed, and responded to, in a series of letters exchanged between Bede Griffiths (a contemporary of Henri le Saux a.k.a. Swami Abhishiktananda who, along with Jules Monchanin, played a key role in establishing the well-known Saccidananda or Shantivanam (Christian) ashram in South India) and Swami Devananda in the late 1980s,[2] as well as a second series of letters exchanged between Griffiths and Ram Swarup around 1990.[3] In their respective correspondences, both Hindu men accusingly labelled Griffiths's and other Christians' blending of Hindu philosophies with Christian practices as an intentional act of trickery and deception, claiming that the Christians' primary concern was to gain converts at whatever cost. Such accusations drew from, and contributed to, the broader sociopolitical debates within India regarding the ethics of conversion – a debate which intensified when, in October 1999, Swami Dayananda Saraswati articulated his now well-known claim that conversion is 'an act of violence' which 'breeds violence' and should not be tolerated.[4] Second, the strong associations of inculturation with Vedantic philosophical thought and contemplative practices were also critiqued by some Dalit Christian theologians. Such theologians gained increased institutional momentum and political visibility from the 1980s onwards and asserted that 'Indianness' (and therefore inculturated Christianity) should not be predominantly or explicitly associated with Vedanta, as if Vedanta were the epitome of Indian culture. This array of Christian theological voices which rejected the association of Indianness with Vedanta (which are now collectively referred to as Dalit theology) emphasizes that Christianity should also reflect the cultural idioms and the subaltern experiences of socioeconomic marginalization of the Dalits, rather than focus predominantly on Brahmanical forms of life.[5] Among these figures are Arvind P. Nirmal (North India) and Vedanayagam Devasahayam (South India) who have popularized the articulations of Dalit theology and are responsible for writing some of its most influential texts.[6] I will return, in slightly greater detail, to the impact that Dalit theology has had on styles of Indian Christianity in Chapter 4 when I discuss the shifts that occurred at STA with the formation of the SoE in the 1990s. At this point in our exploration, this brief discussion of these two significant disputes relating to the normative visions of Hindu identity will have to suffice.

Due to spanning the massive temporal period between 52 CE and the present day, this historical overview of the interactions between Christianity and Indian locales, including the subfield of Indian Christianity, will be an outline of certain distinctive phases. More nuanced explorations of these historical interactions can be found in the magisterial study of Robert Eric Frykenberg,[7] the multiple volumes on the history of Christianity in India published by the Church History Association of India,[8] as well as the works of other scholars of Indian Christianity – many of whom I refer to throughout this chapter. There are also several works which have mapped out the terrain of Christian missionary activity in India.[9] The contents of the subsequent chapters – which focus respectively on Jones's visions for STA in 1930 (Chapter 3); the ways that in the 1990s STA began to develop programmes aimed at new converts to Christianity (Chapter 4); and how the leaders of STA interacted with the WA group in the early 2000s (Chapter 5) – make it especially important for us to understand these competing identities of Christianity as "foreign" and as "inculturated," for these seemingly opposite identities crucially undergird the ethos of STA.

2.2 Associating Christianity with foreignness

2.2.1 The Syrian Christians of India: Their origins and practices

The history of Syrian Christians is documented in detail in various comprehensive and well-written monographs, as well as in numerous volumes on the history of Christianity in India.[10] A brief introduction to the Syrian Christians' origins and socio-ritual practices will provide us with the necessary materials with which to explore the ways that colonial powers and foreign missionaries later interacted with Syrian Christian communities and imperiously sought to establish their own expressions of Christianity as superior to, or more accurate than, those of Syrian Christians, thereby setting in motion certain processes that would later generate the notion that Christianity is a religion of foreigners. When the Portuguese and the British came to India, they brought with them different expressions of Christianity (Roman Catholic Christianity and Protestant or Anglican Christianity, respectively) which, to varying degrees, they endeavoured to impress upon Hindus and other non-Christian individuals, thereby forming communities of converts. But, even more importantly, they used their own expressions of Christianity as a measuring stick with which they normatively assessed, and sought to regulate, the beliefs and practices of both the already existing Syrian Christian communities and the other Indians who had recently converted to their form of Christianity.

During the first fourteen centuries or so of their existence, Syrian Christians grew in numbers not by conversion but rather by reaping the benefits of being a relatively wealthy and well-respected, and therefore socially comfortable, caste-based community whose members were able to consistently reproduce. Though the bulk of their population, to this day, continues to live in present-day Kerala, Syrian Christians did occasionally migrate to other parts of India and expand their ecclesiastical boundaries, as is evidenced by the records which document details such as the number of churches that they constructed in those parts or the different sorts of honours that were given to them, such as the copper plates which were issued by the ruler of Kollam (in Kerala) in 849 CE and which contain some of the most important historical inscriptions regarding Kerala.[11] Syrian Christians share a number of rituals with Brahmanical Hindus, including various rites of passage relating to birth, coming of age, marriage and death, as well as some beliefs and social exclusivities with regards to untouchability and other pollution rituals.[12] It is possible that some Syrian Christians inherited or adopted these wider Hindu classifications of social hierarchy and sought to maintain the status symbols of their upper-caste Hindu neighbours. There is some evidence which demonstrates that they also maintained the upper-caste practice of regarding individuals from the lower castes as ritually impure: for instance, individuals from the lower castes were traditionally not allowed to enter Syrian Christian households.[13] Keeping in mind these resemblances to Brahmanical Hinduism, we can turn now to the ways that European powers interacted during their colonial rules with the Syrian Christians.

2.2.2 The Portuguese colonial influences in Goa

In 1498, some Portuguese Catholic Christians, under their captain Vasco da Gama, arrived at Kozhikode (Calicut) in Kerala. Vasco da Gama incorrectly deemed a local Hindu temple (most likely a Kali temple) to be a Christian place of worship. Scholars have speculated that the devotees at this temple might have been calling out either '*Maari*' (a name of the goddess Kali) or '*Maaṛi*' ('get out of the way'), an invocation which da Gama and his men presumably heard as 'Mary' and interpreted to mean that the people were worshipping the Virgin Mary. Thus, da Gama, too, began to show reverence and instructed his men to join him in worshipping the Virgin there.[14] Da Gama's error of judgement has been documented and explored by a number of scholars, and fuller accounts of it can be found elsewhere.[15] In brief, da Gama not only incorrectly assumed that the Hindu men they encountered were Christians but he also mistook the temple, the religious statues and the practices of worship as being of a Christian provenance. I suggest that there are at least three distinct possible explanations for his error: first, he was simply not intelligent enough to discern significant differences – but this is rather unlikely, given his high rank and responsibilities; second, he was aware that the religious place was not Christian but, for some reason, deviously led his men to believe that it was a Christian place; third, it never occurred to him that there might, in fact, be a deity or a place of worship which was other than, and historically disconnected with, Christianity. I take the third scenario to be the most likely explanation – especially since one must bear in mind that da Gama possessed no language skills vis-à-vis the Indic vernaculars, had very limited foreknowledge of the cultural worlds he was venturing into (for instance, the Portuguese believed that the three biblical Magi came from India, and they did not have any substantial knowledge about India other than a report that the Indians were Christians[16]) and after his long journey of several months at sea he might have had a certain measure of the Portuguese sentiment of '*saudade*' – an aching and longing for the familiar. This nostalgia, even if only at some subconscious level, could have deeply affected his interpretation of the scenes he was met with upon arriving on Indian soil.

This third possible explanation of da Gama's error has also been put forward by Alexander Henn, who suggests that the Portuguese Christians were slow to recognize expressions of Hinduism as being independent of Christianity because they failed to truly see the differences, which they perceived as nothing other than distorted forms of Christian spirituality. Henn explains, 'Ironically, this recognition [i.e. of non-Christian religions such as Hinduism] was delayed in the early-modern period not because the gentiles were, as was done later in classical modernity, conceived as the radical and racial Other, but because they were perceived as hidden and distorted forms of the religious Self.'[17] If we explore this dialectic of the Other as a thinly veiled replica of the Same, then da Gama's apparent embracing of Hindu expressions of spirituality, which he viewed through his Catholic prisms of Marian devotion, is not an example of religious pluralism and tolerance for other religious views understood in the sense of respecting the Other in its Otherness. Rather, it is an exemplary case study of what might happen when one encounters an expression of genuine difference for which our existing world view has not prepared us. In such cases, precisely the glaring differences could paradoxically become oblivious to us because of our cognitive blind spots. Henn summarizes this encounter thus: 'In simpler terms, the problem was how to acknowledge a religion other than Christianity if, by scholastic definition and orthodox belief, Christianity was the only religion or "Truth" possible.'[18] After all, we are inclined – or, if I can be more assertive and speak with Kantian vocabularies, we are primed – to categorically interpret the world only through the experiential and conceptual frameworks that we already have within our grasp. Recently, scholars in the fields of psychiatry and neuroscience too have confirmed that even the most basic elements of human vision (i.e. literal sight) are performed by a 'predictive brain', which takes in those elements of reality that, based on prior experiences, it 'expects' to see in the first place, while effectively blocking out any elements that are unexpected.[19] This biological model of inevitably limited perceptions which are based on former life experiences on European landscapes plays out, on more ethnographic terrain, in da Gama's experience of the individuals whom he 'saw' as Christians at the temple in Kozhikode. In other words, da Gama could not *truly* see the Hindus as anything other than (alternative or covert forms of) Christians, because his former experiences had not prepared or enabled him to envision that anyone other than Christians existed. To borrow the words of Jesus: though 'seeing', da Gama 'saw not'.[20]

It can be interesting to probe deeper into the questions of *how* and *why* da Gama managed to confuse a Hindu community for a Christian one – Henn skilfully prompts his readers to undertake this reflection by guiding them through a range of scholarship which contains substantially different viewpoints on the topic.[21] However, for our purposes, I am more interested in examining how this initial interaction compares to the subsequent interactions that the Portuguese had with religious communities in India.[22] Assuming that da Gama did earnestly believe that the individuals at the temple were practising some form of Christianity, it is noteworthy that his initial response was to join them in worshipping the Virgin Mary (or, at least he assumed that he was joining them in a *Christian* act of worship) rather than to either keep his distance from a practice that seemed to be an utterly distorted form of Christian worship or to vehemently denounce it as infernal or heathenish and in need of refinement and correction. Indeed, while it may be true that da Gama's seeming acceptance of what he encountered was not, in fact, a conscious embracing of Hindu religious practices as understood by Hindus themselves, it still suggests that he was willing to participate in a style of Christian worship that looked remarkably different from his own. Thus, taking a line of analysis different from Henn, my crucial point is this: the fact that da Gama wrongly envisioned the Kozhikode *temple* as a *Christian* place of worship *also* suggests that he possessed some degree of existential and conceptual openness (no matter how ill-informed) towards different ways of practising Christianity. This initial display of openness – no matter that it arose from incorrect assumptions – is particularly interesting because, as I shall demonstrate, the Portuguese did *not* later maintain such hospitality towards doctrinal and ritual expressions of Christianity which appeared to be different from their own.

As time progressed and as the Portuguese colonial presence in India strengthened, it was not just that the Portuguese eventually began to focus on changing the beliefs and practices of the Syrian Christians in India so as to more closely align them with the ways their own Roman Catholicism was practised; indeed, they first went to great lengths to convert Hindus[23] to Roman Catholicism. In 1517, a large group of Franciscans arrived in Goa and, shortly after their arrival, they baptized eight hundred Hindus in the name of Christ; an entire Indian village converted to Christianity in 1524; and by 1539 conversions to Christianity had increased significantly, resulting in a number of villages with Christian churches or chapels.[24] In these earliest years of their colonial presence, the Portuguese methods of conversion were notably less aggressive than what was to come later – they first relied upon 'taking over the care of orphans and using a system of privileges to attract adherents to the faith'.[25] It was only around 1540, Rowena Robinson notes, that these Portuguese Catholics sought to eradicate Hindu culture and Hindu socioreligious existence through launching a campaign against Hindu images, destroying Hindu temples and banning Hindus (particularly the higher-caste *gauncars* – that is, rulers who claimed to be the original inhabitants of the villages – and the priests) from performing religious rites.[26] Expanding upon Robinson's scholarship, Henn has compiled, in substantial detail, the many effective yet subtle ways in which Catholic authorities went about with their 'ferocious iconoclastic campaign against Hindu culture in India'.[27] In the 1540s, evangelization efforts in Goa were augmented by official initiatives such as the Portuguese government's offer to give benefits to missionaries who were able to secure a certain number of Hindu converts to Christianity.[28] At the same time that some conversion efforts were becoming more targeted and forceful, in 1543 the Jesuits established a seminary in Goa in which approximately six hundred male students were taught reading, writing, grammar and catechism.[29] This establishment was possibly a reflection of the Jesuit critique of other European priests who were said to have baptized converts without properly ensuring that they had first received proper catechetical instruction in the ways of the church.[30]

However, no number of Jesuit seminaries and educational efforts could counteract the fact that the Portuguese were already gaining a widespread reputation for fiercely imposing their viewpoints of orthodox Christian belief and practices on the Hindu social forms which they encountered. Contextualizing the eventual use by the Portuguese of more persistent and forceful tactics, Henn provides an overview of the specific ways in which early-modern Christians often violently enforced their religious viewpoints in various cultural contexts in Asia; notable in this regard are the Roman Catholic Church's official stance which banned all forms of *accomodatio* (literally 'accommodating' or tolerating indigenous forms of Christianity) and, in particular, the authoritative doctrinal statements of the Council of Trent (1545–63), which put forth several mandates which explicitly targeted those who were deemed by the Council to have too much overlap with non-Christian forms of religiosity.[31]

It is important for our discussion here to explicitly note that many of the Portuguese Catholics' corrective actions concerning religious beliefs and practices were not focused exclusively on individuals without long-standing commitments to Christian communities (including Hindus outside of Christianity[32] along with those Hindus who had recently converted to Christianity[33]); rather they were additionally focused specifically on the Syrian Christians. An intense scrutiny of religious beliefs and practices, and subsequent attempts at regulation, were carried out by the Portuguese Catholics when interacting with Syrian Christians from the sixteenth century onwards. Through the regulations stipulated at the Synod of Diamper (a diocesan council convened by the Latin rite Catholic Archbishop of Goa in 1599), the Portuguese exerted direct power over Syrian Christians during their age of sociopolitical influence in Goa. The social and religious effects of these regulations are noted by L. W. Brown in his detailed historical narrative, which documents the many ways in which the Portuguese tried to implement their normative understanding of orthodox Christian belief and practice within Syrian Christian contexts – which entailed, first and foremost, adhering to the teachings of the Pope.[34] The Portuguese were quite meticulous and thorough with regards to stipulating the precise ways to believe in, and follow, the one true Christian God; and they wanted to correct (more precisely, to eliminate) the broadly Hindu spiritual notions such as *karma*, *dharma* and others that the Syrian Christians had incorporated into their own Christian practices.[35] To this end, the Portuguese demanded of the Syrian Christians that they present all their spiritual books to the Portuguese for correction. They sought to remove all influences and traces of the wider milieus of Hinduism from these texts, and if they could not be emended, the texts were destroyed.[36] During the Inquisition in Goa (which was established in 1560 and which lasted until 1623) approximately '3,800 cases were tried by the Holy Office in Goa, or almost exactly sixty in a year'.[37] The precise details of the Inquisition (specifically how many individuals were executed and/or died in imprisonment) are not known, since all records have been destroyed.[38] While, as Robinson has demonstrated, it is impossible to fully disentangle the *political* and *religious* threads with regards to the Portuguese motivations for, and methods of, conversion,[39] it is undeniable that the Portuguese authoritarian presence involved a thorough and powerful governing of the religious beliefs and actions of Indians – Hindu and Christian alike.

Widespread discontent with such Portuguese attempts to regulate and govern their own activities and beliefs led many leaders within Syrian Christian communities to take a famous oath in 1653 (the Coonan Cross Oath), vowing to no longer show ecclesiastical obedience to the Pope, to expel all the Portuguese Jesuits from their communities and to follow bishops only from an Eastern Orthodox church.[40] Around twenty-five thousand Syrian Christians are estimated to have taken this oath.[41] This refusal to follow the Roman Catholic Church culminated in a meeting between the Portuguese and the Syrian Christian communities on 23 September 1657 where the two parties discussed the extent to which they felt that Roman Catholic archbishops should be obeyed or have any spiritual authority over the Syrian Christian communities. Consequently, the Portuguese intensified their efforts to bring the Syrian Christian communities into obedience to Rome, and on 22 August 1661 Bishop Joseph succeeded in bringing eighty-four parishes back to communion with Rome – though thirty-two parishes remained without formal obedience to the Pope.[42] Despite the fact that Roberto de Nobili (1577–1656) (an Italian Jesuit, whose allegiance – like the Portuguese – was also to Roman religious authorities, and whom we shall return to below) was advocating, around this time, the acceptance and incorporation of Hindu cultural expressions into his Christian beliefs, practices and preaching, the Portuguese generally rejected these displays of tolerance and consistently attempted to rectify the practices of the Syrian Orthodox communities and to bring them into line with what they deemed to be orthodox.[43]

2.2.3 The British Raj

When the Dutch took over Cochin in 1663, they ordered all other foreign (especially Portuguese) priests and monks to leave the country.[44] However, the period during which the Dutch maintained their power within India is not well documented and the existing sources make it very difficult for historians to gain an understanding of what actually happened.[45] Consequently, we move on to the more extensively recorded and studied interactions between Britons and Indians, roughly between 1800 and 1947, which were also decisive in producing and entrenching a widespread perception that Christianity is a religion of foreigners. The initial split between 'our' Christianity and 'their' Christianity that had opened up in the course of the Portuguese efforts to cast local Indian practices into moulds of Catholic orthodoxy only widened, as we will see, in some of these Indo-British exchanges.

Active proselytization was not an initial feature of British interactions with Indians; most British individuals living in India in the eighteenth century refrained from making any explicit corrections of the doctrines and practices they observed within Syrian Christian communities, and they instead focused their attention on more implicit styles. However, this stance of tolerance began to shift around 1813, when the original East India Company's charter (issued by Queen Elizabeth I on 31 December 1600) was revisited and reworked: a clause was added, which stated that provisions should be made to help people wishing to go to India for the 'religious and moral improvement' of the Indians. Even though any explicit reference to missionaries was avoided,[46] we can note a clear shift in what was deemed to be an acceptable way of interacting with the religious practices of Indians – these were deemed to require moral 'improvement'. Though this wording was an implicit, rather than an explicit, acceptance of missionaries who would be engaged in active proselytization, it was still originally greeted with hostility by British administrators such as Thomas Grenville who declared, 'We are conquerors in India, and I do not like to see a regiment of missionaries acting under and with the authority of unrestricted power.'[47] Such administrators tended to view missionaries as troublesome meddlers who disturbed the local peace and generated social unrest. Even after missionaries became a more visible presence on the sociocultural landscapes of British India, some British missionaries consciously maintained a distinction between active proselytization and other social reformist activities which were focused on improving the everyday livelihoods of Indians. For example, Barbara Ramusack explores the social activism of five British women who lived in India from 1865 to 1945. While Ramusack describes these women as 'cultural missionaries' who often sought to promote Western-European cultural ideas concerning subjectivities like female modesty in the course of enacting their primary goal of educating Indian girls and women, she emphasizes that even those women who held strong Christian convictions consciously refrained from proselytization in order to secure and maintain their position as trusted educators.[48]

Notwithstanding the somewhat lukewarm attitude of the British Government in India towards the active proselytization of the Indians, the rise of British Christian missionary organizations at home corresponded broadly with an intensification of the evangelical attitudes of some Protestant groups in England during the nineteenth century.[49] An early figure in this connection was the English missionary called Thomas Norton from the Society of Asia who arrived in India in 1816.⁵⁰ Norton and his British contemporaries (especially important was Thomas Munro, governor of Madras) were very interested in, and no doubt pleased by, the presence of the Syrian Christians, since the existence of such a long-standing Indian Christian community seemed to prove that Christianity could flourish, and sustain itself, within Indian environments. While the Portuguese had utilized fairly overt forms of correction with regards to the doctrines and the practices of the Syrian Christian communities, Norton and Munro professed that they did not want to directly change the conceptual and experiential forms of Syrian Christianity. They were, in fact, quite interested in preserving the language and the liturgical tradition of the Syrian Christians, and they only sought to strengthen the governance structure of the Syrian Church. In order to ensure that they had the power to authoritatively guide and overrule any decisions made by the Syrian Christian leadership, Norton and Munro strategically placed themselves at the top of the structure; the Syrian Christians were, however, allowed to keep the public seats of power.⁵¹

Towards the second half of the nineteenth century, some British missionaries began to develop stronger measures to explicitly correct the various aspects of Syrian Christianity that they regarded as spiritually erroneous. Brown offers the example of Joseph Peet, an Anglican priest, who between 1833 and 1835 vocally opposed the ways that Syrian Christians in Kerala observed rules of religious purity. Peet not only preached against their observance of such purity laws in socioreligious contexts but also deliberately attempted to defile their purity by touching them after they had completed their ritual washing in preparation for a religious feast. Commenting on Peet's public efforts to stridently eradicate aspects of Indian Christian practices that did not align with Anglican Christian cultural norms, Brown writes that 'there were many such incidents and while they may be deplored as discourteous and unwise it has to be recognised that the missionaries had become convinced that silence on their part would be, in fact, a denial of fundamental Christian truth'.⁵²

Christian convictions similar to those of Peet can be seen around the same time in places like Bengal, where some British individuals consciously steered away from an appreciation of Indian languages, customs and philosophical traditions which had been more common around 1780–1800, and instead dismissed them as primitive, heathenish and corrupt. Some others actively sought to alter Indian customs through administrative interventions.⁵³ From roughly the 1830s onwards, a number of British administrators and policymakers, along with the British Baptist missionaries who lived in Serampore, Bengal (Julius Lipner names William Carey, Joshua Marshman and William Ward as the

'British Baptist trio'), played a pivotal role in promoting English education for Bengalis which, Lipner explains, included 'not only the teaching of English but also the infusion of western ideas along English lines'.[54] Thomas Macaulay's now infamous 'Minute on Education', written in 1835, illustrates the ways in which some administrators believed that they should Anglicize Indians not only for the presumed benefits that would accrue to the Indians themselves but also for the strategic goals of the British colonists who could employ the Western-educated Indians as interpreters. Macaulay notoriously articulated his disdain for Indian literature and culture by succinctly declaring that 'a single shelf of a good European library was worth the whole native literature of India and Arabia'.[55]

This contempt for Indian culture and heritage in the 1830s was a remarkable shift from the effervescent 'Indomania' that had flowed through some British circles roughly five decades earlier, when some civil servants who had arrived in Calcutta around 1780 had developed Orientalist scholarship, which J. J. Clarke describes as being extremely influential with regards to the British gaining a deep understanding of, and also a sensitive appreciation for, Indian customs and traditions.[56] R. Schwab has referred to this intense production of knowledges of the Orient as 'the decisive period in Indic studies'.[57] Around this time, in 1785, the British Governor General Warren Hastings unhesitatingly declared the *Bhagavad Gita* to be 'a performance of great originality, of a sublimity of conception, reasoning and diction, almost unequalled; and a single exception, among all the known religions of mankind, of a theology accurately corresponding with that of the Christian dispensation, and most powerfully illustrating its fundamental doctrines'.[58]

We must therefore ask: What are the structural explanations which could account for this somewhat dramatic shift from a seemingly genuine admiration for, and even tolerance of, Indian (and specifically Hindu) texts and traditions, to an intense 'Indophobia' where a number of British colonial administrators actively sought to overturn the prevalence of Hindu traditions within Indian societies? Peter van der Veer has suggested that these earlier appreciative attitudes of British colonial officials, who had valued Indian knowledges, languages, philosophy and so on, were replaced by an imperial desire to rule and administer India. As the British Self – posited as rational, progressive and spiritual – began to carefully distance itself from its Indian Other – now projected by the British as irrational, reactionary and heathenish – it aimed at actively uplifting Indians through education. In this context, drawing upon the Saidian scholarship of Gauri Viswanathan, van der Veer argues that education became 'religion's primary instrument for conversion and expansion' during the early twentieth century.⁵⁹ While van der Veer concentrates his study primarily on South India, we see a similar development in Bengal around the same time: Baptist missionaries – even those who learned, and published in, Bengali – equally sought to utilize their roles as educators to convey Western values and forms of Christianity and, ultimately, to supplant existing Hindu ones during the first three decades of the nineteenth century. Lipner makes it clear that such missionaries 'deplored Hinduism and its cultural expressions. They subscribed to the view that contemporary Hinduism was socially, morally and theologically irredeemable'.⁶⁰ Some British officials also consistently sought to remove Hindu traditions and practices from public spheres in India. There were several strong displays of 'anti-Hindu rhetoric' which took the form of public protests by Christian Evangelicals in Britain who, starting from around 1817, demanded that the British government in India cease its support of Hindu institutions.⁶¹ For instance, Lord Bentinck (governor general of India, 1828–35) used his political influence to develop several policies which propelled the governing structure towards the conscious modernization of Indian societies.⁶² And, as Richard King (grounding his own argument in Edward Said's *Orientalism*) has so clearly articulated, modernization and Westernization cannot be neatly separated from each other because "'modernity" is intrinsically bound up with the European Enlightenment project. Thus, despite the claimed cultural and political neutrality of the language of "modernization" … [the Orientalists'] methods, goals and underlying values presupposed the supremacy of European culture'. This Eurocentric framework remained operative, King argues, even when European missionaries 'appeared to be promoting the vernacular and the indigenous'.⁶³ We can apply this Eurocentric dismissal of all things culturally Indian not only to some British officials' treatment of Hindus but also of those Indian Christians who seemed to remain too closely tied to Hindu cultural idioms.

In these various ways, we see that – in the case of both Portuguese and British colonial rules – foreign powers frequently deemed various expressions of Indian Christianity to be doctrinally incorrect – indeed, to be *too Indian* – and thus sought to correct them by aligning them more closely with European Christianity. We discussed the ways in which both the Portuguese and the British often endeavoured to establish themselves as the corrective authority which would domesticate the Otherness of the Syrian Christian communities and, more generally, to replace Hindu-inflected beliefs and practices with ones that were more congruent with the respective European Christianities that they held as doctrinally normative. Often, this normalization through colonial power resulted in strategically banning and intentionally eliminating the forms of knowledge which were deemed to be too closely linked to Hinduism. The cumulative result of these interactions is that Christianity gradually gained a reputation in various Indian circles as being associated both with foreign colonial powers and with Western cultures.

2.3 Expressions of inculturated Christianity before STA (pre-1930)

It is against this backdrop of perceptions, representations and images of foreignness that expressions of inculturated Christianity began to emerge from around the turn of the twentieth century. Accordingly, this section moves the focus away from the ways that the Portuguese and the British interacted with various indigenous expressions of Christianity and instead studies specific individuals and institutions enacting and embodying forms of Indianized or inculturated Christianity. Contrary to the passionate statements made by some of Jones's friends and family members who describe him as a great pioneer of inculturation and the founder of Christian ashrams in a more general sense, Jones was not by any means the first to conceptualize and inspire the practices of Christians who sought to live out their faith in cultural forms that would be familiar to (Brahmanical) Hindus. In this exploration of figures of inculturation before Jones, I have included Roberto de Nobili (1577–1656), who came to India from Europe as a missionary, but I consciously limit my discussion of foreign missionaries to him: he is a notable forerunner of indigenization and earns a place in this necessarily brief overview. American missionaries such as John Newton Foreman, Morley Hartley and Samuel (Satyananda[64]) Stokes, among others, who desired to indigenize Christianity in India, are explored in further detail elsewhere.[65] Following my sketch of de Nobili, I focus on two paradigmatic Indians: Brahmabandhab Upadhyay (1861–1907) and Pandita Ramabai (1858–1922). Both of them are also notable forerunners to Jones in imagining, forging and enacting lifestyles that were both doctrinally Christian and culturally Indian; Upadhyay is often recognized as the quintessential Indian figure of indigenization, while Ramabai holds a special place in the context of STA since she is recognized there as a model of Indian Christianity. Sadhu Sundar Singh[66] is another well-known figure of inculturation,[67] and Paul Collins also draws our attention to three Christian priests – Thomas Palackal, Thomas Porukara and Kuriakos Elias – all of whom began to live as ascetics (*sannyasis*) in 1831.[68] There were also some contemporaneous Indian (Protestant) Christian pioneers of inculturation such as A. J. Appasamy, V. Chakkarai and P. Chenchiah who were developing Indianized theologies of Christ.[69] In addition to the lives of de Nobili, Upadhyay and Ramabai, there are also several examples of Christian ashrams that predate the establishment of STA in 1930, and I indicate these below.

In highlighting the many charismatic individuals and institutional efforts which were precursors, with their distinctive missiological methods, of Jones's efforts at inculturation, I do not, however, mean to undermine or belittle the transformative effects that his visions and efforts had on Indianizing the Christian message. To the contrary, I seek to indicate that he contributed significantly to the extensive narratives of indigenization generated by some Christians who had gone before him, and who probably also inspired him at some level. In doing so, he played a crucial role in developing the motifs and the processes of inculturation already present in the pre-Vatican II era. Furthermore, most crucially, as Jones actively sought to create a Christian community which was 'both truly Christian and truly Indian', he operated within the sociocultural contexts created by these forerunners. Importantly, as Chapter 3 shall demonstrate, many of Jones's views relating to what it meant to be 'truly Indian' while being 'truly Christian' echoed the sentiments expressed by these pioneers of inculturation before him. The extent to which Jones consciously inherited their discourses is not known, but, I speculate, the Indian Christian communities and the Hindu societies at large with which Jones interacted would have been informed and shaped by these earlier practices of inculturation. We now turn to some of these individuals who creatively wove together the fabrics of Christian beliefs and practices with Indian cultural expressions.

2.3.1 Roberto de Nobili

When Roberto de Nobili (1577–1656) arrived in South India in 1605, he noted that in nearly eleven years of missionary work, his predecessor Father Fernandes 'had not been able to win to the faith a single high-caste Hindu'.[70] As time went on, de Nobili gradually learned that many aspects of their lifestyles that the Portuguese Christians enacted without much thought or consideration – wearing leather, eating meat, drinking alcohol and so on – were in fact perceived as abominable by high-caste Hindus. This ritualized distaste was not something that Fernandes had ever registered, because he had conceptualized Europeans (especially the Portuguese) as occupying the superior social position with regards to Indians, and he further believed that Christianity was superior to

Hindu Brahmanism.⁷¹ Deeply desiring to welcome high-caste Hindus into the folds of the Roman Catholic faith, however, de Nobili began an experiment in indigenization: Could he adopt a way of life that was acceptable to his high-caste Hindu neighbours, in order to rid them of the prejudices they had developed of Christians? This experiment would involve, among other things, ceasing to interact with Indians from the lower castes in order to maintain his ritual purity in the eyes of the Brahmins. De Nobili also became conversant in some Indian languages (Sanskrit and Tamil), wore the orange robes of a Hindu ascetic and wrote vigorously about the merits of Indian culture and 'the legitimacy of treating it with the same respect afforded to the cultures of ancient Rome and Greece'.⁷² Each of these styles of accommodations – though they were met with varying degrees of success – are early examples of a Christian priest intentionally adopting elements from Indian (specifically, Brahmanical Hindu) cultures in order to be seen as more acceptable and inviting to high-caste Hindus. Even though, as Francis Clooney has pointed out, de Nobili's earliest writings show that he was lacking 'in sympathy for the traditions under consideration and [was] evidently unable to read sympathetically the practices of another tradition'⁷³, de Nobili's interest in, and willingness to, embrace and enact certain idioms of Hindu culture in order to be more effectively at preaching the Christian gospel is a notable early example of inculturation.

2.3.2 Brahmabandhab Upadhyay

We now turn to Brahmabandhab Upadhyay (1861–1907), whom Lipner has described as having made a 'pioneering attempt to Indianize Christianity'⁷⁴ and who is often depicted as an exemplary model of indigenized Christianity. Upadhyay was born in Calcutta (Kolkata) and sought to live out the ideals of an ascetic.⁷⁵ Upon converting to Catholicism, he continued to identify as a Hindu because he understood Hindu *dharmic* teachings to be fully compatible with Catholic doctrine. Importantly, Upadhyay was attracted to certain Catholic doctrines more than to the institutionalized hierarchies of Catholic communities – he argued that, while Catholic teachings were inspired by God, they had been warped by the inherited ecclesiastical traditions of the Catholic Church.⁷⁶ Upadhyay therefore wished to take the teachings of Catholicism and dress them in 'Hindu garments', and his primary allegiance remained to Catholic teachings about Christ rather than to the institutional structures of the Catholic Church.⁷⁷ Interestingly, Lipner argues that Upadhyay did *not* simply seek to 'implant Christian concepts in Vedantic soil' but instead sought to construct 'more or less exact correspondences between Vedantic ideas and Thomistic ones so that Vedanta in some respects may be seen as a form of crypto-(neo-)Thomism and Shankara as St Thomas in disguise. This is a mode of transplantation, not of implantation'.[78] Lipner elaborates upon how Upadhyay sought 'to show that the *sat, cit,* and *ānanda* of classical Vedanta as a description of ultimate reality corresponded more or less exactly to the understanding of the nature of God of Catholic *natural* [sic] theology, that is, neo-Thomistic reasoning about the essence of the divine being'.[79] According to Lipner's reading of Upadhyay, then, any discussion of Upadhyay in the contexts of inculturation should be shaped by the understanding that Upadhyay himself might have resisted a notion that is implicit in some definitions of inculturation – that one religion (Christianity, in this case) could be shifted to a different culture beyond its European epicentre, and, with time, would take on certain new attributes and aspects in that new culture. In contrast to the claim that European Christianity was being transplanted *into* Indic soils, Upadhyay – at least at certain points in his own journey which are recorded in his writings – viewed Vedanta as a veiled form of Thomism and thus already containing Catholic truth. In other words, some quintessence of Christianity, no matter how obscured, had always been present in India; any expression of Christianity which was clothed with distinctively Indic cultural idioms was therefore not altogether new.

Of course, Upadhyay was theologizing in a context before Said and other postcolonial scholars from the 1970s and 1980s, whose sound critiques of the power dynamics with which Orientalism operates forced subsequent scholarship to reconsider any assertions that two distinctive religions are, more or less, the same (or at least challenged the tendency of making such identity-claims too hastily). This historical location places Upadhyay in a camp rather different from present-day comparative theologians like Francis Clooney,[80] Michelle Voss Roberts[81] and others who so beautifully look to two distinct traditions with the hope that one will shed light on the other while maintaining and preserving the distinctive features of both traditions. It should also be noted that Upadhyay was not focused on the generalized categories of *Christianity* and *Hinduism* but, more specifically, on *Roman Catholicism* and *Advaita Vedanta*, and his terminologies frequently reflect this relatively narrow focus.

All this to say that Upadhyay's passionate interest in both Roman Catholicism and Advaita led him to live a lifestyle which embraced a hybrid combination of both Christian and Hindu teachings and practices – he actively sought to combat the notion that Christianity was exclusively a religion of foreigners and was necessarily packaged with the trappings of European cultures. Upadhyay's rejection of the foreignness of Christianity is further seen, quite unambiguously, in his plea that Christian preachers consciously refrain from doing anything that might further reinforce the perception that Christianity was a religion of foreigners and a destroyer of the Indian cultures. Along these lines, in 1894 Upadhyay wrote that 'the itinerant missionaries should be thoroughly Hindu in their mode of living. They should, if necessary, be strict vegetarians and teetotalers and put on the yellow *sannyasi* garb…The missionaries should be well-versed in Sanskrit, for one ignorant of Sanskrit will hardly be able to vanquish Hindu preachers'.[82] And, a few years later, Upadhyay wrote that the Catholic Church must find a way to 'make Hindu philosophy hew wood and draw water for her', by which he implied that Hindu philosophies would offer conceptual tools which Christianity needed in order to flourish in Indian contexts.[83] Reiterating this conviction, Upadhyay wrote in 1898 that 'it is the *sannyasi* alone who is capable of presenting to our countrymen the mysteries of the Catholic faith'.[84] As much as Upadhyay felt that the habit of the *sannyasi* should be worn by Catholic missionaries who wished to communicate their faith, he also advocated for a metaphorical 'dressing' in which Catholicism is consciously 'donned' not in 'European garb' and 'alien dress' (which, Upadhyay asserts, 'repels [his Indian] countrymen') but in a 'Hindu garment' in order to be 'acceptable to the Hindus'. That is, the missionaries should present a Catholicism that is deeply imbued with the cultural idioms that would resonate with (Vedantic) Hindu experiences.[85]

2.3.3 Pandita Ramabai

Pandita Ramabai (1858–1922), whose photographed portrait hangs in one of the main rooms of STA, is embraced and eulogized there as a figure who did not abandon her Indian cultural identity while embracing the salvific doctrine of Christianity in which Jesus Christ is regarded as the unique means of spiritual transformation, salvation and redemption.[86] Because of the ways she is revered within the spaces of STA as well as is championed more widely as an exemplar of inculturation and also as a notable Indian Christian woman, her religious narrative merits some discussion.

Ramabai grew up in a Brahmin family where she was exposed to very traditional forms of Hinduism. Her father was well versed in Sanskrit and Ramabai learned to read Sanskrit at a young age. Not fully satisfied with the forms of Hinduism she had been exposed to through her childhood upbringing, Ramabai later sought out the teachings of the Brahmo Samaj in Calcutta before being exposed to Christianity there. The Christianity she encountered initially seemed utterly foreign to her, and she struggled to understand how Indians could embrace such a distant religion. In spite of this distaste, she was deeply drawn to the very active engagement of some Christians with social justice projects and especially their caring for widows and orphans. When Ramabai began to notice the everyday forms of suffering around her, she simultaneously observed that Christians seemed to show more mercy to the sufferers than did her fellow-Hindus; indeed, Ramabai concluded that Christianity as a religious system responded more humanely to suffering than did Hinduism.[87] Consequently, Ramabai began to understand Jesus to be someone who broke through social barriers and crossed cultural boundaries in order to serve people with goodness and kindness; she was particularly struck by stories within the Christian scriptures in which Jesus shows a desire to help those who had sinned, and moves beyond his society's boundaries in order to conduct acts of service towards those who were less fortunate. This sort of context-specific and scripturally rooted understanding of God's restoration of people who have been hurt, oppressed, marginalized or mistreated through their social systems would later become a prominent feature of Dalit theology, as we will see in Chapter 4.[88] In 1883, Ramabai set sail for England and was introduced to the work of the Sisters of the Community of St Mary the Virgin among the sick and infirm women in London. Prompted to thus reflect on the condition of such women in Hindu society, and in the light of her reading of John's Gospel, she became convinced that Christ was the Saviour who could 'transform and uplift the downtrodden womanhood of India and of every land'.[89] Inspired by such Christian teachings, Ramabai soon opened a girl's home (the Sharada Sadan or 'Home of Learning') for the education of young child widows who were of Brahmanical parentage and for other high-caste women.[90] The Sharada Sadan was a testament to the great value that Ramabai placed on education, but it can furthermore be considered in order to better understand Ramabai's own navigation of Hindu and Christian identities.

As her exposure to Christianity developed, and as her Christology became more nuanced, she began to identify as a Christian but vowed to keep the Brahmanical purity laws in her school and to not officially teach any Christian doctrine. This assurance to the girls' parents that her school would remain an environment where the Hindu students would also continue to observe their religious purity was crucial for its success. Ramabai's respect for Brahmanical purity laws can be understood as an expression of her respect, more broadly, for India's many religious traditions; her admiration and reverence for non-Christian traditions is expressed in her 1883 essay 'Indian Religion' in which she applauds some missionaries for their willingness to learn from 'the sacred writings of India ... which God has given to us in past ages', and she further asserts that this willingness to draw upon ancient Indian sacred texts will 'help my countrymen to see more of the divine truth'.[91] A year later in 1884, arguing that the inscription of a cross that was to be displayed on the premises of the mission in Poona should be in Sanskrit and not in Latin, she wrote: 'Do you think that [the] Latin language has something better in it than our old Sanskrit? I stick fast to Sanskrit, not because I think it to be sacred or the language of the gods, but because it is the most beautiful, and the oldest language of my dear native land.'[92]

During the early years of managing the Sharada Sadan, Ramabai herself continued to observe Brahmanical purity laws, and she went to great lengths to defend what she saw as the good and noble aspects of Hindu philosophy and practice.[93] Yet, at the same time, Ramabai claimed that she could not resist her urge to openly express her Christian faith, which she described as the spiritual force which had completely transformed her life. Accordingly, she found various ways to incorporate her Christian faith into the forefront of the school's activities: every day she led her own daughter in Bible study, and over time some other girls slowly joined the discussion. Many of the Brahmins with whom she had previously maintained affiliations began to publicly voice their dislike for Ramabai's clear avowals of Christianity, and around 1891 many of the guardians who had entrusted their young girls to Ramabai's school promptly withdrew their wards due to allegations of proselytization.[94] It is likely that their refusal to accept her active embracing of some aspects of Christian faith, combined with the strident rejection of other Brahmins who disapproved of her Christian affiliation, led to Ramabai's own subsequent rejection of Brahmanical rituals and philosophies. Ramabai became particularly focused on the theology of the atonement in her later years, and scholars in the field of Indian Pentecostalism generally attribute the spread of Pentecostal Christianity to the Mukti revival in Maharashtra, which Ramabai fervently led.[95] And yet, as Ramabai eventually came to view her Christian faith as a progressively stronger transformative force within her own life, she grew increasingly distant from, and even hostile towards, her Hindu socioreligious background. Eventually, Ramabai reached a point where she derogatorily referred to Brahmins as 'heathens' who were in need of the atoning sacrifice of Jesus Christ if they wished to be made right with God – despite the fact that she had actively resisted such views in her earlier years as a Christian. As Jan Peter Schouten points out, these developments in her later years as a Christian rendered the prospect of dialoguing with Hindus impossible.[96]

2.3.4 Institutional expressions of Indianized Christianity

Not only were there various individuals who acted as the forerunners of enacting an Indianized Christianity, but also there were several institutional efforts during the first two decades of the twentieth century which sought to infuse Christianity with Indian cultural idioms.[97] We know that there were discussions relating to Christian ashrams in Protestant contexts in 1910 which were initiated by S. K. Rudra,[98] and also among other non-Catholics in April 1912 at a meeting of the National Missionary Society in Delhi[99] – and there could have been earlier, undocumented instances. The earliest institution of a Protestant ashram was in 1917 in Satara by N. V. Tilak, but the ashram did not last very long due to Tilak's death only two years later.[100] The first Protestant ashram which lasted more than a few years, Christukula, was founded in 1921 in the town of Tiruppattur in Tamil Nadu, South India.[101] An even longer-lasting and better-known Protestant ashram, by the name of Christa Seva Sangha, was founded in 1922 by Jack C. Winslow,[102] and a few years later the Christu Dasa ashram was founded in 1929 by P. John Varghese in Palghat, Kerala.[103] These various Christian ashrams, and a number of others which were formed after 1930 – including the numerous Catholic ashrams which began to emerge in the 1950s – have been documented and explored in great detail elsewhere.[104] For example, Cornille notes that there was an increase in the number of Catholic ashrams in the 1970s, and their interactions with one another were facilitated through an inter-ashram newsletter called *Ashram Aikiya*.[105]

Further, though the historical records are somewhat murky, scholars have speculated that around the 1920s the Catholic missionaries in North East India (around Assam, Nagaland and various hill stations in the Khasi-Jaintia hills) began to develop a 'greater sensitivity' to the tribal cultures with whom they interacted, thereby accounting for an increased number of conversions when compared to earlier Protestant practices which had been less driven by inculturation.[106] Other scholars have explored the various ways that inculturation was cultivated through the merging of Western and Indian musical traditions – in terms of both lyrical content and musical structure – and subsequently used in Christian contexts.[107] All these styles demonstrate that, in the decades leading up to the establishment of STA in 1930, there were available on the ground various examples of Christianity which had sought to incorporate Indian cultural idioms into its beliefs and practices.

More recently, some scholars have also pointed to the fact that from the 1950s onwards many efforts of inculturation involved conceptualizing Jesus as the true guru. For example, Cornille points to an excerpt from Henri le Saux's diaries from 1955 to indicate how he came to view Christ as his Hindu guru. Le Saux writes, 'The Christ whom I have first known and loved in his historical life in Jesus and later in his epiphany in the Church, has appeared to me at the end of time (of my time) in Bhagavan Sri Ramana.'[108] Cornille's focus on the guru-disciple relationship as an avenue to exploring patterns of Christian inculturation has been developed by other scholars. For example, Christopher Shelke focuses on the devotional writings attributed to a number of different poet-saints, including the Maharashtrian mystic Ramdas (1608–1681), and explores several guru-disciple relationships. In this discussion, Shelke draws a strong correlation between the doctrine of the Holy Spirit and the notion of the true guru (*Satguru*).[109] Nearly two decades after Cornille's volume, Schouten traces Christology in India over the last two centuries and provides a comprehensive survey of the prominent Indian-formed Christologies, thus demonstrating the varying and intricate ways through which some Indians have sought to understand and incorporate Jesus as a guru into their world views.[110] Schouten's work is particularly relevant to our discussion because his study does not highlight Vatican II as the historical moment out of which inculturation originates. Rather, Schouten studies a number of individuals who predate Vatican II, and who have contributed to the dialogue between Hindus and Christians and/or to embodying inculturated Christianities in India. Similar individuals are also the focal point of Bob Robinson's book *Christians Meeting Hindus*.[111]

2.3.5 Inculturating a particular kind of Indianness

These concretizations of Indianized and inculturated Christianity sought to show that Christianity could exist in India in a way that was not necessarily foreign. That is to say, expressions of Christianity should not be thought to be limited to Western archetypes or Westernized expressions. In doing so, their proponents combatted the earlier impressions of Christianity that had resulted from the colonial rules of Portugal and Britain. At the same time, these efforts to embody a type of Christianity that was distinctively Indian, rather than foreign, were rather single-mindedly focused on *one* particular kind of Indianness that was largely representative only of a relatively narrow strand of Hinduism. In order to understand the somewhat complicated and interlinked historical, social and political currents of the 1920s and the 1930s, we also need to look more broadly beyond the sociohistorical narratives of Indian Christianities. Specifically, we must note that these decades witnessed the emergence and the consolidation of certain forms of hard-line nationalist movements (later often clubbed together and referred to under the term 'Hindutva'). There are a number of pivotal moments which punctuate the timeline in which socioreligious identities were being actively reconstituted and reconfigured: V. D. Savarkar's *Hindutva* tract was published and distributed in 1923; the Rashtriya Swayamsevak Sangh (later associated with the Sangh Parivar) was established in 1925; in 1928 there was a purification (*shuddhi*) ceremony in Goa in which a large number of Roman Catholics expressed their interest in returning to Hinduism; and so forth. Alongside these sociopolitical shifts, we also notice the increasing representation of Advaita Vedanta as the essence of Hindu spirituality by some prominent members of the Hindu intelligentsia, partly in response to Christian missionary critiques, throughout much of the nineteenth century, of Hindu lifeworlds as idolatrous, superstitious and heathenish.

The philosophical and the soteriological teachings of Advaita Vedanta had already been actively imported to some Western countries after Swami Vivekananda's addresses at the World Parliament of Religions in 1893, and since then they had become increasingly well known in certain circles across the United States, Canada and Europe.[112] This increasing popularity post-1893 was not, however, the first time that Advaita Vedanta had become a topic of immense interest for Western scholars; rather, a keen interest in Vedanta and, more generally, Hindu spirituality can be traced to the period of European Romanticism, in which German scholars in particular displayed a great fascination with, and deep respect for, Vedantic philosophies. Influential scholars such as F. W. J. Schelling (1775–1854) 'expressed great interest in and support for Indian and Oriental studies'; indeed, Schelling believed that India's sacred texts were 'superior' when compared to the Bible.[113] This affinity for India's spiritual philosophies was asserted with even more conviction by Friedrich Schlegel (1772–1829) who wrote that '[e]verything, yes, everything has its origins in India'[114] and believed that India was 'the primary source of all ideas'.[115] While these transnational translations of philosophy and spirituality that took place between India and Western countries cannot be explored in detail here, it is important to note that these intellectual influences from outside India contributed to establishing Advaita Vedanta as the quintessence of Hinduism. Several Hindu intellectuals, social reformers and political figures began to present Advaitic spirituality as the quintessence of the religious traditions of the world, and as the 'higher Hinduism' which was superior to the diverse cultic and 'folk' practices within India. Indeed, R. D. Ranade delivered a series of lectures in Calcutta in 1929 on the topic of Vedanta in which he presented Vedanta as 'the culmination of Indian thought'.[116] It was against this backdrop of a self-assertive Hinduism shaped with Vedantic elements that Indianized expressions of Christianity were gradually configured and enacted, and it is therefore not surprising that these expressions were heavily informed by Vedantic and Brahmanical vocabularies, norms and ideas. Further, as we shall see in more detail in Chapter 3, these Brahmanical configurations resonated with what Jones deemed to be 'the right way' of bringing the gospel to Hindus.

2.4 Conclusion

Few people would deny the assertion that 'no human is an island' or that 'no action occurs in a vacuum', but at the same time, without the effort of excavation, we are rarely aware of the various social, historical, political, cultural and other influences that shape our opinions, thoughts and behaviours. Striving to achieve such awareness is important – not only because the individual's perspectives are interesting and valuable in themselves but also because self-awareness is the first step in enabling a critical self-reflexivity. When we become aware of not only what we are doing but also of the various external factors which influence us to think and act in the ways that we do, we increase our capacity to reflect upon these external influences on our actions and consequently to decide the extent to which we wish to pursue and engage with them. This effort of intentional self-awareness featured prominently in Chapter 1 in our discussion of methodological bracketing and BIR, with respect to the generalized practices of anthropology as a discipline, but, more specifically relevant to our exploration of STA, this chapter, too, has offered just this sort of contextual excavation. Through exploring the activities of Portuguese Catholics and British Protestants in India during their respective countries' colonial rules, we have seen the ways that Christianity gained a reputation within India as being a religion exclusively of foreigners. Through considering cases in which European individuals (both as ruling officers and as missionaries) interacted with Syrian Christian communities, we saw how both the Portuguese and the British often took measures to assert themselves as the corrective authority and, consequently, stamp their (Eurocentric) versions of Christianity as the normatively correct way of being Christian. At times this imperial stance resulted in the eradication of all religious practices and beliefs that were considered by them to be too closely linked to Hinduism, for only Western Christianity was deemed acceptable. Thus, as Sister Vandana, a Catholic nun who led the Christian ashram Jiva Dhara, and who wrote several books on the topic of inculturated Christianity, has highlighted, 'the "foreignness" of the Gospel presentation in Asia has long been a stumbling block' for individuals who might otherwise be interested in Christianity.[117]

Following the overview of the foreignness of Christianity, we looked at a number of examples of inculturation (by foreign missionaries, Indian Christians and different institutional religious groups within India) which consciously incorporated various Indic cultural idioms into their expressions of Christianity, thereby embodying forms of Christianity which were deeply influenced by, and also accommodating of, Indian culture. Ranging from Roberto de Nobili, Brahmabandhab Upadhyay, to Pandita Ramabai, and various institutionalized efforts, we see many examples of inculturated Christianity which predate 1930; importantly, these embodiments of Indianized Christianity were heavily influenced by, and inflected with, particularly Brahmanical strands of Hinduism. It is only in more recent years that many scholars have been challenged with the reality that Hinduism (let alone Indianness) is not limited to one particular style – works like Francis Clooney's *Theology after Vedanta* (1993), for example, consciously avoid any attempt at a generalized dialogue between Vedanta and Christianity.[118] In the beginning and middle of the twentieth century, however, this type of critical awareness had not yet permeated writers on Hinduism, and Indianness was often unequivocally associated with, or even identified by, a Brahmanical and/or Vedanta-inflected Hinduism. Keeping this historical trend in mind, Chapter 3 will explore in more detail the ways that E. Stanley Jones himself, and the development of STA in particular, was shaped by, and also contributed to, these Vedanta-inflected embodiments of Indianized Christianity.

3

The origins of Sat Tal Christian Ashram and E. Stanley Jones's 'Ashram Ideals'

3.1 Dr E. Stanley Jones: The founder of Sat Tal Christian Ashram

When the American Methodist missionary Dr E. Stanley Jones (1884–1973) began to visit the Kumaon foothills in the outer Himalayan region of Uttarakhand (northern India) around 1915, he would often walk along a series of roughly trodden footpaths towards a large plot of land called Sat Tal. Sat Tal, named after the seven (*sat*) freshwater lakes (*tal*) which surround the region, was significantly smaller than its closest town (Nainital) and had little going on within it. Even today, over one hundred years later, Sat Tal is home to only a few buildings other than STA: it has a small post office, a handful of tea stalls where one can – albeit inconsistently – purchase one's favourite snacks and other odds and ends, one tiny church (kept locked and unused for most of the year), and a YMCA. Today, STA and the ashram's estate occupy the majority of the Sat Tal region. But in 1915, what is now STA was a (largely unsuccessful) tea plantation owned by a retired British engineer named Mr Evans. The tea plantation spanned around 300 acres, and Mr Evans and his wife rented out the estate's cottages to individuals (mostly foreign missionaries) who wanted to escape to the hills from the heat of the Indian summer and rejuvenate themselves alongside the freshwater lakes and the remarkably diverse wildlife. From the Nainital hill station to Sat Tal was about 12 miles on foot, and Jones greatly enjoyed the walk.

Jones, who frequently travelled across the country to some of the biggest and busiest cities in order to preach the gospel after his arrival to India in 1907, found refuge in the idyllic calm of the Kumaon foothills. Along with his wife Mabel, Jones had moved to Sitapur (in the present-day state of Uttar Pradesh) in 1911 in order to take care of several institutions affiliated with the American Methodist Church.[1] Excluding his international travels and travels across India (both mission-related), and his furloughs in the United States, he lived in Sitapur for over three decades, and the stresses of his work took a severe toll on his mental health – especially in his earlier years of work.[2] Throughout his time as a missionary in India, Jones repeatedly experienced what were then described as 'nervous collapses'. These forced him to return to the United States on furlough at least twice in order to recover from his physical and mental fatigue.[3] Some of Jones's biographers have suggested that these 'nervous collapses' would have been psychologically classified in today's medical vocabulary as some sort of anxiety disorder.[4] Knowing this small yet important detail about Jones's life might help us make sense of why he so often took to the hillside: the engineer's tea plantation was even more remote than the bustling town of Nainital, and its small private lakes offered a pleasant space for physical and spiritual rejuvenation. When living in Sitapur, Jones began to journey to Sat Tal's hills for three months every summer and would swim in one of the freshwater lakes, *Garud Tal* (formerly called *Panna Tal*), whenever the weather allowed. He writes fondly about the several summers that he, his wife and daughter spent at Sat Tal while the land was still owned by the Evans, and one can imagine that – despite professing later that he had never imagined that he would own the place, let alone develop an ashram there – Jones found in the hills of Sat Tal some of the comforts of home.

3.1.1 Jones's emphasis on the person of Christ

When Jones was not recuperating in the relative calm of Sat Tal, he was actively evangelizing both in Sitapur and elsewhere in India. Having had his own life positively transformed when he committed himself to Christ's teachings as a seventeen-year-old in the United States, Jones was a passionate Methodist who wished to share the Christian gospel with whomever would listen to him.[5] Reflecting on his earlier years as a young evangelist in India, Jones confessed that he had been a bit naive in his ideas about other people's receptivity to the gospel – he had unreflectively assumed that everyone with whom he spoke would quickly and eagerly respond to Christian teachings, and adopt them as their own. Instead, he realized that many individuals already inhabited specific religious frameworks which guided their beliefs and actions, so that Jones's explanations of what he deemed to be the key doctrinal points of Christianity did not, he discovered with surprise, seem to offer anything unique or necessary to their religious lives. Jones was pushed into this understanding first-hand while trying to evangelize a Hindu man during his first Indian train ride – the man found Jones's stories compelling, and even seemed to listen with genuine interest, but at the end of the conversation retorted that he had similar stories in his own religion, and the man left the train without showing any interest in learning more about Christianity. Baffled, and battling his disappointment, Jones was forced to reflect on his assumptions regarding evangelism. This early realization is an important moment which prompted Jones's first substantive shift in the way he approached evangelism. Specifically, Jones began to realize that trying to instill the specific *teachings of Christianity* was not nearly as important as communicating the *person of Christ*. Consequently, he began to emphasize the soteriological impact of an encounter with the living person of Christ; he deeply believed that individuals who thus encountered Christ would be so enamoured with, and drawn by their own need for, Christ that they could do no other than begin to follow Christ's teachings. This shift in focus from doctrine to person, as Jones often indicates in his writings, continued to mature throughout his years as an evangelist. At various points, he recentred himself through this focus of a personal Christ, and allowed its spiritual gravity to become expressed in his evangelical approaches in different ways.[6] Ultimately, Jones reached a point, whereby in 1925 he asserted (quoting from his journal from 1917) that 'Christianity must be defined as Christ, not the Old Testament, not Western civilization, not even the system built around him in the West, but Christ himself'.[7] Around this same time, the emphasis of the *person* of Christ rather than the *tradition* of Christianity was also professed by figures such as Ram Mohan (Rammohun) Roy in his book *The Precepts* (1920)[8] and by Gandhi (whom we will return to in Section 3.1.3), and this emphasis of Christ, rather than Christianity, continued to be articulated by several Hindi spiritual figures, such as Swami Prabhavananda who wrote *The Sermon on the Mount according to Vedanta* (1963). Of course, in the light of two millennia of doctrinal disputations in Christian religious history, this plain equivalence between *Christianity* and *Christ* is either disturbingly ambiguous or wonderfully ambiguous, depending on one's level of existential comfort with loosely held definitions without clear creedal formulations. This equivalence effectively transforms the question from '*what* is Christianity?' (and, consequently, 'what does one's life look like as a Christian within Christian socioreligious milieus?') to '*who* is Christ?', so that the consequent question is: 'What does one's life look like when following Christ and becoming existentially conformed to Christ?' But I shall lay aside for now Jones's highly personalist definition of Christianity and remain focused on sketching Jones's evangelism.

3.1.2 Dialoguing with educated high castes

For the first fifteen or so years of working as a missionary in India, Jones concentrated his evangelism on individuals from the lower socio-economic classes – individuals who, using the vocabulary common to his time period, he referred to interchangeably as 'low castes', 'untouchables' and 'outcastes'.[9] It was only in the 1920s that Jones began to specifically tailor his evangelical efforts towards individuals whom he described as the 'educated high castes'.[10] Jones's intentional engagements with educated individuals drew upon his academic strengths and ministerial training – Jones had attended school at Asbury College (now Asbury University) in Wilmore, Kentucky, from 1903 to 1906 during which he became a licensed preacher, and was 'an enthusiastic and able student'.[11] Numerous people, at different times throughout my fieldwork, narrated the following story about Jones which neatly encapsulates this marked shift from evangelizing primarily to lower-caste individuals to engaging with higher-caste individuals. In the 1920s, when Jones was speaking with an educated upper-caste Hindu government official at one of Jones's recreational activities, the officer asked Jones why foreign missionaries focused all their attention on converting lower-caste individuals. Why, the official wondered, did the missionaries not preach also to the Brahmanical Hindus and others who came from more educated backgrounds? Jones informed the official that he and other missionaries had presumed that Brahmins did not want what the missionaries were offering, to which the official replied, 'We do want you, if you come in the right way'.[12] For Jones, this conversation was a revelatory moment which, combined with his initial shift in focus to the person of Christ discussed above, transformed the style of his missionary efforts after the 1920s. Among other changes to his evangelizing methods, Jones established round-table conferences (1917–20)[13] in order to promote personal interactions and focused dialogues between Christians, educated Hindus and others, and he later founded STA in 1930. We have thus far highlighted two distinct shifts in Jones's approach to evangelism: first, he desired to speak of, and indeed offer to others, the *person of Christ* rather than proclaim particular *doctrinal formulations* of Western Christianity; and second, he realized that this sharing of Christ need not be limited to individuals from lower-caste backgrounds. As the Hindu government official had confirmed for Jones, Brahmins and other educated individuals might indeed receive the missionaries' gospel – if only the missionaries managed to come 'in the right way'.

But what exactly *was* this 'right' way? Evidently, as is suggested in the official's comment, the way in which foreign missionaries had brought the message of Christianity to the untouchables (or Dalits and OBCs in current terminologies of the Indian nation state) was not 'the right way' to bring the same message to Brahmins. Chapter 2 highlighted the ways that various 'Hindutva' movements which emerged in the 1920s and 1930s, along with several other factors that I outlined there (Section 2.3.5), shaped the ways that the philosophical teachings of Advaita Vedanta were consciously presented to both national and international audiences as the true expression of Hinduism and, indeed, as *the* true way of being Indian. 'Indianness' was thus being strategically refracted through the prism of this very particular, though highly influential minority, strand of Hinduism. And thus, I contend, as much as Jones was directly influenced by this particular conversation with the Brahmin at the recreational club, he was also inescapably shaped by his cultural locations within these various broader sociopolitical discourses which were conceptually equating 'Indianness' with 'Vedanta'.[14] Shaped by these direct and indirect influences, Jones determined that 'the right way' of bringing the gospel to Hindus would necessarily entail going about it in a way that resonated with Vedantic, Brahmanical styles.

3.1.3 Inspiration of the spiritual model of Gandhi

Jones also had to grapple with the emerging figure of Gandhi who was regarded by some of his contemporaries – Indian and foreigner alike – as a Christ-like figure, and Jones himself frequently described Gandhi in Christian terms.[15] We know that Jones found Gandhi's practices and teachings regarding non-violent resistance to be both highly inspirational and spiritually uplifting – he claimed that Gandhi's resistance gave him a 'deeper appreciation of the cross as a universal validity'[16] – and he was thus genuinely interested in learning from Gandhi. Inspired by Gandhi's lifestyle, Jones 'wore a khaddar dhoti [traditional Indian garb] on his visit to [Gandhi's] ashram and went barefoot' when he first visited the ashram.[17] Scholars have also noted that Gandhi himself, and later Gandhian ashrams, had a significant influence on the establishment and development of many Christian ashrams.[18] It is thus possible that Gandhi's ashrams (the first of which, Satyagraha – later named Sabarmati – was established in 1915) influenced Jones's own development of STA – perhaps some of the other founders of the Christian ashrams mentioned in Chapter 2 were influenced by Gandhi. Whatever may have been the nature and the extent of Gandhi's influence on the notion of a Christian ashram, Jones sought out Gandhi for specific advice concerning how

Christianity might be understood and appreciated by Indians as a truly Indian religion rather than as a religion of foreigners. Jones's first meeting with Gandhi occurred, according to Jones's own recollection, 'soon after [Gandhi's] return from South Africa [in 1915]'.[19] One of Jones's biographers, however, dates this meeting to 1919.[20] No matter the precise year when this meeting took place, it is worth highlighting that it occurred, as Jones explicitly points out, significantly before Gandhi had developed a public viewpoint concerning conversions to Christianity in India[21] – Gandhi's discourse surrounding conversion as an undesirable and even unethical or immoral act did not materialize until well over a decade later.[22]

But, when Jones approached Gandhi around 1920, Gandhi's public opinion on conversion was still relatively ambivalent. Apparently without regards for pleasantries, Jones directly presented his key question to Gandhi:

> How can we [Christian missionaries] make Christianity naturalized in India, not a foreign thing, identified with a foreign government and a foreign people, but a part of the national life of India and contributing its power to India's uplift? What would you, as one of the Hindu leaders of India tell me, a Christian, to do in order to make this possible?[23]

(The reader will, no doubt, have already noted that Jones's repetitive use of the descriptor 'foreign' suggests that Jones was keenly aware of Christianity's strong reputation as a religion of foreigners – something Chapter 2 explored in detail.) Gandhi responded, '

> First, I would suggest [that] all of you Christians, missionaries and all, must begin to live more like Jesus Christ. Second, practice your religion without adulterating it or toning it down. Third, emphasize love and make it your working force, for love is central in Christianity. Fourth, study the non-Christian religions more sympathetically to find the good that is within them, in order to have a more sympathetic approach to the people.[24]

In this response, we see that Gandhi made no effort to convince Jones that his main desire – to 'make Christianity naturalized in India' – was fundamentally flawed or spiritually unnecessary. Instead, Gandhi provided Jones with advice that further strengthened Jones's spiritual commitment to preaching the *person* of Jesus, and offered some guidance which likely not only reinforced Jones's general resolve to create STA but also presented Jones with a model of what spiritual life at an ashram could look like. In the present day, the individuals at STA who knew Jones best continue to affirm that Gandhi had exercised a profound influence on

Jones's desire to build an ashram. In 2016, Dorothy Firr (a former manager of STA, a close companion of Jones and a frankly remarkable nonagenarian woman who remains actively involved in STA and other endeavours) explained to me that one main reason that Jones wanted to build an ashram was

> because he was a close friend of Gandhi. And Gandhi had Hindu ashrams in Gujarat ... people always came to Gandhi's ashram and Gandhi always was insistent that they work. People should work [in order to] break down prejudices, ... break down the caste system. [Because] the outcastes weren't treated like people, but they are all people! Brother Stanley [like Gandhi] also wanted people to work. Everybody. And he led by example – Brother Stanley cleaned the latrines![25]

Additional features of the present-day STA ashram, such as the month-long daily programme that Jones implemented at the 'Summer Ashram' (and, in later years, at the 'Winter Ashram'), were specifically modelled on Gandhi's ashram.[26] This discipline includes following a daily rhythm of rising early for personal meditation, attending morning meditation (*dhyan*) with the group, eating meals together and participating in at least one hour of assigned work; I return to these details below and also in Chapter 4. The remainder of the day at STA during the SoE programme consists of group spiritual teachings, personal time, prayer time, and meals, and the evening concludes with 'fellowship', during which hymns are sung and/or testimonies are shared.[27]

3.1.4 STA's ashram ideals

Considering these three distinct lines of force – Jones's desire to share the living person of Christ rather than the specific doctrines of Western Christianity, the encouragement he received during his first Indian train ride to approach Hindu Brahmins with the gospel, and the advice and the spiritual model of Gandhi – it is not surprising that Jones eventually established a Christian ashram. First, ashrams in Hindu contexts often focused on the charisma and the personality of the individual guru rather than on subscribing to a specific set of doctrinal claims in the way of religious institutions.[28] Therefore, ashrams, it would have seemed to Jones, could facilitate sharing and teaching about the person of Christ, thereby incorporating a guru-focused spiritual practice which is common to many Hindu spiritual traditions.[29] Yet, rather than declare himself as a human guru (a declaration which would not have appeared out of the ordinary to some of his Hindu audiences) Jones instead proclaimed that it was Jesus, and not

Jones himself, who was the true guru of STA. Although Jones, as we shall see in Chapter 4, is often spoken of by present-day ashramites as a remarkable and noble spiritual teacher, and is sometimes even given reverence as if he were their guru, Jones never elevated himself to this honorific status; he instead preferred the identity of a 'Brother', and frequently referred to others as his brothers and sisters.[30]

Second, ashrams were deeply embedded in the cultural heritages of some aspects of Brahmanical Hindu cultures, and were traditionally regarded as abodes of serenity, holiness and spiritual gravity. And, as we see in *The Christ of the Indian Road* – published five years before establishing STA – Jones was already conversing with some itinerant Hindu ascetics and had visited specific ashrams such as that of Rabindranath Tagore in Shantiniketan, near Calcutta.[31] The significance of the ashram for Jones's mission is often highlighted by Jones's family members: thus, when Eunice Jones Mathews, Jones's daughter, was interviewed in 1974 about her father's work in India, she spoke about the influences that had led Jones to establish STA. She explained, 'It bothered Daddy that among the Christian community so many new Indian Christians had abandoned their cultures to take on a Western veneer. My father very much wanted to bring back as much of the Indian culture into Christianity and bring the Christian community back into their own culture …The Ashram was an answer for him.'[32]

And so Jones, along with Reverend Yunas Sinha and Miss Ethel Turner, sought to purchase the roughly 300 acres of land from the tea plantation owners in 1929, and began transforming the land into STA. According to the 'Ashram Ideals' that he penned in 1930, Jones desired for STA to espouse vegetarianism, group meditation, Bible study, prolonged silence, service ('working with the hands'), creativity and simplicity.[33] Taking these desires into account, I have identified three key themes that are present not only in these 'Ashram Ideals' but also throughout Jones's writings and sermons. Importantly, he stipulated that (1) he wanted the ashram to be 'truly Christian and truly Indian'. He also wanted (2) all individuals 'who sincerely desire to find God' to be welcome at STA, regardless of whether they were of the Christian faith, a different faith or even 'no faith'. And (3) he envisioned the ashram as a 'miniature Kingdom of God', where individuals from a myriad of different spiritual and religious traditions would not simply seek out ready-made answers handed to them but would instead '*be* the answer' by living out a noble spiritual life inspired by, and centred on, Jesus. Each of these three features of Jones's vision for STA is fundamental to the spiritual environment he established at STA; thus, I will consider each of them in turn. In Section 3.2, my focus shall be on the first of them, and the discussion will set the stage for Chapter 4; I shall return to the latter two features in Chapter 5.

3.2 The quest for the 'Truly Christian and truly Indian' at STA

Of course, Jones's aim to create a community which was both Indian and Christian must be understood within the larger context of the somewhat complicated relationships between Indian cultures and the Christian faith which had developed over the preceding centuries – a relationship that Chapter 2 explored in some detail. But we should not interpret the vision of Jones only as a historically shaped quest to combat the perception of Christianity as a foreign and foreigners' religion; we also need to understand how Jones conceptualized the key terms *Christian* and *Indian*, and how these understandings, in turn, shaped each other. The question of what precisely counts as either *truly Christian* or *truly Indian* is, of course, dependent on the individual figure or institutional authority who is staking the claim to authenticity. As Harold Coward asks pointedly, 'What does it mean to be a Hindu? Or a Christian? ... Who decides? ... According to which criteria?'[34] The debates relating to true or authentic expressions of Christianity versus incomplete, or even completely erroneous, expressions are not limited to our discussion of STA or even, more broadly, to inculturated Christianity within Indian contexts; rather, anthropologists have demonstrated that such contestations over fidelity and identity are, in fact, a rather common phenomenon within Christian contexts.[35] These negotiations over membership are, as I argued in Chapter 1, especially distinctive of certain Protestant contexts where the distinctions between insider and outsider are clearly marked out in terms of the acceptance or the rejection of creedal formulations.

3.2.1 'Truly Christian'

Jones's concern that the ashram be recognized as truly Christian can be understood in the light of these contested socioreligious identities. Indeed, Jones wished that STA would be recognized by others as a distinctively *Christian* ashram, but the crucial question, of course, was: Christian by *which* or *whose* criteria? For Jones, as we have seen, the defining features of Christianity extended beyond any specific doctrinal or institutional-ecclesiological context, as he certainly did not wish to merely import the forms of Western Christianity that he had grown up with – even his own Methodism, though he was associated with this denomination throughout his missionary work, was not something that he wished to transplant into STA's spiritual soil.[36] And yet, Jones was adamant that STA was – beyond any shadow of doubt – deeply Christian. In his autobiography, Jones writes clearly,

> some might surmise [that] because we have a Hindu term that therefore the Christian Ashram is an amalgamation of Christianity and Hinduism. Nothing could be further from the reality. The Christian faith, being life, assimilates. The Christian faith reaches into the culture of every nation and takes out things, which can be assimilated into its purpose, but in doing so makes something entirely new and different.[37]

I am not here primarily interested in addressing the various ways that Christian systematic theologians or scholars working in the fields of critical religion and Orientalism would critically evaluate Jones's assertion that 'the Christian faith ... assimilates'.[38] To be sure, this declaration might be critiqued today as a form of Christian epistemic violence, or even cognitive imperialism, which refuses to foreground the alterity of Indic world views and instead seeks precisely to *assimilate* them to a Christian standpoint.[39] However, Jones himself would have been unaware, just like Upadhyay in Chapter 2, of such important critiques of Western *re*presentations of Eastern world views like Said's – which were formulated in the late 1970s – so we must keep in mind that the paradigm-assessing resources that Jones had available to him were somewhat limited. But, equally crucially, I am not here evaluating Jones through the lens of Orientalism because my interest in this chapter lies elsewhere: I instead offer a phenomenologically sensitive and interpretive account of *why* and *how* Jones sought to navigate the terrains of Indianized Christianity while being deeply committed to the person of Christ. In other words, Jones's emphasis that the spiritual core of STA is indeed Christian, and STA is not a mere 'amalgamation of Christianity and Hinduism', raises the following question: precisely what did it mean to Jones himself for something or someone to be *Christian* at all?

We know from Jones's own writings that his views concerning Christianity changed substantially during his time as a missionary in India, and he consciously set aside some of the doctrinal convictions that he once held dearly. However, in spite of these changes, Jones consistently regarded his Christian faith as the dominant framework through which he interpreted his life and the world around him. Time and time again, it was the *person* of Jesus on whom Jones focused his attention, and he believed that this personal Christ, removed from the specific trappings of Western Christian cultures, could be passed on to Indians. In stark contrast to many other missionaries during colonial times, including the 'British Baptist trio' of missionaries mentioned in Chapter 2 (Section 2.2.3), Jones was not interested – at least not consciously – in presenting Indians with a form of Christianity that was deeply bound to its Western cultural expressions. This vision of an Indianized Christianity for Indians is made clear in Jones's influential book *The Christ of the Indian Road* (1925), which not only was an immense success amongst missionaries in India and in other mission fields but which also became a bestseller in the United States.[40] In it, he asserts, 'I am frank to say that I would not turn over my hand to westernise the East, but I trust I would give my life to christianise [sic] it. It cannot be too clearly said that they are not synonymous.'[41] And, in the same book, he argues that India is able to 'take from Christ' in a way it could not do earlier because only now is it 'able to disassociate [Christ] from the West'.[42] Thus, we see that from Jones's own Christ-formed standpoint, the *assimilative* power of Christianity, as much as that word might grate on our post-Saidian subjectivities, indicates not so much a reduction of all human religiosity to Christianity but their spiritual elevation into a new life in Christ. To repeat Jones's words: 'The Christian faith, *being life*, assimilates'.

This same sentiment of the life-giving Christ whose transformative power was being stifled by institutional Christianity was expressed earlier by the well-known Indian Christian poet Narayan Vaman Tilak (1862–1919).[43] And, of course, similar sentiments had been expressed by figures such as Upadhyay and Ramabai, whom we encountered in Chapter 2 (Sections 2.3.2 and 2.3.3). It was this conviction that the categories of 'Christianization' and 'Westernization' were not synonymous or congruent which enabled Jones to consider establishing a Christian ashram which would be deeply imbued with an Indian ethos.[44] And yet, at the same time, Jones held on to certain convictions regarding the theological uniqueness of Christ, and he never veered away from this Christocentric standpoint.

3.2.2 Situating Jones within broader discussions of the foreignness of Christianity

I believe it will help us to make sense of Jones's own understanding of Christianity if we stand back for a while from the 1920s and sensitively resituate him within some of the broader historical discussions regarding the foreignness of Christianity in India. As Chapter 2 demonstrated, Christianity had gained a reputation within some Indian public spheres of being exclusively a religion of foreigners; I argue that we can conceptualize this view as occupying one far end of a spectrum of views regarding whether or not Christianity in India is, or can ever become, sufficiently Indian. There are, however, several scholars from a variety of disciplinary backgrounds who occupy the opposite far-end, and who have articulated a counterargument which, I think, is important to consider in this discussion – not the least because these arguments force us to reflect critically on the claim that Christianity outside European milieus should be conceptualized in terms of the conceptual binary of *either* foreign *or* native. Social scientists Chad Bauman and Richard Fox Young reject the notion that there is one normative Christianity to which Indian expressions of Christianity should be compared.[45] In asserting this notion, they decidedly veer away from the missions-focused scholarship that had focused largely on the question of whether, and to what extent, the various forms of Christianity found across different non-European cultures were deemed acceptable to European missionaries. Crucially, Bauman and Young instead champion the notion that 'Christianity' has never historically existed as a monolithic religion. Scholars who work in the field of Early Christianity similarly agree that the definitional problems relating to precisely what makes an individual or a community 'Christian' have been present since the first century, thereby adding more historical basis to the sociological claim that Christianity is not one singular belief or social formation.[46]

In this context, the theologian Jaroslav Pelikan has argued that throughout the centuries Christ has been interpreted through multiple images which have been inflected with – and which, in turn, reflect – specific sociohistorical idioms; thus, in different social contexts we see Christ described as the 'King of Kings', or the 'true image of God', the 'Universal Man', the 'Teacher of common sense', the 'Liberator' and so forth.[47] From the perspectives of such a historical understanding of the multiple images of Christ and of Christianity, by consciously refusing to privilege one particular iteration (whether cultural, temporal or denominational) of Christianity over others, the various versions of, and variations on, Christianity which exist throughout the world (including the many inculturated expressions scattered throughout India) would neither neatly fit into one putative norm nor would they be castigated as deviations from such a norm. According to this viewpoint, in short, rather than being a *prescriptive* norm, the original and the early expressions of Christianity are primarily *descriptive* or *programmatic* models of what Christianity could look like – but they are not exhaustive or definitive of Christianity itself.

Where might Jones have placed himself on this spectrum of, on one side, conceptualizing Christianity as *either* foreign *or* native in the way that became commonplace in some public spheres of India (of course, with the resounding agreement that it was foreign!) or, on the other side, asserting that Christianity could be seemingly infinite in its diverse iterations, through its processes of – borrowing the phrase from the apostle John – 'taking on flesh' of different cultures, landscapes and time periods? I place Jones somewhere in the middle of this conceptual continuum. We have seen that Jones fundamentally rejected the idea that Christianity was exclusively a religion of foreigners: he desired to create a sociocultural atmosphere within whose hospitable spaces Indian Christianity could be practised. Furthermore, as Jones makes clear in his writings, he did not want to hold onto teachings merely for the sake of hallowed tradition; he was prepared to take on any practice that might enable him to draw closer to Christ, just as he was also willing to discard anything that he felt might hinder this spiritual closeness. Thus, he wrote in an almost iconoclastic tone,

> We must fearlessly go over our faith, our methods, our organizations, our programs, and our spirit, and ask concerning each one the question: 'Does it unlock anything? Does it unlock reality, does it fit into the soul of India, does it bring me to God and to people, is it really redemptive, is it according to the mind of Christ?' And we must be willing to lay aside rusted keys that no longer fit into things and no longer bring us to vital touch with Christ and life.[48]

But at the same time, the potential boundlessness of Christian expressions suggested by the scholars who argue against any normative core whatsoever to Christianity would likely have seemed to be too much of a doctrinal stretch for Jones. Numerous Christian theologians throughout the ages have claimed that there *is* a central structure to the Christian faith, which is defined through the scriptural bases of 'one Lord, one faith, one baptism',[49] even though, of course, they have interpreted the fundamental concept of 'one' in quite divergent ways. Writing in this vein, we know from Jones's public reaction of disappointment to the *Rethinking Missions* report,[50] for example, that Jones thought that some attempts at presenting the gospel in an inculturated style went too far; he felt that some Christian missionaries had effectively abandoned some of the most important components of the message of Jesus by being seemingly endless in their openness to the various expressions of human faith.[51] Jones's stance on the necessity as well as the limits of inculturation would have resonated with the theology of Indian Christians such as Kali Charan Banerji (incidentally the uncle of Upadhyay) who, some decades before Jones arrived on the scene, had already distinguished in 1892-3 between 'substantive Christianity', that is, certain foundational doctrines which remain invariant and 'adjectival Christianity', that is, specific styles of ecclesiastical organizations and creedal confessions with which the former are clothed.[52]

So, we might ask at this stage, how did Jones demarcate between what could be 'laid aside' and what was essential, or even normative, to the Christian faith? What, if anything, made one mode of belief and spirituality distinctively *Christian* while making something else fall outside the Christian faith? And what precisely did Jones want to express institutionally in making the ashram 'truly Christian'? Jones's standpoints on these questions are important for us to understand, not the least, because, as we will see in Chapter 4, there remains even today a deep ambiguity surrounding these topics among some of the ashramites of STA.

3.2.3 Being Christian as surrendering to Jesus

One note that is consistently struck in Jones's own writings and sermons is that the sum and substance of Christianity is Christ himself; for Jones, Christianity was therefore grounded in the continual practice of an ongoing self-surrender to Jesus.[53] Indeed, we recall Jones's declaration that 'Christianity must be defined as Christ'.[54] In other words, instead of viewing Christianity in terms of a sociohistorical phenomenon or an ecclesiastical system or a doctrinal structure, Christianity is to be seen as a way of being-in-the-world which is vitally shaped by, rooted in and oriented to the personal encounter with the living reality of Christ. In his PhD thesis on the thought and work of Jones, Paul A. J. Martin cautions his readers, however, from oversimplifying Jones's understanding of Christianity, and argues that 'Jones's distinction between Christ and Christianity was not as radical as it sounded at first'.[55] Martin then proceeds to articulate the various ways that Jones 'insisted that the Gospel record about Jesus was substantially historically accurate'.[56] In other words, while Jones indeed emphasized individuals' need for an encounter with a personal Christ, he was still very much rooted in mainstream Christianity which consistently teaches that the figure of Christ is defined by his salvific actions and words as recorded in the New Testament narratives. It was the Old Testament, rather than the New Testament, from which Jones distanced himself. I have heeded Martin's cautionary words and not oversimplified Jones's distinctions between Christ and Christianity; nonetheless, at the same time, it is undeniable that Jones did, time and time again, emphasize that he understood that the heart of Christianity in its truest form can be distilled down to the person of Jesus. Thus, I seek to understand what Jones thought about the person of Jesus, and how this crucial belief played out in Jones's own personal life.

One of the most tangible demonstrations of Jones's unwavering focus on the person of Jesus is the style of greeting that Jones established for STA: Jones would hold up three fingers as he verbalized the affirmation 'Jesus is Lord'. This quickly took the place of other customary greetings such as 'good morning' or 'hello', and the action on its own could also serve as a mode of greeting amongst ashramites even during silent hour.[57] To this day, many ashramites still hold up three fingers when they greet one another, saying either '*Yeshu Masih hai*' or 'Jesus is Lord', and the ashram is decorated with various figurines, paintings and photographs of three fingers held up in this manner. There is even a large print of Jones in his later years, holding the posture. Jones's constant efforts to thus affirm the Lordship of Jesus is explained throughout his writings, where he emphasizes that the earliest Christian creed was simply 'Jesus is Lord', and he interprets this confession to mean that self-surrender to Jesus is the earliest Christian attitude and practice. Indeed, Jones spoke, somewhat paradoxically, of bondage to God as the highest form of freedom, and taught that the way to achieve such freedom was through becoming bound to Jesus in an offering of self-surrender. As readers who are familiar with the New Testament may pick up on, there are clear resonances of this motif with the claims of being a bondservant (Greek: *doulos*) to Jesus Christ – an avowed identity with which Paul, Timothy, James, Peter and Jude all describe themselves.[58]

This particular theological paradox of bondage as freedom is, furthermore, not unique to Christian contexts. As one example among many, the cowherd maidens (*gopis*) in the paradigmatic *Rasa Lila* narrative of the *Bhagavata Purana* (10.29.1–4) declare that they have been 'captured' by their beloved Lord Krishna, and are thus enraptured by and attuned to him, but it is through these devotional processes of entanglement, which oscillate through moments of painful separation and joyful union, that they become free.[59] I am not aware of Jones's familiarity with the pervasiveness of this paradox of bondage as freedom across religious traditions. Jones definitely engaged with spiritual teachings outside of Christianity in his own discussions of bondage and freedom. Specifically, he engaged with certain Buddhist philosophical teachings in order to emphasize the need for Christians to become bound to Jesus. After outlining (and agreeing with) the Buddha's teaching that desire (*dukkha*) leads to suffering, Jones went on to proclaim that the solution to becoming free from suffering was not, as Buddhism teaches, the dissolution of desire but rather the reorientation of desire to Christ. Thus, in 1933 Jones wrote, 'There is no possible way to get rid of one desire except to replace it by a higher desire. One does not get rid of desire by its suppression, but by its expression in a higher form.' When our love, Jones continued, becomes 'fastened upon a personality like Christ, [it] rises into a higher form and is redeeming ... The unsatisfied desire is therefore removed, not by its extinction, but through its satisfaction. The love of the lower is cast out by the love of the higher'.[60]

3.2.4 The spiritual supremacy of the living Christ

This above passage is just one of many examples through which Jones makes it abundantly clear that he believed that true richness of life could not be found without Jesus, while also demonstrating how Jones could skilfully interweave certain aspects of Christianity into an Indic world view. Jones's emphasis on the centrality of the person of Jesus is also seen in the round-table conferences at which he facilitated interreligious dialogues from 1917. When reflecting on these dialogues in his written work, Jones notes his gratitude to the participants for having taught him about Hinduism and Indian culture through these exchanges, and he further professed that elements of his own Christian faith had been altered through these interactions.[61] He describes his participation as a form of 'sympathetic listening', and we can understand him as having entered into dialectical exchanges with the Hindus who attended these sessions.[62] Throughout these dialogues, Jones required that individuals (when it was their turn to speak) did not argue vociferously with others and further stipulated that they must not attempt to convince others to follow their own religion, nor were they permitted to enter into intellectual arguments about questions of doctrine or historicity. Individuals were not even allowed to speak 'abstractly' or to 'merely discuss religion'. Rather, individuals must share, from the resourceful wellsprings of their personal experiences, what their religion had done for them.[63] In the midst of regulating these terms of discussion so as to encourage individuals to speak of their own personal experiences, through creating an environment where he would share his own experiences of Jesus with others, Jones would also unabashedly seek to demonstrate that Jesus offered something unique to all humanity for spiritual life. It must be made clear that Jones's Christ-centred world view did not allow the possibility that any other religious pathway was as soteriologically efficacious as the Christianity that he had himself embraced. In this vein, in 1935 he wrote, 'I am persuaded that the Christian religion ... has more of the Kingdom of God within it than any other system. It has within it the noblest ideals, the finest character, and the most self-giving service to the human race of any religious system.'[64] Jones earnestly desired to contribute to creating and participating in a 'miniature Kingdom of God' (I shall return to this in Section 3.5), and he wanted to do whatever he could to inspire and enable others to equally participate in fostering such a community. Yet, to Jones, this God-centred community would be best achieved when striving to enact the theological ideals encapsulated within Christianity, and, consequently, this goal would be most effectively reached through striving to become more like the person of Jesus.

Jones's perception of Christ as the supreme and unique personal God is further seen through the ways in which he occasionally reinterpreted the religious lives of his dialogue partners through Christocentric prisms. For example, though Jones was no doubt aware of plenty of examples of individuals whose lives were vitally shaped by unwavering devotion to a deity other than Jesus – *bhaktas* (devotees) were one of the six classifications that Jones himself retroactively applied to the individuals who had frequented his round-table conferences[65] – he remained adamant that devotion to anyone other than Jesus was simply not as spiritually transformative an experience as was devotion to Jesus. Jones's substantiation for this claim is based on his personal reflections on anonymized individuals who, according to him, did not undergo the same type or degree of spiritual transformation as individuals who are devoted to Christ – this conviction consistently forms the basis for his arguments in most of his books. For Jones, it was Jesus alone who could imbue individual lives with positive spiritual significance and effect salvific transformations, and it was the spiritual teachings of Jesus alone which could 'heal a society' and 'give life' to individuals and communities. Consequently, it was only Jesus who was fully worthy of being the supreme object of our self-surrender.[66] Despite respecting – and even, as we noted above, learning from – some of their points of philosophy, Jones described non-Christian religions with terms such as 'inadequate'[67] and 'bankrupt',[68] and insinuated that even their most redemptive qualities were, in fact, the result of 'an importation from Christian sources'.[69] He thus felt that India was plagued by 'a spirit of almostness' in which individuals, through their various religious beliefs and practices, had come so close to realizing God and yet very few of them had actually arrived at this goal.[70] Referencing Jones's consistent declarations of Christianity as the supreme religion, Martin therefore notes that 'in spite of the many inclusivist tendencies in Jones's thought, a bedrock of exclusivism remained'.[71]

Jones's view in this regard was, of course, not unique to him; Catherine Cornille has identified T. E. Slater (1840–1912) as 'one of the first advocates of this fulfillment theory' which asserts, in Slater's words, that 'the Christian Gospel thus offers all that the Vedanta offers, and infinitely more … Christ includes all the teachers'.[72] According to this fulfilment theology, human beings have certain innate religious yearnings which can be satisfied by a series of 'lower' religions which are progressively replaced by the 'highest' one, namely, Christianity, into which they 'evolve'. We can see this view quite clearly in Jones's assertion above regarding the 'almostness' of non-Christian religions.[73] According to this view, the lower religions are ordained by God for the purpose of gradually training human beings to receive the fullest revelation in Christianity.[74]

3.2.5 Christian-in-the-making

Lest, however, we hastily characterize Jones as a domineering religious man who championed all expressions of Christianity while wholly repudiating all non-Christian ones, I want to make it clear that Jones also felt that the lives of a significant number of Christians were equally characterized by a lack of intimacy with God as indicated by their absence of a sense of fellowship with Christ.[75] Indeed, Jones readily admitted that Jones himself, Western civilization and the Christian church were all in continual processes of becoming reformed into a more Christ-like existence, and he explained all of their shortcomings as the inevitable result of the world not yet becoming fully conformed to Christ. It was only Jesus, Jones proclaimed, who was impeccably beyond reproach. Thus, Jones writes,

> I will have to apologize for myself again and again, for I'm only a Christian-in-the-making. I will have to apologize for Western civilization, for it is only partly christianized. I will have to apologize for the Christian church, for it, too, is only partly christianized. But when it comes to Jesus Christ, there are no apologies upon my lips, for there are none in my heart.[76]

This antipathy towards top-heavy ecclesiastical organizations is also reflected in Christian writers such as Kierkegaard for whom the organized structures of Christendom diverted individuals from a genuinely Christian existence, which should be shaped by a salvific transformation through the wholehearted emulation of the suffering of Christ.[77] The focus here is on the 'raw Christ' – the person of Jesus himself – and not on the Christ who is refracted through creedal formulations, social formations or ecclesiastical organizations. All of this reveals, once again, that for Jones to be authentically *Christian* – that is, to truly become transformed through spiritual intimacy with Christ and, through this ongoing process of Christ-centred discipleship, to realize God – necessitated conscious, unwavering and complete self-surrender to the person of Jesus so as to enter a state of ongoing transformation. Jones desired that all individuals, including those who already inhabited Christian contexts, would make conscious efforts to 'vertically convert' themselves (a process which Jones distinguished from 'horizontal conversion', i.e. moving from one religious identity to another[78]) by way of making Christ the central point in every aspect of their life.[79] In other words, for Jones the real conversion is not so much the lateral ('horizontal') shift across socioreligious identities but the inner ('vertical') turn to the living Christ.[80]

Ensuring that STA was a *Christian* ashram, then, meant for Jones more than it being simply a place where Christians happened to gather, for he was insistent, in the anti-ecclesiastical tone of Kierkegaard who declared that 'Christendom is a prodigious illusion',[81] that individuals and institutions who identify as Christians might not, however, be fully committed to Christ. STA was also more than just a place where Christian doctrine happened to be taught. In claiming the ashram to be resolutely *Christian*, I therefore understand Jones to have been signalling his desire that STA would be a place where individuals would learn to surrender their everyday worldly selves fully to Jesus and to actively cultivate patterns of Christian discipleship. From this reflection, I interpret STA's daily practices like morning *dhyan* (which, as I shall elaborate upon below, took the form of a forty-five-minute period of individual contemplation of a selected biblical passage) and *shramdaan* (a one-hour work period in which individuals worked wherever help was needed in the ashram) as spiritual tools aimed at enabling individuals to become more Christ-like. Consistently throughout his writings, Jones argued that commitment to Christ was to be displayed through the ongoing transformation of one's attitudes, instincts and practices[82] – and so the virtues cultivated through such transformation were both the means to reach that end of Christ-likeness, and simultaneously they were the expressions of approaching that end.

3.2.6 '… and truly Indian'

Having explored some dimensions of what Jones meant by his claim that STA should be 'truly Christian', we can now begin to explore what he meant by his claim that it should also be 'truly Indian'. I have already outlined the various ways that Jones was influenced by his wider socioreligious milieus to associate Indianness specifically with forms of Brahmanical Hinduism and Advaita

Vedanta. Like many of his time, Jones did not think of 'Indians' as Muslim, Sikh, Jew or any other religious identity. We might think of Jones's thought patterns through a series of conceptual equivalences in this way: to be truly Indian was to be culturally Hindu, and to be culturally Hindu was, in turn, to be familiar with Brahmanical cultural idioms which have Vedantic undertones. Ergo, a *true* Indian is an individual whose life is shaped by Vedantic notions, values and experiences. Although Jones's writing does, at times, demonstrate an understanding that Hinduism contained many different sects and philosophies,[83] he often wrote and preached in ways that used the term 'Hindu' to refer exclusively to individuals from educated and higher-caste backgrounds who were clearly aligned with Brahmanical, Vedantic philosophies and practices. Such Brahmanical descriptions are epitomized in Jones's description of Jesus as 'the Christ of the Indian Road', in which Jones envisions that Brahmins would imagine Jesus to be wearing the garments of an ascetic.[84]

We find some further evidence that Jones's understanding of Hinduism was deeply reflective of Brahmanical qualities in the ways in which he taught other foreigners – especially his close friends and family – about Hinduism. Acharya James K. Mathews, Jones's son-in-law and the man whom he appointed in 1971 to be his successor as the chief Acharya of STA, was, by his own admission, profoundly influenced by Jones. Thus, when interviewed in 1974, Acharya Mathews proclaimed an understanding of Hinduism which had strikingly Brahmanical resonances: "The Hindu spiritual ideal is self-cultivation. It is self-control. It is finally self-negation. The further you go into Hinduism, the more withdrawn you become from the world, and the more you concentrate on yourself and your identification with God."[85] This understanding of Hinduism is saturated with notions of world-renunciation and rigorous asceticism (*sannyasa*) that simply do not play a significant role in many devotional and folk expressions of Hinduism. Importantly, it is not that this understanding of Hinduism is incorrect (insomuch as there certainly are expressions of Hinduism which match Mathews's description) but it is grossly incomplete, for it reductively equates the diverse socioreligious traditions of Hinduisms with specific strands of Brahmanical Hinduism, as if there were no other diverse expressions on the ground. On the contrary, there are many Indians who self-identify as coming from Hindu family backgrounds but who have no affinity with the 'high' forms of Brahmanical Hinduism, and who would instead see their Hindu social lifestyles as robustly world-affirming. There are also many Indians who hold no familiar ties with any branch of Hinduism. In fact, as Chapter 4 shall explore in greater detail, STA witnessed an increasing entry of individuals who clearly did not affiliate themselves with Brahmanical Hinduism in the 1990s, when it established its one-month long SoE programme with heavily subsidized rates so as to allow all individuals, irrespective of their socio-economic status, to visit the ashram. Nonetheless, looking back at 1930, when Jones envisioned STA as 'truly Indian', it is clear that he sought to imbue it with specifically Brahmanical idioms that would seem acceptable and familiar to Hindus from such backgrounds.

Along these lines, Jones stipulated in his 'Ashram Ideals' that 'the dress, the food, the manner of eating would be Indian. As we expect Hindus to come and share life with us for longer or shorter periods the food would be vegetarian'.[86] Jones thus encouraged men and women to wear 'traditional Indian clothing', and there are many photos in the STA archives which show Jones himself dressed in such Indian garb, sometimes with a garland of flowers around his neck – though there are also just as many photos of him dressed in a suit and tie while walking around the ashram grounds. But we can notice how Jones, in his succinct use of the term 'Indian', again equates Indian identity with Brahmanical Hinduism – the adherence to a vegetarian diet is not something that all Hindus deem to be an important dimension of their lifestyle, and surely it is not a spiritual marker of the various other Indian religious individuals, for example, many Muslims, Sikhs, Christians and Jews throughout India. As for the vegetarian food, it is possible that Jones was aware of the ways in which some non-Christian Indians feared that beef-eating Christians might actively coerce them into eating meat, and that he wanted to avoid even the slightest suspicion that such an incident might occur at STA.[87] But this stipulation of an 'Indian diet', just like that of the wearing of an essentialized 'Indian clothing' – both reminiscent of the *accomodatio* of Roberto de Nobili which we discussed in Chapter 2 – was possibly due to Jones's intention to create a sociocultural atmosphere which would be familiar to Brahmanical Hindus and within which they would feel welcomed, all the while exploring and, Jones hoped, embracing the teachings of Christ.

3.3 Ethnographic moments: The quotidian contestations over 'truly Christian and truly Indian'

Having now painted, with broad brushstrokes, some of the features with which Jones envisioned the social backdrop of STA in order to make it 'truly Christian and truly Indian', I turn to my ethnographic fieldwork to demonstrate some of the ways that Jones's ideals from 1930 unfold in present-day lived experiences.

Thus, I offer 'thick' descriptions of three phenomena: the morning meditation (*dhyan*), the practice of individual labour (*shramdaan*) and the (non)-vegetarian cuisine served at STA. As the reader will observe, the last of these three is rather distinct from the first two. While the first two can be broadly seen as present-day phenomena which embody Jones's founding visions, the third, as we will see, disrupts this pattern due to the ways that the lived-out realities of the current practices surrounding the occasional supply of non-vegetarian cuisine contradict what Jones had envisioned for STA. But, rather than interpret the third as indicative of a failure to live out Jones's founding vision, I argue that this rupture ultimately bolsters the point that the first two phenomena begin to demonstrate: namely, that the STA community's embracing of Indian cultural idioms occurs only when such practices are thought to enrich the Christian ethos of STA. As such, 'Christian' occupies the place of the primary substantive identifier for which 'Indian' becomes a descriptive adjectival qualifier – a concept that we saw in Chapter 2 in the context of discussing inculturated Christianity (Section 2.3), and which we will return to in more detail in the theoretical framework that informs Chapter 5. In other words, I argue that, in Jones's vision, STA ashramites are primarily *Christians* who are Indians, and not *Indians* who merely happen to inhabit Christian spiritualities. We recall that Jones himself emphasized that STA is first and foremost a *Christian* ashram. Thus, my aim is to highlight some of the various ways that some STA ashramites navigate the processes of being both 'truly Christian' and 'truly Indian'.

3.3.1 *Dhyan*

Though we will only consider *dhyan* briefly, it is important to have some sense of this aspect of spiritual practice at STA. Etymologically, the Hindi word *dhyan* comes from the Sanskrit root *dhyai* which means 'to think of', and *dhyan* is today often translated into English as 'meditation' – at STA, *dhyan* encompasses scriptural reading, silent meditation and sharing one's reflections with the group. Depending on the size of the group at any given time, the morning *dhyan* either takes place in a small room in the Midlakes building (the main building at STA and one of the few original buildings from when the grounds had been a tea plantation nearly one hundred years ago) or in the spacious chapel. Both rooms feature several artistic renditions of STA's iconic 'Jesus is Lord' motto, and the chapel is especially well decorated with uplifting spiritually themed art pieces.

During my fieldwork in 2016, most individuals removed their shoes before entering the building for *dhyan* – an action of respect and reverence which is practised in many other religious contexts throughout India. We focused on one chapter from a biblical text each day – the *dhyan* during my fieldwork was centred on the Gospel of Matthew and then, when we finished reading through it, the Gospel of John. We usually spent about fifteen minutes in silent reflection before being invited to share any of our reflections with, or direct our questions to, the wider group. The reflections varied in depth and type depending on the individuals who were present; during the SoE, which I focus on in Chapter 4, individuals often picked up on phrases and verses which highlighted the power of Jesus, especially his healing power while, at the Winter Ashram that I attended, the theme of healing was rarely mentioned.

3.3.2 *Shramdaan*

We can also consider STA's practice where all individuals participate in an hour-long *shramdaan* (work period) and other forms of labour. The word *shram* (etymologically related to the word *ashram* – 'no work') can be translated as work or labour and the word *daan* (also often used at ashrams to refer to monetary donations) can be translated as generosity; *shramdaan*, then, is the voluntary giving of oneself through the act of labour. In spite of the fact that STA refers to the hour-long period as *shramdaan* on its written schedule, many of the ashramites at present-day STA simply use the English phrase 'work period', even when conversing in Hindi. Today at STA there is, at least among some of the ashramites (particularly those who have been coming to the ashram for a long time, and especially those who knew Jones personally), an eager enthusiasm to join and participate in the long-standing tradition of STA's work period. Through their keen involvement, what can appear as a mere quotidian action is also combined with their conscious intent and thereby holds the spiritual potential to be transformed into a religious act; in other words, labour is not simply a physical exercise but is a spiritual activity.[88] In order to understand this distinction, it would be useful to first articulate some of the precise reasons why Jones desired everyone at STA to do their own dishes. On one level, washing one's own dishes is a simple and straightforward practice of STA to circumvent the need for paid labour. At this level of interpretation, the act of washing dishes would be viewed as a daily chore and a 'mere routine' which some social scientists have contrasted with a ritual.[89] Yet, at another level, seemingly mundane actions such as washing one's own dishes and participating in the one-hour daily 'work period' were intentionally implemented as ashram rules by Jones for the purpose of removing any sociocultural prejudices associated with the traditional orders of

Brahmanical social hierarchy, in which those who are thought of as ascriptively 'lower' would have to serve those who are ascriptively 'higher' in socio-ritual and socio-economic status.[90] Washing dishes is thus a labour of love in which one lovingly offers one's self to the ashram.

Anthropological discourses on ritual and performative action offer some helpful insights into this discussion. I argue that Jones, and the subsequent Acharyas, envision labour as an action through which certain understandings regarding both the spiritual value of labouring as well as the conscious rejection of social stigma surrounding certain types of labour could be ritually encoded and expressed. In anthropological discussions of ritual action, Victor Turner's definition of ritual as 'a stereotyped sequence of activities involving gestures, words, and objects, performed in a sequestered place, and designed to influence preternatural entities or forces on behalf of the actors' goals and interest' often enters the discussion.[91] However, Fiona Bowie, drawing upon the work of Audrey Richards from the 1950s, cautions anthropologists from developing too narrow and overly nuanced definitions of what counts as ritual; she instead asserts that the study of ritual should be broadened to include actions that do not immediately strike one as particularly meaningful or symbolic, and which are not limited to intentionally attempting to influence a supernatural or 'preternatural' realm.[92]

More useful for our understanding of dishwashing at STA in ritual terms is Bobby C. Alexander's definition of ritual, in which ritual is conceptualized broadly as a 'performance' through which everyday acts are transformed into something meaningful and potentially powerful.[93] Interpreting ritual as a kind of cultural performance or drama allows Alexander to emphasize that 'enacting' (which he compares to 'acting' and contrasts with 'just pretending') 'contradicts neither the notion of belief nor the practice of theatrical acting'.[94] Thus, in addition to playing a role in actively *reimagining* the cognitively inscribed order of social status, physical labour was also described by Jones as a selflessly performed act that allowed the individual to become more like Jesus through an active surrender of the sense of a hierarchized self. That is to say, the everyday act itself – unlike the ritualized actions usually focused on in the context of Turner's definition of ritual – was only made powerful through the inward self-surrender of the individual performing the action. Thus, this spiritualized activity of washing dishes can be viewed as a recurring event through which every individual – often three or even four times daily[95] – concretely participates in a physical enactment of both the rejection of social hierarchy and the intentional practice of selfless action as a means of ongoing re-formation and reorientation to Christ who is himself often described by the New Testament as a 'servant'.[96]

Although individuals were clearly informed of the expectation that they would each wash their individual dishes at the beginning of their stay at STA, this point was not highlighted time and time again – and, through being loosely enforced, this created an opportunity for individuals to determine the extent to which they would participate in the labour. While some ashramites (predominantly, I noted, the men whose wives or mothers accompanied them) did at times nonchalantly shirk the task of washing their own dishes, a number of individuals were adamant about their desire to 'religiously' wash their own dishes after every single meal and teatime. I recall here Uncle William's response when I once offered to wash his dishes along with my own, sometime during the October 2016 Winter session. Uncle William – a long-time ashramite of STA and someone who had heard Jones deliver public lectures in Mumbai – was in his mid-eighties and on that day he seemed particularly low in energy. After I offered, he looked me squarely in the eye and told me, 'I informed you early on that you would become like my daughter. And so, *as my daughter whom I love*, you can wash my plate today. But tomorrow, I will return to washing my own. You know, Dr Stanley Jones also washed his own plates! It's the way of the ashram!' This sort of confessional declaration epitomizes the awareness that offering selfless labour was a way of imitating the beloved founder Jones (who himself had sought to imitate Christ). Further, it demonstrates that Jones's desire for social statuses to be equalized and for all individuals to participate in labour in communitarian settings has been successfully embraced by some ashramites. Indeed, Uncle William emphasized, his sanctioning of his plate to be washed by someone else was not because he viewed himself as ascriptively higher to others; such surrendering itself was, instead, another expression of his ongoing cultivation of the labour of love.

3.3.3 (Non-)vegetarian cuisine

We can also look at the practices surrounding food and eating at STA in order to come to a better understanding of some of the precise ways that STA inherited and sought to promote Jones's vision of STA as 'truly Christian and truly Indian'. As early as pre–Second World War,[97] anthropologists were particularly interested in food and eating habits because food reveals, and sometimes also reaffirms, significant details about the social cohesiveness of a cultural group.[98] Indeed, as Eliot Singer argues, the act of eating is 'not just an instrumental behavior for obtaining nutrients' but it is also 'a means of expressing beliefs, ideals, and ambitions'.[99] Just as through the physical ingestion of food, the *biological* health of one individual is maintained, through the participation of specific individuals at a shared meal, certain *social* boundaries are established and defended. Indeed, the consumption of food is a truly socio-biological event: the types of material food that are prepared and eaten, as well as the socialized actions and activities that occur leading up to, during and after the 'breaking of bread' are particularly revealing about the self-understanding of a given group. When we consider the food practices of STA we see, strikingly, two somewhat incongruous phenomena: (1) Jones envisioned the ashram as serving vegetarian food so as not to ward off (Brahmanical) Hindus; and yet (2) STA today regularly serves eggs, fish and meat – all of which are clearly considered to be 'non-vegetarian' in an Indian context of diet.

This conspicuous dissonance surrounding the practice originally envisioned by Jones and the present-day lived-out negotiations hinges on vegetarianism – a dietary choice that, as I shall elaborate upon below, is inseparable from religious practice and identity in various Indian contexts. This association of 'vegetarianism' and 'religion' was clearly evident at STA. For example, in a series of pre-fieldwork administrative emails with Mr Kabir Likhna, the estate manager of STA, I inquired about whether STA currently followed a vegetarian diet. In his reply, Kabir informed me that the ashram did cook a lot of vegetarian food but pointed out that it also served fish and meat occasionally. 'Not to forget', he added pointedly, 'that it is a *Christian* Ashram.' He followed up that sentence with a kind and jovial assurance that I, a vegetarian, would still 'get my veggies'. But his explicit assertion to me that STA is 'a *Christian* ashram' – in the context of an inquiry about vegetarian food – was quite striking. To outsiders to Indian sociocultural contexts, it might not be immediately evident that he was implicitly working through a chain of conceptual equivalences: 'Vegetarian food = *Hinduism*; STA is a *Christian* ashram; therefore, STA also serves fish and meat.' And, thus, non-vegetarian food was regularly available from STA's kitchen.

3.3.4 Considering Indian practices alongside Christian identity

Holding these three ethnographic descriptions in mind, we can proceed to explore the episode relating to (non-)vegetarian cuisine in further detail since, as I indicated above, it ruptures the pattern established by the previous two phenomena – here, the present-day reality directly contradicts Jones's envisioned ideal. First, it might be helpful to summarize some key points about vegetarianism within Indian socioreligious contexts more broadly. As Parvis Ghassem-Fachandi highlights in his book chapter which explores responses to meat and meat-eating in central Gujarat, vegetarianism has been articulated by some members of various right-wing Hindu affiliations as the most noble choice of diet.[100] Fully aware of this association between vegetarianism and religious purity, ashrams – that is, Hindu ashrams – have typically followed strict vegetarian diets not only because vegetarian cooking is a simpler and more affordable way of cooking/eating for large numbers of people but also because ashrams were populated by upper-caste Hindus who viewed non-vegetarian food as impure. Apart from following a strict vegetarian diet, some Hindu ashrams would additionally avoid certain foods which are understood to excite passion, hatred and anger – most commonly including spicy food, garlic and onion.[101] The justification for avoiding such items is to facilitate the generation of an internal environment in which the seeker can focus on the spiritual life, and not consume foods which are understood to evoke vicious emotions.[102]

Moving on from this theme, I consider the non-vegetarian cuisine cooked and consumed at STA as a practice that asserts and re-affirms that STA is unequivocally *Christian* and, as such, is not bound by such Hindu ideologies concerning food purity. I do not mean to suggest that STA offers non-vegetarian food with the same militant fervour as the various social groups and individuals who have recently engaged in 'beef-eating protests' as a way of enacting what C. Sathyamala refers to as 'a political act of subversion' opposed to the current ban against slaughtering and eating beef.[103] Indeed, STA was careful to always clearly label their food as either 'veg' or 'non-veg', and to always have a 'veg' option available whenever non-vegetarian food was being served. As I learned throughout my fieldwork, for many at STA the decision to cook non-vegetarian food was nothing other than a practical choice which allowed meat-eaters to eat meat while ensuring that vegetarians could still follow a vegetarian diet. That is to say, there was no specifically anti-Hindu vehemence to ensure that meat must be consumed – although, as a vegetarian myself, I was often at the receiving end of individuals' genuine confusion, utter bafflement and jovial mocking regarding why a vegetarian diet would be maintained by individuals who did not otherwise adhere to Brahmanical purity laws. Throughout my many conversations with Acharya G. (the resident Acharya of STA during my fieldwork), for example, he never once communicated even the slightest indication that STA's non-vegetarian cuisine had anything to do with consciously subverting Hindu ideological equivalences between food consumed and embodied spirituality. Indeed, when I asked him if he could recollect the timeline or the rationale for introducing non-vegetarian food into STA, he simply shrugged his shoulders and offered this rather mundane explanation as his best theory: 'Maybe around the same time we stopped using oil lamps and got flush toilets ... probably because the ashram had more money? It is the same with us having sweets after dinner – people like to eat well.'

And yet, I argue, the absence of a clear adherence to vegetarianism at STA effectively serves to establish a boundary line – conceptual as much as social – between that which is normatively Hindu and that which is normatively Christian. This is an iteration of a broader phenomenon that is well accepted by various social theorists: the self, and indeed the group that one self-identifies with, is determined dialectically in relation to others; we define who we are through the transactional processes of seeking to clearly delineate who we are not.[104] Self-*identity* is thus the obverse of *other*-construction.[105] To be clear, the STA management was acutely aware that their inclusion of non-vegetarian food rejected the Brahmanical practices of eating vegetarian food – the very practices that Jones was aware of and thus had laid down that the ashram would serve vegetarian food.

Although, as I shall explore in greater detail in Chapter 4, many of the original features of the ashram have changed over the years (and, specifically, some of the more Brahmanical dietary characteristics have become less palatable, literally speaking, to the ashramites as the social demographics have changed), I find it striking that vegetarianism was one of the first features of STA's 'Indianness' to be cast aside. By lumping together non-vegetarian food with after-dinner sweets, the non-vegetarian diet is conceptualized as a welcome luxury and a pleasant treat – not as an element which potentially obstructs the atmosphere of 'Indianness' conceived as 'Vedantically Hindu'. I wonder if this somewhat casual slippage is because the strict adherence to a vegetarian diet was never conceptualized as a spiritual practice which had the potential to positively transform individuals through making them more Christ-like. After all, other 'Indian' elements of STA such as the morning *dhyan* or the *shramdaan*, as I have discussed above in Sections 3.3.1 and 3.3.2, did actively promote Jones's vision of STA to be a place where individuals would live out a life of obedience to Christ. But, in contrast to these other practices of contemplation and action, I speculate that vegetarianism was simply not conceptualized as having this type of transformative potential.

Keeping in mind the extent to which Christianity had been perceived by many Indians as being a religion of foreigners (Chapter 2), I contend that the initial success of STA was vitally dependent on Jones's effort to weave together

Christian and Indian aspects so that they might both peacefully co-exist in the lifeworld of STA. In such a way, cultural idioms that signified 'Indianness' were permitted – and even encouraged – to be a part of spiritual life at STA provided they did not impinge upon one's Christian existence. Thus, practices like *dhyan* and *shramdaan* continue to be embraced by STA leadership even if, as we shall see in Chapter 4, they are sometimes met with differing views by the individuals who come to STA. And yet, as suggested by the instance of (non-)vegetarianism, these very Indian aspects had a certain dispensable quality to them, and thus had the potential to be discarded when they no longer seemed to serve the purpose of deepening one's Christian faith. I think that many at STA conceptualized vegetarianism as, to use one of Jones's own analogies, a 'rusted key' which could be 'laid aside' once it was revealed to no longer 'unlock' a closeness to Christ. 'What', Acharya G. once pointedly posed to me in casual conversation, 'did eating veg food do for one's spiritual life?' The Acharya's reluctance to embrace spiritual practices that did not seem to explicitly bring individuals closer to Christ is one that we shall see again in Chapter 5 in the context of adopting a prolonged period of silence.

By considering phenomena such as the morning *dhyan*, *shramdaan* and the (non-)vegetarian cuisine, we can note some of the embodied ways through which Jones attempted to inform and inflect the atmosphere of STA with characteristics of both Christianity and Indianness. But, by exploring the ways that each of these three practices are negotiated in the lived realities of ashramites today, we can further observe that, in the effort to be 'truly Christian and truly Indian', it would seem that each identity is not pursued with an equal vigour. Rather, 'truly Christian' is given preference and is, thus, placed as 'higher' than 'truly Indian' – something that is not entirely surprising when considered in the light of Jones's own equation of Christianity with Christ, and, subsequently, of Christ with life.

3.4 'All who sincerely desire to find God'

We can now sketch an overview of the second and the third visions that Jones had for STA when he established it in 1930 (Section 3.1.4). The reader can recall that Jones wanted it to be a place where all individuals (regardless of their faith affiliation, or lack thereof) who sought God would be welcomed into the spiritual community of STA. Just as in the case of understanding what Jones precisely meant by STA being 'truly Christian and truly Indian', we must also ask here: What did Jones understand 'sincerely desiring' and 'God' to mean?

Must the act of *seeking* – part and parcel to *finding* – follow a specific pattern or protocol? Was 'God' to be used as a synonym for 'Jesus' –that is, the personal Christ whom Jones dearly loved and preached about? These questions, as we shall see, will become vitally important in Chapter 5 and, thus, I shall return to them in more detail later on. For now, one point regarding Jones's view of 'sincerely desiring to find God' will have to suffice: Jones was clearly aware of the vast ways that various individuals attempted to seek God, and, referring to the various religious expressions in India alone, Jones observed, 'I have found India God-stirred, but still seeking. There is not yet that sense of finding.'[106] Thus, Jones believed the majority of Indians to be plagued by a state of continual seeking without finding – an 'almostness' in their questing, as we have seen (Section 3.2.5). Jones contrasted this with Christians who, he was convinced, had attained their 'finding' via Christ, even though they were Christians-in-the-making who had to become progressively more conformed to Christ.

3.5 'Becoming the answer' by living out a miniature kingdom of God

Noting the ways that India was 'God-stirred, but still seeking', Jones further wanted the very community of STA to 'be the answer' (as opposed to simply seeking answers) by living out a miniature kingdom of God. Earlier in this chapter (Section 3.2.4) I discussed Jones's statement that 'the Christian religion ... has more of the Kingdom of God within it than any other system' in the light of his conviction that Christianity (rooted in Jesus) was morally and spiritually superior to other religious traditions and spiritual leaders.[107] And yet, Jones's statement contains additional nuances that I had to set aside from our discussion until now. The full quotation reads:

> I am persuaded that the Christian religion, *even as it is now organized with all its faults*, has more of the Kingdom of God within it than any other system. It has within it the noblest ideals, the finest character, and the most self-giving service to the human race of any religious system ... I repeat that the Christian religion *in its ideal state* would be [synonymous with the Kingdom of God], *but I am not dealing with that ideal system*.[108]

I have used italics to emphasize the eschatological nuances contained in this viewpoint: namely, Jones conceptualized Christianity (i.e. as taught and modelled by Jesus Christ) as an ideal state which diverse historical Christian expressions (i.e. the socioreligious expressions that Christians indwell and are limited to) can never reach. We have seen this theme elsewhere in Jones's writings (we recall that he described himself as a 'Christian-in-the-making') and there are, of course, a host of other Christian theologians who have articulated more or less this same viewpoint – from the Apostle Paul in the first century to, as we have seen, Kierkegaard. But, since we wish to gain an understanding of what Jones meant by his desire for STA to be a 'kingdom of God in miniature', it is especially important to note that Jones associates the eschatological *ideal* (i.e. the fully perfected version) of Christianity with the phrase 'the Kingdom of God'.

Jones, who graduated from Asbury theological seminary in 1907, was perhaps shaped by the influential writings of the distinguished Princeton theologian Geehardus Vos, who wrote in 1903 about the teachings of Jesus concerning the Kingdom of God in which he distinguished between the 'present' and the 'future' Kingdom of God; he indicated that the immanent 'manifestation' in historical time was only 'partial' and would come to fulfilment in the eschatological future.[109] Vos described the activities of Christian communities as being part of an 'internal kingdom' which still required them to go through 'a lengthy process'[110] of spiritual transformation.[111] This eschatological theme had also been highlighted by John Nicol Farquhar, one of the most well-known Christian missionary figures in India in the 1910s and the 1920s, and someone with whose arguments Jones was familiar. Farquhar had argued that there are many riches in Christ which are yet to be unearthed and many of Christ's teachings are not properly understood and appropriated, and this process of discovery requires the efforts of the entire 'human family'. It is only when the biblical promise that all the nations shall be brought under Christ reaches its eschatological fulfilment that the 'religious genius' of India, reformed by Christ, will come alive in his light.[112] Jones resonated with Farquhar's missionary approach – in 1925 Jones described it as 'a vast improvement on the old method [of attacking the weaknesses of other religions]'[113] – but he additionally wanted to go beyond it by actively setting up an environment where, through open, non-aggressive dialogue, he could introduce individuals to 'the positive presentation of Christ'.[114] Thus, for Jones, we see that the Kingdom of God that he wished to establish at STA was conceptualized as both the transhistorical ideal of Christianity (or, at least, the conscious act of striving towards that ideal) and a dialogical environment through which Christ could be presented in historical contexts to particular individuals. These theological nuances, as we shall see in Chapter 5, are of the utmost importance to understanding some of the present-day dynamics that unfold at STA.

3.6 Conclusion

This chapter explored some of Jones's motivations for, and methods of, endeavouring to ensure that STA was truly Christian and truly Indian. Because of the ways that concepts like 'Christian' featured so prominently in Jones's formation of his 1930 'Ashram Ideals', we were thus prompted, in turn, to seek to understand how Jones understood what it meant to be Christian, and how he conceptualized the relationship between Christianity and Western society. As we saw, Jones's proclamation that he was *Christian* was just as consistent and resolute as his proclamation that *Christianity* was not limited to its Western expressions – for Jones, Westernization and Christianization are not synonymous processes, just as spiritual rootedness in Christ and Christian identity are indelibly linked. My ethnographic vignettes indicate that this particular desire to make STA 'truly Christian and truly Indian' continues to be played out in STA through several embodied expressions, including *dhyan*, *shramdaan* and (non-)vegetarian cuisine. Subsequently, we asked the following question: Did Jones imagine 'Christian' and 'Indian' as two individual identities peacefully coexisting alongside each other, or was it a fusion or merging of the two identities into one cohesive form? We saw the various ways that Jones prioritized the *Christian* identity over and above any other identity marker. Along with his aim of 'truly Christian and truly Indian', Jones also envisioned STA as a place where all individuals 'who sincerely desire to find God' would be welcomed, and where a 'miniature Kingdom of God' would be lived out. As we shall see in the forthcoming chapters, these three foundational visions are put to the test during the decades following his articulation of them in 1930. Specifically, the formation of the SoE in 1991 would challenge the understanding of what the hybridity of both 'truly Christian' and 'truly Indian' looks like – a theme that I explore in more detail in Chapter 4.

4

The School of Evangelism and its challenge to the ideal of 'truly Christian and truly Indian'

4.1 Introduction

Sometime around 5.30 am, the first bell of the morning rang and, somewhat resentfully, I cast off the woollen blanket from my tired body and prepared to step out of bed. I could almost picture the watchman grinning mischievously as he rang the bell in the darkness, making it CLANG CLANG CLANG and echo throughout the otherwise quiet hills. Even the songbirds had barely woken up. My hands fumbled underneath my pillow, searching for my torch, and when I found it I robotically turned it on and began to scan the room for spiders. It was early September and, in the persistent monsoon rains, more than usual of these creepy-crawlies were inclined to make their homes within any dry shelter they could find. My room, uninhabited for weeks before my arrival, appeared to be an especially welcoming place for the palm-sized spiders that thrive in Sat Tal's tropical climate. I knew I was safe as I slept – one day before leaving Delhi for the ashram I had purchased a mosquito net which was really more like a tent – but I always performed my ritual scan before working up the courage to exit my mosquito-free fortress.

But spider-scanning was not supposed to be my first morning ritual. Indeed, according to the ashram's schedule, I was supposed to have woken up well before the 5.30 am bell for my own personal meditative practice.[1] The 5.30 am bell was then to serve merely as a warning or preparatory reminder for individuals to join the group's morning meditation (*dhyan*) at 6 am in the small chapel-like room in the Midlakes building. In my first few weeks of living at STA, still relatively unaccustomed to the practice of personal meditation, if ever I woke up before the first bell, I used the time to go on an early morning jog, or to wander through the hills with my phone, searching for an adequate mobile connection in order to be able to load and read my emails. Despite my fervent, far-and-wide seeking for a 3G signal, one could hardly call my quest meditative. I was evidently not the only one who slept in until the first bell rather than waking up early for personal meditation: many a time, as I walked briskly to the group *dhyan* to avoid being late, I was joined by several men from Rajasthan who stayed in a cottage near my own room and who rubbed the sleep out of their eyes as we stumbled groggily to *dhyan* together.

This experiential disjuncture between that which is *normatively expected*, or *prescribed*, and that which *actually happens* is a reoccurring phenomenon often observed (and, indeed, theorized upon) by ethnographers; events rarely occur in the precise ways that one envisions them.[2] Through articulating the minute and sometimes mundane events of the SoE, the present chapter explores the disjuncture between that which is expected to occur and that which actually occurs by offering four phenomenologically sensitive ethnographic descriptions which highlight two different layers of disjuncture. A first layer is seen in the ways in which the development of the SoE in the 1990s contrasted starkly with some of Jones's original visions for STA (see Chapter 3, Sections 3.2, 3.4 and 3.5). The SoE was developed in the 1990s under the leadership of the newly appointed Acharya V. and the guidance of the former Acharya T., who wished to create a programme aimed at teaching and equipping individuals about some of the basic tenets of Protestant Christianity. The programme, which was launched in 1991[3] and attracted a handful of individuals who were working as independent evangelists, was dubbed 'the School of Evangelism' and celebrated its twenty-five-year anniversary during my fieldwork in September 2016. In direct contrast to the round-table conferences envisioned by Jones (see Chapter 3, Section 3.2.4) where individuals from different religious contexts were invited to speak about their personal experiences, the SoE is aimed specifically at individuals within Christian contexts and takes as its starting point the assumption that individuals can be reasoned into a Christian world view. This shift in focus, along with heavy financial subsidies from a Methodist church in Delhi so as to keep the costs of attending the SoE low, correlated with a noticeable change in the type of individual who came to STA: many of the SoE participants are from lower socio-economic backgrounds and/or come from low-caste Hindu families.[4] As I elaborated on in Chapter 3, Jones envisioned creating a spiritual community in which (Brahmanical) Hindus could feel culturally at home – and he did, with varying degrees of success, manage to create such an atmosphere at STA. But the sociocultural demographics of some of the SoE students, and their increasing presence at STA over the last three decades or so, is a sharp contrast to the

Brahmanical and Advaita Vedanta–inflected Hindus envisioned by Jones in his 1930 'Ashram Ideals'.

In addition to highlighting and exploring some of these demographic contrasts, this chapter simultaneously explores a second layer through which the disjuncture between that which was expected and that which has actually occurred is manifested: the expressions of Christianity that are highlighted and taught by the spiritual teachers of STA are noticeably different from the ones spoken of by the SoE students. Notable differences in conviction, belief and practice between teachers and students are – at least to some degree – often expected due to generational shifts, but for cultural anthropologists these differences are especially fascinating and thought-provoking. These on-the-ground variations of Christianity variously accentuate and give shape to the differing ways that Christianity can be conceptualized, spoken of and practised; furthermore, the ways through which these divergent expressions of Christianity are expressed often reveal important aspects of the relational dynamics between the teachers and the students. In other words, through paying close attention to some of the differences between the teachers and the students at the SoE, we not only 'see in action' multiple diverse expressions of lived Christianity but we can also use these differences as a sort of focal lens through which to gain a deeper understanding of teacher-student relationships at the SoE.

Thus, both the disjunctures – between (1) Jones's envisioned Hindus and the SoE students, as well as those between (2) the Christianities expressed by the SoE students and the teachers – will be discussed in this chapter. It might be helpful to think of the former as a diachronic disjuncture relating to varying demographic contexts across time and the latter as a synchronic disjuncture. These two types of spatio-temporal disjunctures, of course, cannot be fully disentangled from each other – not only because the first disjuncture has an obvious effect on the second due to the timelines involved but also because the latter sometimes points back to the former, especially as the SoE teachers purposely reference Jones's original visions for STA when justifying their present-day actions and beliefs. Nonetheless, it is useful to conceptualize these two disjunctures as distinctive threads, even if only as a functional manoeuvre to facilitate our ethnographic exploration.

To investigate some of the reasons which led to the development and the execution of the SoE, and to further explore some of the ways that these disjunctures play out on the ground, I sketch four ethnographic vignettes, each of which is pivoted on one of four key themes: labour, conversion, music and healing. Anthropologists who are familiar with the wide array of ethnographic literature focused specifically on even one of these four themes might contend that combining so many themes into one single chapter is, at best, overambitious. However, I am not purporting to conduct a thorough anthropological analysis of all or any of these themes; more modestly, I consider them together as distinctive features which are symptomatic and indicative of the wider socioreligious disjunctures contained in the SoE and highlighted in the previous paragraph. It is these underlying broader disjunctures themselves – not the specific expressions of difference – that I wish to highlight here. But, first, it is important to provide some contextual background information regarding the macrocosmic sociopolitical influences that led to, and were correlated with, the development of our microcosm of the SoE.

4.2 Contextualizing the development of the SoE within its sociopolitical and historical contexts

According to the recollections of the former Acharya V., who was the resident Acharya at STA during 1989–2009, the inspiration and impetus for the SoE originated with the former Chief Acharya Bishop Mathews – Jones's son-in-law whom Jones appointed as the chief Acharya of STA when Jones stepped down in 1971. Acharya V. recounted to me the manner in which he was approached by Acharya Mathews in 1991.

> [Acharya Mathews] asked me, 'Brother V, will you start this school of evangelism?' He provided a little money – approximately $1000 USD – and it was a challenge for me, and so I approached some organizations who could join with me. [Others] started sending their evangelists, and in this way the financial burden was shared. In the beginning it was a three-month programme, [and] the programme was designed for voluntary gospel ministry rather than being something that is job oriented. The gospel ministry was our focus. … And ever since we started, the SoE is going on – without any break. Without any break at all! I travelled to Kerala, to Bihar, to Rajasthan, Punjab, Madhya Pradesh, Gujarat, all over [to recruit students], and during my period [as resident Acharya], more than five hundred students came from over fourteen provinces! … And those students are now working in different ways. Some are freelance evangelists. Some have joined some organizations. Some five to six evangelists are working under a Methodist church. Every year students are coming.[5]

In addition to narrating the story of founding the SoE, in the same conversation Acharya V. further pointed out that, leading up to the formation of the SoE, there had been a steady decrease in the number of individuals who showed interest in coming to STA to participate in the other programmes offered there. He recalled trying to start a programme called *Adhyatmik Paricharcha* (which he described as 'a spiritual dialogue for Hindu people') in 1989, but in spite of advertising it widely across a number of different cities, only five or six individuals came to participate. And, even before Acharya V. was appointed as the Acharya in September 1989, his predecessor Acharya T. had experienced similar difficulties with holding a captive audience for the *satsangs* (truth-gatherings) that he had tried to implement around 1980. Eventually, Acharya T. ceased his *satsangs* completely due to a lack of participation, and he consequently advised Acharya V. against starting his own *satsangs*, speculating that there would not be enough interested audiences to sustain them.

These points were mentioned only briefly by Acharya V., and were offered as a sort of tangential evidence in support of his main view: that other Acharyas were not sufficiently gifted to maintain the same size or style of audience that Jones had seemed to attract effortlessly. As one of the many avid supporters of Jones and of STA, Acharya V. was not alone in attributing the decline of interest in STA to the loss of Jones as STA's Acharya. Many long-term ashramites of STA speculated that some of the most significant socioreligious changes over the last few decades – especially the decreasing interest in interreligious dialogues at the round-table conferences and the dwindling number of non-Christians, as well as Christians, who sought out STA for the spiritual environment offered through its programmes – were instigated by the loss of Jones, first, as STA's official leader in 1971 and, second, at his death in 1973. Such individuals spoke of Jones as having proverbially left behind shoes that were too big for any other Acharya to fill: Acharya V. called him a 'spiritual giant', and others like Acharya G., Auntie Eleanor and Dorothy Firr referred to him with similar descriptions, suggesting that he possessed a quality and depth of charisma which could not be matched by subsequent generations of leaders.

Although it is true that Jones possessed a certain knack for drawing people together, I contend that the significant shifts in the general climate of interreligious relations in India since the inauguration of STA in 1930, and during the subsequent years that Jones spent as the spiritual leader of the ashram, are equally important. Consequently, when exploring both the general decline of active interest in the programmes offered at STA and the development of the SoE, there are two vital factors which must be considered simultaneously. On one level – which focuses microcosmically on STA with a sort of tunnel vision – there is indeed the loss of a truly charismatic and talented spiritual leader who was replaced by generations of leaders who, while immensely passionate and well intentioned, did not seem to be able to match Jones's charisma. STA can therefore be understood in Weberian terms to have encountered its steady, and seemingly irrevocable, decline as a direct result of the shift in leadership and the subsequent loss of charisma.[6] While Jones's charisma might have been, to use Weber's expression, 'characteristically *unstable*'[7] insomuch as its supposed stability and power rested on the inevitably finite existence of a single, fallible human person, it allowed the ashram to grow and flourish – that is, until Jones ceased his leadership.[8] And yet, on another more macrocosmic level – one which recognizes the wider contexts within which STA inevitably operates – there were various sociopolitical changes in India during the decades leading up to 1990 that indirectly affected the operations of STA; more specifically, the Christian-Hindu (that is, Christian-Brahmin) interreligious relations that Jones had envisioned would flourish at STA were generally suffering from a decline in interest. Therefore, it seems plausible to me that, even if Jones had been able to continue indefinitely as the spiritual leader of STA, the shifting sociopolitical environments of northern India more broadly would have overtaken him, and created hurdles, or even impassable barricades, that would have undoubtedly complicated his efforts to maintain the spiritual environment that he so actively strove to create. To understand the reasons for the development of the SoE, therefore, we must hold together both of these micro and macro lenses in tandem.

4.2.1 Hindu nationalism and critiques of inculturation

Picking up a point we first encountered in Chapter 2 (Section 2.1) let us therefore study some of these sociopolitical contexts which influenced, however indirectly, individuals' receptivity to, and interest in, a Christian ashram and the various inculturated expressions of Christianity that STA sought to embody, enact and impart. Shortly following the establishment of STA in 1930, a number of different princely states in British India began to pass legal acts which prohibited conversion in their provinces. Thus, the Raigarh State Conversion Act (1936) mandated that any individual who was interested in converting had to first submit an application to the designated officials.[9] Other states began to enact their own anti-conversion legislation even before political independence (1947), including Patna's Freedom of Religion Act (1942), Sarguja's State Apostasy Act (1945) and Udaipur's Anti-Conversion Act (1946).[10] Furthermore, Gandhi (who, we recall from Chapter 3 (Section 3.1.3), had crucially influenced Jones's desire to establish a Christian ashram and had expressed a somewhat lenient opinion of conversion during his meeting with Jones in 1917) was becoming increasingly articulate in the 1940s about his concerns regarding conversion to Christianity in India. By the 1940s Gandhi was asserting that conversion should not be pursued or enacted – not the least because, he argued, Christianity offered no spiritual worth that Hinduism did not also offer.[11] According to Gandhi, conversion was an unwise attempt to change an 'integral part of one's self'[12] and might lead to physical violence.[13] Additionally, after the assassination of Gandhi and following India's Independence from Britain in 1947, the states of Orissa and Madhya Pradesh enacted anti-conversion legislations in 1967 and 1978, respectively, which re-enforced and strengthened the impact of the similar laws that had been initiated elsewhere in the 1930s and the 1940s.[14] Furthermore, a number of organizations were formed which Chad Bauman has recently described as being 'spawned' by the right-wing Indian nationalist Rashtriya Swayamsevak Sangh ('National Volunteer Organization', known more commonly as RSS), including the Akhil Bharatiya Vanvasi Kalyan Ashram (ABVKA) in 1952, the Vishwa Hindu Parishad (VHP) in 1964, the Bharatiya Janata Party (BJP) in 1980 and the Bajrang Dal in 1984.[15]

I consider these above-mentioned post-Independence legislations and organizations as the beginnings of a third wave of Hindu nationalism. According to Barbara Metcalf and Thomas Metcalf, Hindu nationalism emerged as an active presence in late colonial India towards the end of the nineteenth century – manifested largely in the form of cow protection movements, mostly in Uttar Pradesh and the Punjab – which we can consider as the first wave of Hindu nationalism where certain sociocultural markers of Hindu identity were foregrounded.[16] As I indicated in Chapter 2 (Section 2.3.5), a second wave of Hindu nationalism emerged in the 1920s which sought to reclaim and reinstitute the Hindu essence (*hindutva*) of the subcontinent, and these have since been referred to as the 'Hindutva' movement. These later offshoots of the RSS – beginning in 1952, rapidly gaining momentum in the mid-1980s and continuing into the present – seem to be a part of what Metcalf and Metcalf refer to as the 're-organization' of the Hindu right, which sought to regain the public support that it had effectively lost in the late 1940s after the assassination of Gandhi.[17] Further, we can recall from our discussion in Chapter 2 (Section 2.1) that, in the decades leading up to the inauguration of the SoE, there was also, especially amongst some nationalist Hindus, an increase of public criticisms of the character and the motives of those Christians who sought to practise different forms of inculturated Christianity.[18]

4.2.2 Increased public visibility of Dalits

In addition to the formation of several organizations which supported, in varying degrees, the promotion and the execution of Hindu nationalist ideologies, there were also significant changes in the political and socio-economic environments in India during the 1960s and the 1970s – these have been explored in great detail by Diego Maiorano.[19] Crucially, Maiorano argues that during these two decades a number of rural and relatively impoverished Indians (who collectively formed a substantial proportion of the population) began to place significant demands and pressures on the leading politicians. Such pressures had the political road paved for them by important figures like B. R. Ambedkar, who was India's first law minister and who had actively fought for the civil liberties and the political rights of India's untouchables (today usually designated as Dalits) since 1927.[20] These increasingly vocal demands of Indians from the lower socio-economic backgrounds led to an increased political focus on national economic goals such as 'abolishing poverty', while also substantially raising public awareness regarding the needs, aspirations, desires and rights of groups of Indians who had been historically oppressed for centuries.[21] And, importantly, these two decades also witnessed a significant growth in styles of Pentecostal faith both internationally and also in India specifically,[22] as Pentecostal denominations began to emerge alongside (and sometimes replace) older establishments of Roman Catholic and Protestant Christianity in India.[23]

I outline these various sociopolitical shifts of the 1940s–80s as some of the macro contributing factors to the decline of attendance at the microsite of STA since Jones stepped down from leadership, and also to the general decline in interest in the inculturated expressions of religiosity that STA offered, as detailed to me by Acharya V. Offering more historical basis to my argument, the declining attendance was not unique to STA; various other Christian ashrams that existed in India during those decades also experienced a similar decline, making it difficult to argue that STA's decline was entirely due to the loss of Jones alone as their charismatic leader.[24] Therefore, I submit, it was not *just* the loss of Jones as the spiritual leader that was responsible for the declining interest; there were several other factors which were far beyond the direct sphere of influence of the STA leadership. It was in this context of a general decline of interest – punctuated by public accusations against Christian conversion as well as a growing public awareness of the aspirations and visions of individuals from the lower castes – that STA developed a programme aimed at attracting a different kind of audience. And, indeed, echoing the words of the former Acharya V., 'every year students are coming' to the SoE.

During my fieldwork in 2016, twenty-six students attended the SoE programme, bringing it almost to its full capacity. A large group journeyed from Rajasthan, and others came from equally distant places like Varanasi, Agra, Delhi and Ajmer, while some other students came from relatively nearby places like Moradabad, Haldwani and Sat Tal's neighbouring town of Bhimtal. These students did not know any of the others before coming to STA (the one exception being the two married couples) but they quickly became friendly amongst one another, and from the stories they told me about their upbringing, and by noting their professions and/or their fathers' professions, I sensed that they shared a similar social status. And, importantly, almost all of them had grown up in Hindu families, so that they can be classified as recent converts – a point that will become especially relevant in our discussion below. Some of these recent converts like Suhasini and Anil thus came to STA's SoE programme to learn more about the basic tenets of Christianity. However, the Rajasthanis, whom I return to below, came on slightly different terms due to receiving financial sponsorship from churches in Delhi: individuals were selected to come each year by a village pastor. Accordingly, the Rajasthanis themselves were not always eager to be at STA, and though they respectfully attended the classes taught at the SoE, many of them instead longed to learn practical skills that they could employ in their villages – the most real-world of Christian skills, they explained, were related to healing (*changayi*). Indeed, many of the SoE students began their affiliation with Christianity and with Jesus after personally experiencing, witnessing or hearing about a story of healing which had taken place in their village. In this way, healing of one kind or another played a fundamental role in the lives of many of the SoE students – especially, as we shall see, the group from Rajasthan.

4.3 Disjunctures on the ground

Having now contextualized the development of the SoE within its broader sociopolitical contexts, I move to explore the four themes – labour, conversion, music and healing – which collectively demonstrate two significant disjunctures that structure the SoE. Specifically, as I indicated, there are significant differences between (1) 'the expected' Brahmanical-influenced Indians as envisioned by

Jones and 'the actual' individuals for whom Brahmanical Hindu philosophies and practices were neither relevant nor appealing, and (2) the viewpoints and/or practices of my fellow SoE students and of the leadership of STA. I consciously avoid focusing on the actual teachings which were explicitly conveyed during the SoE's formal instruction periods. As the daily schedule suggests (see note 1 of this chapter), two structured lessons were held each day, and the lessons covered a range of topics including the history of Christianity, Old Testament, New Testament, Christian mysticism, Hinduism (and 'speaking with Hindus', by which was often meant 'Evangelizing to Hindus'), Islam (and 'speaking with Muslims', with a similar qualifier), among others. My disinclination to focus on the substantive content of these lessons is not because there is nothing interesting or relevant to say about them – on the contrary, much could be said! – but it is rather because many SoE students repeatedly expressed to me that they themselves were generally disinterested in the lessons, and did not find them useful for their daily lives. For example, my friend Suhasini, whom we first met at the beginning of Chapter 1 as she professed her boredom with the SoE classes, confided in me that she felt that the doctrinal and scriptural materials covered in the lessons seemed to add unnecessary layers of complication to a teaching which, she had felt, was rather simple; she was baffled and irritated that a clearer message, for example, 'Jesus loves you, and has saved you. Follow him', was not more central to the teachings. Suhasini herself embodies some of the highly personalist dimensions of the spiritual quest of the founder Jones, which we studied in Chapter 3. Adding further support to Suhasini's perspective, Uncle Pratyush once candidly told me that the bookish teaching material of the SoE classes are 'of little use in the village' – the lessons that he and other evangelists needed to instead learn, he asserted, were more musical songs about Jesus and how to pray more confidently for healing. Of course, the students' clear disinterest in the lessons could in and of itself merit further exploration but, taking my lead from the SoE students, I will not focus on that motif here. The four themes I have selected to focus on – labour, conversion, music and healing – are ones I chose after a careful revision of all of my fieldnotes related to the SoE, onto which I employed a thematic structure akin to grounded theory;[25] after considering my qualitative data, these four themes were, for me, undeniably present.

4.3.1 *Shramdaan:* The spirituality versus the materiality of labour

When we finished eating our meals, we washed our dishes in the washing area located around the corner from the dining hall. The washing area included a bin for food scraps, a cold-water sink for rinsing and three steaming tubs of water for washing. We scrubbed our metal dishes dutifully as hungry monkeys peered through and pawed away at the screened-off windows, looking longingly at the food scraps in the bin. But few individuals washed their receptacles as a solitary task; most of the SoE students spontaneously enacted a sort of assembly-line system in small groups of three or four. One person would perform the initial rinse in the sink, another would wash, a third would rinse again in the two rinsing buckets and the last person would put the dishes on the drying racks. During this process of washing, rinsing and putting away our dishes, we would chat and laugh with one another, and we sometimes even hummed a tune or sang. As an alternative to this assembly-line system, I also noticed that some SoE students participated in a sort of informal shared washing, and it was especially common amongst individuals who frequently sat together. Not unlike the 'rounds-buying' culture that permeates the UK pub scene, this second style of shared washing (what we might call 'rounds-washing') relied on the fact that all the participating individuals would eventually take their turn as the washer and would consequently enjoy several turns of not-washing for each time that they had washed. I often saw certain individuals taking away one, two or even three additional sets of dishes with them in order to wash; this allowed them to able to sit back and relax for the next two or three meals, while someone else took away their dishes to wash.

To scholars unaccustomed to the minute details that ethnographic research often focuses on, these washing-up descriptions might seem uninterestingly trivial but it is often the most mundane events which reveal highly significant aspects of social and cultural dynamics. Indeed, I submit that these two styles of washing – both of which revolve around an approach that is 'communal' (in the literal sense of being shared amongst others within a *communitas* in Victor Turner's sense, and not in the Indian sense which often connotes group territorialism and intergroup violence) rather than solitary – are worth focusing our attention on. The reason why the washing up is so noteworthy is that it is a stark contrast to both the envisioned ideals of STA (we can recall from Chapter 3 (Section 3.3.2) that Jones desired all individuals to participate in labour specifically as a spiritual discipline). This raises the following question: Why was there such a marked difference between the envisioned practice of solitary washing at STA (which a significant portion of the regular, and more fervent, ashramites would keenly follow – we can recall my exchange with Uncle William) and the ways that the SoE students did their washing up in a collaborative manner?

I speculate that the SoE students were not trying to 'cheat the system' and actively dismiss Jones's vision for spiritual transformation vis-à-vis labour; the SoE students did not consciously reject any deeper spiritual reasons for labour. Instead, I suggest that their non-participation in what Jones had conceptualized as a fundamental aspect of spiritual life at STA was much more of a passive rejection – indeed, many students seemed unaware that there was anything that they were rejecting in not pursuing the trajectory of solitary washing as an outer expression of an inner spiritual practice. In contrast to many of the regular ashramites who came to STA outside of the SoE programme, physical labour in and of itself at the SoE offered no significant 'rupture' from these students' regular life nor did it offer them a means through which they could prove that they did not view labour as something that should be exclusively relegated to individuals from a lower caste – they *were* from lower castes, and labour was thus already a commonplace activity in their daily schedules outside of STA. Many of the men from Rajasthan, for example, worked as day labourers and thus regularly performed physically taxing manual labour.

The same disinterest towards investing labour with any spiritual significance was also evident in the hour-long morning work period (*shramdaan*) which we already encountered in Chapter 3. Much like the washing of individual dishes, some of the tasks assigned during the work period were ones which would have otherwise required the care of paid labourers (e.g. cleaning toilets, cutting vegetables, watering the many potted plants and herbs around the main building) but other tasks seemed less necessary (e.g. sweeping the fallen leaves or pine needles from various parts of the forest into piles, only to have them blown away by the wind and, then, to sweep them again the next day – a truly Sisyphean labour!) and were perhaps allocated simply for the purpose of ensuring that everyone participated in some mode of labour. In the case of these acts of labour which seemed to be unnecessary from a strict task-completion perspective, it was not uncommon for the students – especially the ones from Rajasthan – to slip away from the group and instead go on a walk, take a nap or hand-wash some of their clothes. It is clear, then, that labour was not conceptualized by the SoE students in the same ways in which we encountered it in Chapter 3; indeed, it was *not* seen by the SoE students as a physical practice which was imbued with spiritual meaning and transformative power.[26] Instead, they conceptualized labour as a practical necessity and a mundane task; it was an everyday chore which required completion and, as such, which could be done with varying degrees of efficiency. Cooperation – either through assembly-line teamwork or through taking turns with the washing – was largely a practical means of speeding up the process, and thus the act of labour in general did not serve the spiritual purpose that Jones had imagined it would; 'the envisioned' and 'the actual', in other words, were drastically different.

4.3.2 Conversion: Motivations for, and hesitations of, following Jesus

One morning following *dhyan*, Suhasini told me that the morning's scriptural passage contained some verses which she did not like and had questions about. I looked at Suhasini, made a fierce sword-chopping motion with my hands, and in Hindi I asked, 'The verse that says Jesus will not bring peace, but will do this [gesturing with the motion] to families? Is it that verse that you didn't like?' She nodded, looking distressed, and replied anxiously, 'Peace will not be brought? This is Jesus's teaching? This is Christianity? No, no, I am not satisfied with this. I am not satisfied.'

'Suhasini', I started, 'I think these are very difficult verses. And I will tell you that I too do not like them. Because I think God should bring peace, isn't it right? But there is more to be understood about these verses. They have a – ' here I hesitated, unable to explain 'broader cultural and literary context' in my limited Hindi. 'Wait. Let's ask the Acharya.' We tracked down Acharya G. on the verandah of the main building, where he was sipping a cup of chai. After we greeted him, I smiled and told him that Suhasini and I had a question about some verses from *dhyan* that we did not like. He looked at me, bewildered, perhaps thinking that I was mixing up my Hindi vocabulary. 'You do not *like* them or you do not *understand* them?' He clarified in English. 'Perhaps it is both!' I replied, 'We do not understand them fully but what we understand we do not like.' I opened up my Bible and read him the verse: 'Do not suppose that I have come to bring peace to the earth. I did not come to bring peace, but a sword. For I have come to set a man against his father, a daughter against her mother, a daughter-in-law against her mother-in-law – a man's enemies will be the members of his own household.'[27]

Acharya G. asked me what I understood those verses to mean, and I rattled off how, during my high school years of avid church attendance and again in my undergraduate years of Biblical Studies, I had received various teachings about some of the nuances within ancient Greek rhetoric regarding concepts like love and hate: how 'hate' is relative to how much one loves something else. In this understanding, when the Bible says that one's own family would become one's enemies, it is a matter of rhetorical priority – whom would you prioritize if you were forced to choose: your family *or* your God? Accordingly, I told Acharya G.

that I thought the passage means that our love for God should be so great that, if it came to it, we must tear ourselves from our family rather than deny our faith, but that is not to say our families should not matter to us at all or that we should not want to have good and healthy relationships with them. 'Isn't it so?' I asked in conclusion.

Acharya G. had been nodding along while I was offering my explanation, but now he turned to Suhasini, '*Aur? Tumhara interpretation kya hai?*' ('And? What is your interpretation?'). Not having followed our English-language conversation, Suhasini replied, in Hindi, that she had absolutely no understanding regarding what the verse was about, and she asked him to provide her with one. He began to explain the passage to Suhasini, drawing examples from Suhasini's and her husband Anil's respective family members who are still Hindu – despite years having passed since Suhasini's and Anil's conversions to Christianity. 'Your families are not angry with you and Anil that you are both Christian', Acharya G. explained in a matter-of-fact tone, 'but some Hindu families would be angry that you have converted. They would be very, very upset! And so, this verse speaks about choosing your priorities – whom do you love more: your family or Jesus? This verse says that it should be Jesus!' The Acharya was emphatic before drifting off in thought, 'But, in your case, you do not have to choose – and this is a good thing.'

This dialogue between Suhasini and Acharya G. compels us to examine some of the wider sociohistorical currents related to the vexed matter of conversion in India, which is vastly important to the SoE, not only because some of the teachings of the SoE focused on how to converse with individuals from Hindu or Muslim faith contexts with the hope of teaching them more about Christianity but also because many of the students identified as recent converts themselves. As we have indicated in Chapter 2 (Section 2.1) conversion has been articulated by some Hindu figures as a culturally undesirable and even morally inappropriate action wherein certain individuals use their spheres of power and influence (e.g. access to education, medicine or financial means) as a form of allurement to convert others – the culmination of this viewpoint can be seen in Swami Dayananda Saraswati's claim that conversion is an act of violence.[28] Gandhi also furthered some Indians' suspicions that conversion was simply a fraudulent and unethical practice conducted by opportunistic Christians by arguing that Dalits and other uneducated individuals who converted had 'no mind' and 'no intelligence' with which to grasp the spiritual significance of their conversion but who were instead supposedly driven by socio-economic impulses.[29]

These controversies surrounding whether conversion is an ethically acceptable practice have been considered through different analytical lenses. According to one standpoint, conversion debates between Hindu and Christian communities are often 'rooted not only in divergent analyses of the historical material on conversions but also in competing theological truth-claims about the nature of the ultimate reality and the human possibility of attaining this reality'.[30] Some of these multiple ways through which conversion can be considered are highlighted by Rowena Robinson in her broader analyses of Hindu-Christian relations in sixteenth-century Goa.[31] The majority of scholars considered by Robinson wrote between 1935 and 1960, but these debates continue in the present. Some recent scholars have focused more on the theological world views presented by different communities and religious traditions, and have explored the ways that individuals, either through implicit or explicit coercion or entirely through their own motivations, have altered their cosmological viewpoints from their formerly held tradition to their newly held one. For such scholars, conversion is considered primarily as a theologically motivated change that happens internally in the mind of the individual.[32] Approaching conversion through a different analytical lens, other scholars have instead primarily examined the social, political and other external motivations for conversion.[33] Of course, it goes without saying that these 'internal' motivations and 'external' pressures that lead an individual or group to convert from one tradition to another cannot be neatly or fully isolated from each other; both the internal and the external dimensions interweave, sometimes seamlessly, in an individual's life story – indeed, we see this inseparability of internal and external factors in some ethnographic literature.[34] Nonetheless, it is a helpful analytical tool to conceptualize these 'internal' and 'external' factors of conversion as conceptually distinct, not only to aid our scholarly discussion of the ethnographic materials we present here but also because it seems that Jones himself possessed a rather dichotomous understanding of these two factors.

As we saw in Chapter 3 (Section 3.2.5), when Jones spoke and wrote about 'conversion' he occupied himself primarily (albeit not exclusively) with what he called 'vertical conversion' – an inward movement which he conceptualized as becoming more spiritually aligned with the teachings of, and more devoted to the person of, Jesus Christ. In fact, he went to great efforts to distinguish between (inner) conversion and (outer) proselytization. Thus, in his book aptly entitled *Conversion* (published posthumously in 1997), Jones clearly asserted, 'We have seen that conversion is not to be confounded with proselytism which Jesus repudiated, for proselytism is the changing from one group to another group without any necessary change in character and life.'[35] Such mere proselytization, Jones emphasized, held the risk of being 'a perversion – a using of the church as a means to one's own ends, those of gaining social recognition'.[36] In this vein, referring to his own life story and detailing the various stages of his conversion, Jones wrote: 'I [initially] underwent a half-conversion ... my label had been changed but not my life. I had been horizontally converted but not vertically.'[37] For Jones, his own 'half-conversion' had come about through his regular attendance of a Christian church, thereby being part of a community of Christians and, in turn, taking on the social-institutional 'label' of a Christian. But all this business of religious identification and self-labelling through being part of a community, Jones argues, falls under the realm of 'horizontal' conversion, and still falls short of the deeper self-transformation that is intrinsic to, and expected of, 'vertical' conversion. This 'vertical' conversion was the ultimate goal, whereas 'horizontal' conversion might *either* deter individuals from realizing, *or* help them to realize, this goal, and thus by being so unpredictable, it should be less a focal point of one's quest than the spiritual ascent through a 'vertical' conversion.

Indeed, Jones occupied a puzzling, if not seemingly paradoxical, position in his view of whether 'horizontal' conversion was at all a favourable moment in spiritual life. We can look at Jones's relationship with Gandhi as an example: Jones often affirmed that Gandhi (who never self-identified as a Christian) 'manifest[ed] a Christian spirit far beyond most of the rest of us'.[38] This sentiment seems to suggest that for Jones being Christian was more integrally related to one's inward state ('vertical' conversion) than to one's outward identity affiliation as a social category ('horizontal' conversion).[39] At the same time, however, Jones did long for Gandhi to identify as a Christian by avowing his personal commitment to Christ as Lord and Saviour. Thus, in a letter to Gandhi, Jones wrote, 'I thought you had grasped the center of the Christian faith, but I'm afraid I must change my mind. I think you have grasped certain principles of the Christian faith which have molded you and have helped make you great – you have grasped the principles, but you have missed the Person.'[40] To return to a central theme in Chapter 3, for Jones, truly knowing 'the Person' – that is, the soteriological Christ who ultimately saves – and not remaining at the penultimate threshold of doctrinal 'principles' would be best facilitated through indwelling Christian communities and maintaining Christian identifications; Jones lamented the fact that Gandhi never did outwardly identify as a Christian, speculating that 'much of the blame [for

Gandhi's lack of "horizontal" conversion] must fall on us as missionaries'.[41] Therefore, as I understand Jones, 'horizontal' conversion was conceived, soteriologically speaking, as less vital and less transformative than the crucial moment of 'vertical' conversion, but it still could be a pedagogical tool which could be used to prepare, verify, magnify, sustain and strengthen one's own 'vertical' conversion. For this reason, much like any other event or process that Jones interpreted as a positive movement 'toward Christ', Jones welcomed 'horizontal' conversion too as functionally valuable.[42]

However, born into low-caste Hindu families, many students of the SoE were confronted with certain realities of 'horizontal' conversion that Jones had not anticipated – or, at least, had not squarely addressed in his writings. As we shall see below (Section 4.3.4), some SoE participants spoke of being beaten up and/or socially ostracized on account of their newly developed affiliation with Christianity. Such acts of violence directed at Indian Christians is, as Chad Bauman's recent monograph has extensively demonstrated, 'disproportionately' directed at individuals from lower castes.[43] In addition to describing the ways that they were sometimes violently targeted due to their Christian practices, some SoE participants furthermore voiced their concerns about how baptism and any official declaration of Christian identity might affect their children's access to education quotas reserved for Hindus from low-caste backgrounds. In India, a certain number of educational reservations and job quotas are set aside – albeit not without controversy[44] – for Dalits due to the state's recognition that their social and financial status, shaped by historical injustices, is likely to have impeded their ability to pay for their children's school or to secure an administrative job themselves; however, if a Dalit officially converts to Christianity they cannot often access these quotas.[45] Against this sociopolitical backdrop, it is crucial to note that baptism, for Jones, was not a necessary part of Christian identity and he even allowed unbaptized individuals (whom he referred to, in the descriptive term coined by his contemporary Kandiswamy Chetti, as 'informal Christians') to fully participate in Christian activities – including the simple communion held at STA each Sunday.[46] Though he did at times baptize individuals at STA, he did not view baptism as essential for salvation – which is only possible through a 'vertical' *conversion* to Christ.

If we keep in mind Jones's own understandings of 'vertical' conversion as soteriologically superior to 'horizontal' conversion, and, at the same time, recall his desire for 'horizontal' conversion to still occur, we can explore how the lived-out realities of the SoE students compare to Jones's envisioned desire. At this point it is important for us to recall that, for Jones, Hinduism was epitomized by

Advaita Vedanta philosophy and expressed through certain Brahmanical cultural idioms. Thus, for Jones, individuals could conceivably convert 'vertically' while still holding on to their previous social identities – that is, so long as their Hindu-influenced identity markers did not get in the way of deepening their newfound relationship with Jesus; Jones found both Pandita Ramabai and Sadhu Sundar Singh to be exemplary models of this 'naturalization' (see Chapter 2, Section 2.3.3). Yet, for many students of the SoE, the moment they officially assume a Christian identity they are forced to contend with both social and legislative losses through forsaking their access to certain government benefits available through quotas.

This returns us to the conversation between Suhasini and Acharya G. regarding the biblical passage in Matthew that Suhasini (along with myself) 'did not like'. Contained in the subtext of the Acharya's explanation to Suhasini regarding Hindu families who adamantly opposed conversion to Christianity was the question 'If one had to choose between any worldly thing or Jesus, which should they choose?' The answer for Acharya G., unequivocally, was Jesus'. Whether one was asked to choose between Jesus and one's Hindu family, or whether one was – as was the case for several of the students of the SoE – forced to choose between identifying as a Christian and maintaining one's legislative access to educational quotas and job quotas,[47] Acharya G.'s answer was consistently to choose Jesus and Christianity. Indeed, when some of the men from Rajasthan expressed their concerns about losing their educational quotas, Acharya G. candidly informed them of his own reliance on God's provision throughout his life choices, including accepting a lesser salary so as to be able to continue doing what he felt was God's work. 'Jesus', he once quipped, referencing a biblical passage that we had meditated on in a morning *dhyan* 'should always be chosen first. Seek ye *first* the Kingdom of God.'[48] Though I did not hear Acharya G. or any of the teachers actively distinguish between 'horizontal' and 'vertical' conversion *à la* Jones, they seemed to view 'horizontal' conversion just as, if not more, important than 'vertical' conversion. While Jones seemed to conceptualize 'horizontal' conversion as a natural and desirable outcome of 'vertical' conversion (e.g. in the case of Gandhi, it was only after sensing Gandhi's personal transformation so that Gandhi had become, in Jones's vision, a Christ-like individual that Jones began to actively hope for Gandhi also to self-identify as Christian), the teachers of the SoE seemed to conceptualize the inverse: 'horizontal' conversion was a necessary precursor to 'vertical' conversion, since it was 'horizontal' conversion which would ensure that correct doctrine was being taught which could, in turn, enable the self to be transformed. This theme, as we shall see when discussing the life story of Vihaan, was a point of significant disagreement between the SoE teachers and students.

4.3.3 Music: Christian worship and learning to clap on beat

One day during our afternoon lesson, Mr D. abruptly paused his lecture and began to discuss something which, from his manner and tone, seemed to have caused him immense unease for quite some time. Standing at the front of the classroom, he let his gaze wander around the room, making eye contact with several of the men from Rajasthan. 'The music at the evening fellowship hour is not good. You are not clapping correctly. You are all just clapping whenever you choose, and no one is following the rhythm. One claps here, another claps here, a third gives two claps close together – it is not good at all. Maybe in [Hindu] temples (*mandir*) it is fine to do that, but we are singing Christian hymns.' He went on to explain, in an animated way, the practice of clapping on beat to the dominant rhythm and proceeded to spend about five minutes demonstrating to the class how to clap along to a single beat. The entire class clapped with him, and a few of the men seemed to be holding back grins and laughter. When the spontaneous lesson in clapping had finished, Mr D. returned to the topic of that day's lesson.

From one angle, this incident exemplifies one of the many ways that a leader can try to instill a shared identity amongst a group through teaching or enforcing specific actions, or ritualized performances, which ultimately strengthen the identity of the group by reinforcing boundary lines which clearly dictate who is in and who is out of the group. The formation of group identity (or, we might more accurately say 'the negotiation of group membership', since anthropologists did not explicitly use the term 'identity' until the late 1970s when A. L. Epstein[49] wrote about the formation of ethnic identity) is something that anthropologists have focused on in great detail in recent decades. However, I am primarily concerned here not with how the practice of clapping on beat could represent as well as reinforce a shared identity nor, even more minutely, with how the very action of forming one cohesive and united sound might unite the group – though those who are familiar with chanting and other practices focused on monophonic music could weigh in about the way that this style of clapping, too, enhances the cohesiveness of a group. Rather, I am focusing on a different angle of Mr D.'s effort to make the group clap correctly: effectively, he was teaching them how to correctly enact *Christian* worship. Implicit in his explanation was the idea that there was a correct standard of Christian worship from which the SoE students were deviating. More specifically, he presented the idea that the way to correctly worship Jesus was to do so in an orderly fashion, and he directly contrasted this style of worship with the unregulated manner of worship that, he claimed, occurs in Hindu temples.

To say nothing of the energetic clapping, even the use of the bells and the drum – instruments which the Rajasthani men had brought with them from their villages – during the fellowship hour was initially met with hesitation and reluctance by the STA leadership. The leaders, apart from this specific intervention by Mr D., usually tolerated the loud style of worship led by the Rajasthani villagers, but they rarely joined along in it. While the leaders and some of the students opted for music from the Methodist hymnals, or sang relatively newly composed melodies from Western churches whose English lyrics had been translated into Hindi, the men from Rajasthan sang tunes which, they explained, had been sung in their local villages for generations. These songs were often in Bagri (the mother tongue of the group from Rajasthan) though some of them were in standard Hindi. The melodies were monophonic and often followed a sort of call-and-response style, where the lead singer sings a line followed by the rest of the group who repeats the line after them. Drumbeats, bells, finger cymbals and clapping reinforced the metric-feel pulse. (Most of the songs featured 1/8 and 2/16ths repeating percussive patterns with emphasis on the strong beats; almost all of them were wonderfully upbeat, featuring a metronymic pulse of 72–8.)[50] In less musicological terms, they are the kind of songs which readily prompt spontaneous foot-tapping, hip-swaying and fist-pumping; 'the Bagri Boys' (as I took to calling them in my fieldnotes) always sang them with full energy. Uncle Pratyush explained to me that one of the reasons why they used a call-and-response style of singing is that, often, the singing crowd would be a mix of literate and illiterate people; and illiterate individuals would not be able to follow along with a written text such as the hymnals used in many churches. The Rajasthani *bhajans* were a stark contrast to the hymns, and sometimes evoked giggles from the non-Rajasthani students who seemed unfamiliar with such triumphantly vigorous and upbeat tunes.

Often, immediately following the song, Acharya G. would request a translation or explanation of the songs that were in Bagri – one was always dutifully provided, usually by Uncle Pratyush. Towards the end of the SoE programme, I also approached Uncle Pratyush and asked him to provide me with a Hindi translation of some of the Bagri *bhajans* that they had sung most frequently. With him dictating, we wrote out the lyrics of a handful of them. I present three of them here:

1. *Tayaari karo.* (Begin the preparations.)
   Yeshu paas aane wale hai.[51] (Jesus is going to come.)
   Bhakti karo. (Devote yourselves.)
   Dua karo. (Pray.)
   Mahima karo. (Glorify.)
   Prashansa karo. (Praise.)
   Prarthna karo. (Pray.)
   Burai chodo. (Shun wrong deeds.)
   Bible padho. (Study the Bible.)[52]

2. *Mai prarthna karke* (I pray) *teri raah dekh raha hoo tu*[53] (and wait to see you).
   Mai mahima karke. (I glorify.)
   Mai prashansa karke. (I praise.)
   Mai ghutna tekke. (I kneel.)
   Mai haat jodke. (I join my hands in prayer.)
   Mai dandavat karke (I prostrate myself)
   Mai sir jhukake (I bow my head.)

3. *Yahova charwaha mera hai* (Jehovah is my shepherd.)
   Yahova bhakti karave (Devote yourselves to Jehovah.)
   Yahova paapan maafi aale (Jehovah forgives all our sins.)
   Yahova maanda me hadaare, langde, lulu, gunge (Jehovah heals the ill among us: those who are crippled, lame and dumb.)

These *bhajans*, which express worship to Jesus, contain some striking resonances with the more traditional *bhajans* from Hindu *bhakti* religious contexts such as those attributed to medieval poet-saints such as Tukaram, Mira and Kabir. Specifically, the use of certain verbs, as well as the use of '*teri*' and '*tu*' so as to use the most informal of the three possible ways (*aap, tum,* and *tu*) to address another person in Hindi is seen in both the traditional *bhajans* and these ones in Bagri. This level of informality is comparable to the choice, in French, to '*tutoyer*' rather than '*vouvoyer*' someone, but it holds even more weight here since it is the Hindi '*tu*' (the most informal possible) rather than '*tum*' (used for a level of casual informality among friends) which is chosen here. To address God as '*tu*' conveys a deep sense of intimacy – comparable to that of lovers – where the use of formalities would seem amiss.

And yet, from my reading of them, these Bagri *bhajans* also contain distinctive features which, I think, can be better understood by considering them alongside some key themes articulated by Dalit liberation theology.[54] Such visions creatively use the local languages, mythic narratives, symbolic patterns and cultural lifestyles of Dalits to express their experiences of being crushed, their hopes and agonies, and, most fundamentally, their faith in the living God who is with them in their suffering and who will liberate them from their bondage. There is much in these Bagri *bhajans* which strongly resonates – in every sense of the term – with these concerns of Dalit theology in which 'pathos is the beginning of knowledge', for it is on the way of suffering that individuals come to know Christ who participates in their suffering.[55] Thus, in these *bhajans*, there is a clear focus on the anticipation of the return of Jesus as the healer of broken, diseased and unhealed humanity. In the first *bhajan*, the line 'Jesus is going to come' is repeated after each exhortation to an action. And, in the second *bhajan*, the line 'I wait to see you' is repeated in the same manner. The majority of the lines, even those which are descriptive of the poet-speaker's actions, can be read as prescriptive ways in which one should act in order to prepare for the coming of Jesus. These songs, then, are not descriptive in the same ways that some *bhakti bhajans* are – in which the poet-speaker often laments passionately about her seemingly unrequited love for her Lord[56] – but they are a fervent call to action and an assertion of God's coming. The Bagri *bhajans* also contain, as demonstrated in the third song, declarations of the power of Jesus: Jesus is not only a remover of sins but also a physical healer who can cure all sorts of ailments.[57] One entire song (not provided here) was devoted to proclaiming the biblical story in which Lazarus was raised from the dead; Jesus's ability to heal even the most severe of infirmities, and to restore good to all situations, was a recurring theme. We will return to this focus on healing in Section 4.3.4 of this chapter.

Interestingly, when I asked Uncle Pratyush about who had composed the *bhajans*, he simply told me that the melodies themselves had already existed – he explained that the villagers had merely replaced a few of the words and, of course, crucially added 'Jesus' to the various refrains. He elaborated,

> With these songs which use our local, tribal languages, we praise Jesus Christ and sing about his miracles, how the Lord Jesus gives vision to the blind, gives ears to the deaf, enables the lame to walk, and gives life to the dead. All of this we sing about so that we might give glory to the Heavenly Lord. We play various instruments like the drums, harmonium, guitar, cymbals and sing along and clap our hands while chanting God's name. We praise and glorify God, and we can feel his presence when we sing; we become peaceful, healed and blessed.[58]

Uncle Pratyush also told me that these songs are more generally sung in the villages for a multitude of other purposes, including for entertainment or alongside any rituals or any cultural or traditional shows.[59]

I interpret these two details shared with me by Uncle Pratyush – the fact that (1) these particular *bhajans* had been created by infusing pre-existing ones with Christianized themes by simply altering the lyrics, and that (2) these same *bhajans* were then used in a variety of social and ecclesiastical settings – as examples which encapsulate and demonstrate the mutability and the malleability of religious devotional motifs as conceptualized by many of the SoE students. For them, the motifs were intrinsically flexible – hence Suhasini's puzzlement and dissatisfaction over biblical passages that called for choosing Jesus *over* choosing one's family – and also energetic; a proclamation and celebration of the miraculous deeds that God had done for the people of God. Reverence for God was not solemn or orderly in the manner of some regulated church services; it was largely an enthusiastic call to God where the joy of the singers spilled over and out of the vessels that tried to contain it.

But, if we recall this section's opening vignette which described the teacher Mr D. endeavouring to instill in the SoE students a particularly 'right' way to worship by clapping orderly, we note that the SoE students and the teachers held rather different views of worship. Mr D's reference to this Hindu style of worship is particularly revealing of the fluid nature of *bhakti* that often criss-crosses Hindu-Christian binaries in rural and small-town India. Discussing one form of devotional songs which draw on materials from the Sanskrit Puranas and the epic narratives in the Radhavallabha tradition, Guy Beck notes that it involves an 'intimate interaction between the lead singer and the responders', and is structured by the responsorial singers who repeat the lines of the principal singer (*mukhiya*). These participants assume the roles of Krishna and the cowherd women, and the musical performance progresses through their interactive 'play', which is not simply a meditation on the eternal *Rasa-Lila* dance but a vicarious participation in its transcendental movements.[60] Perhaps reflecting some of these participatory motifs from their folk Hindu milieus, for the SoE students too, worship was indeed not only an expression of gratitude to God but it was also itself a transformative act, as expressed by Uncle Pratyush's assertion that it is through singing the songs that they *become* 'peaceful, healed and blessed'. And, as the attentive reader might have already noted, this entire process of worship was deeply grounded in the process of healing: songs could include either a vivid proclamation of the healing one had already received or a declaration about the healing power of God, and the act of singing itself had the potential to bring about healing in individuals. Thus, keeping this somatic focus of healing in mind, we turn to our fourth and final theme: testimonies of healing.

4.3.4 Healing, faith, knowledge (*changayi, viswas, gyan*)

After dinner and evening chai, we returned to the main building for the fellowship hour, during which we sang a selection of songs until eventually one person (selected in advance by the Acharya) shared his or her testimony. Terms like 'the hope of glory' (*mahima ke asha*), 'salvation' (*uddhar*), 'healing' (*changayi*), 'the kingdom of God the Heavenly Father' (*parmeshwar ke raj*), 'the Holy Spirit' (*pavitra aatma*) and 'baptism of the spirit' (*agni baptisma*) were frequently invoked by those who shared their testimony and/or offered prayers following another's testimony.

The majority of the Rajasthanis, as well as a number of other students, began their testimonies by describing how they used to operate within a strictly Hindu sphere of religious belief and practice but, through their recent exposure to Christianity, they have begun to adhere to Christian practices. They started with phrases like 'I was a Hindu' or 'I come from a Hindu family', and then proclaimed that, following a series of events, they or their entire family now possess faith in Christ. These personal testimonies, though they varied with respect to the exact details of their circumstances, followed a very similar pattern. When referring to the events and the circumstances which had brought about their transition from strictly Hindu beliefs and practices to specifically Christian ones, individuals spoke of having experienced disturbances and troubles (*pareshani*) in their family situations which placed great stress upon each of the family members. These *pareshani* included social dynamics such as alcoholic fathers who drank away the family's finances (some of the men spoke of their own former alcohol and cigarette addictions) and domestic abuse, and some individuals also indicated that there had been suspicions of spirit (*bhut*) possessions which made them visit village folk healers (*Tantriks*) in search of relief and cures. A larger number of the individuals gave vivid accounts of combatting various illnesses and diseases – ranging from persistent headaches, to boils and lesions on the skin, to partial paralysis – and of struggling to make ends meet financially, where these difficulties had often materialized through scarcities of water and food for either their crops and livestock or their immediate family members. While these negative circumstances continued to plague the individuals and their then-Hindu families, there was often a nearby Christian pastor or devout family in the village who offered to pray for them and encouraged them to start joining the Christian gatherings so that they could also begin to pray to Jesus for themselves. Individuals explained that, sometimes immediately upon receiving the consolation of prayer from others and sometimes only after starting to pray regularly for themselves, their *pareshani* and *bimari* (illnesses) were removed and they were given *changayi* (healing), which further increased their *viswas* (faith) in *Yesu Masih* (Jesus Christ). For this transformation, they offered their gratitude to God (often referring to God as *Prabhu* and sometimes as *Parmeshwar*), thanking God for bringing them *shanti* (peace) and improving their situation by providing for their needs. Some of the individuals had since received baptism (some referred to this rite of passage with the Hindi (and Hindu-inflected) term *diksha*, though most simply used the English word *baptism*) and, though the majority of the SoE group was not baptized, a few of them spoke specifically about having ceased their visits to the *Tantriks* after commencing Christian prayer.

What is particularly intriguing about these testimonies are the conceptions and the images of Christianity that are portrayed through them. To be sure, these students of the SoE do articulate some sense of a distinction between their Hindu pasts and their current Christian practices, but the precise activities and beliefs which demarcate (or not) their identity *either* as a Hindu *or* as a Christian do not always seem to suffice for the spiritual leaders of STA who demand more precisely drawn contours. As far as the STA leaders are concerned, many of the SoE students reside in an undesirably ambiguous middle ground of dangerous in-between liminality of Hindu and Christian. A conversational exchange between Acharya G. and an eighteen-year-old Rajasthani man, Vihaan, exemplifies the ways that the students of the SoE and these leaders held on to rather different understandings regarding precisely what the Christian faith consists of and looks like and, more specifically, whether Vihaan himself was to be viewed as someone in-between and, thus, not yet fully or properly Christian.

We can start with a brief summary of Vihaan's life story, which he narrated to our group on the same night that prompted the conversation between him and Acharya G. One evening, Vihaan began his testimony by indicating that he had grown up in a Hindu family which had many *pareshani* and *bimari* and had no *shanti*. He spoke of experiencing persistent aches in his body and, in spite of the various treatments that he sought out, he never seemed to be able to recover from them. Further, Vihaan's family were cowherders, and a scarcity of water (they had dug two underground wells but both failed to produce a sufficient water supply) forced them to spend from their savings to buy tanks of water for the cattle; this expenditure had a drastic impact on the family's financial status. Knowing about the family's troubles with maintaining a sufficient water supply, a pastor offered to pray for Vihaan and invited him to join in Christian fellowship. Vihaan accepted the pastor's offer of prayer, joined the fellowship and also invited his own family to come along with him. After praying to Jesus, the pastor instructed Vihaan's family to dig a third well in a place that he claimed God had told him would produce water, and – sure enough – this well produced an abundance of water, enabling the family to care for their cattle, share water with their neighbours and even begin to grow some vegetables. Vihaan's family was delighted, and gave thanks to God for their newfound ability to save 10 INR/day (around 0.10 GBP). With their worldly problems resolved, the family stopped attending the Christian fellowship until Vihaan's elder brother fell seriously ill. The family tried to care for him at home, but when his condition continued to worsen, the family took him to the church in order to request the pastor to pray for his recovery. After the pastor's confident prayer to Jesus, Vihaan's brother began to recover quite rapidly; his recovery reinforced the family's faith in Jesus, and Vihaan proclaims that he has remained steadfast in his faith ever since. Following this testimony, which received ample applause and loud vocalizations of 'Hallelujah' from the rest of the group, Acharya G. directed some questions at Vihaan.

Acharya G. (AG): You said that you left and then came back into faith, what do you mean by coming into faith?
Vihaan (V): By faith I mean that with prayer I was healed of my health issues, and this is the reason that we came into faith.
AG: Yes, what do you mean by you came into faith? What faith? What do you have faith in?
V: I mean faith in the Lord, after he healed us of something that I thought was impossible, and gave me peace.

At this point, Uncle Pratyush (P) from Rajasthan jumped in to offer a modified explanation to the Acharya on behalf of Vihaan. And, moments later, Uncle Rahul (R), the pastor who had advised Vihaan's family about the wells, himself joined in.

P: [Vihaan] has not completely mentioned that he was discouraged to embrace Christianity by his family members, thus he was sceptical. And then again there was trouble, like his elder brother fell sick and then he finally was firm on his decision

AG: But Vihaan, do you read the Bible? Have you read its entirety?

V: I haven't yet read it completely.

AG: No?! You must read it, your faith will increase by hearing and reading God's word, the more you read, the more you'll understand (*samajh*) and your faith will become stronger (*tumhara viswas badhega*). Healing is only healing ... it is important, of course – but knowledge of the Lord is very important. (*Changayi sirf changayi ... zaruri hai – lekin Prabhu ka gyan bahut zaruri hai*).

V: Yes, I'm learning from my phone. I have a track which has the recording of the Bible so I can hear it in Hindi. I am uneducated but I can pray very well, just like my friend whom you heard praying yesterday. I am learning about the Bible even though I cannot read it. The Lord does really great work.

AG: Very good, very good. Son, I know there are lot of problems where you stay, and so healing is very important, and through this the Lord shows you faith but you must increase your knowledge (*gyan*) and wisdom (*buddhi*), through reading the Bible. For example, it's said in the Bible that Jesus died for our sins.

R (interrupting): Yes Sir, he's a new addition, it's not been very long, I'm helping him to learn. They had a lot of problems, especially with water, they had to call for tankers. When I went to his house, God led me to show him a place where he could get water in his house, and after that he is having no problem with water, after the prayer. There was enough water for the fields and even to give to others, that's how their faith increased even more. That's how the entire family came into faith; they are eight to-ten of them. The bore ring well incident really increased our faith. God is great and where there is prayer God shows God's power.

This dialogue demonstrates a significant difference between the Acharya and Vihaan with regards to how they perceived what it meant to have Christian faith. What, then, is faith? I dare not attempt to answer this theologically, but I can answer it ethnographically. That is, I can draw upon my qualitative research to reveal and demonstrate the distinct views that the STA leaders (Acharya G.) and the SoE students (Vihaan) had concerning faith.

For Vihaan, faith was the natural end result of both experiencing a physical healing and obtaining a practical provision which were attributed to the miraculous intervention of Jesus. Because Jesus provided and healed in a way that Vihaan had no other way to account for (and in a way that other *Tantriks* and Hindu deities had not accomplished), he was filled with faith in Jesus. Upon possessing this faith, Vihaan continued to express it through offering gratitude to God and maintaining a personal practice of prayer and *bhajan* singing within a context of Christian fellowship. When Vihaan spoke of his faith leaving him, he did not speak of any change of belief in the divine power of Jesus; he only indicated that he had stopped attending the Christian fellowship – that is, he had ceased his own practice of praying to, and *bhajan* singing in praise of, Jesus. Given the ways that Vihaan spoke about his faith both during his testimony and during other conversations with me throughout his stay at the ashram, it might be helpful to think of his faith as the result of a sort of inferred confidence in God's abilities – that is, faith was the consequent expression of gratitude through prayer and Christian fellowship. The starting point of Vihaan's faith was witnessing the power of Jesus, but this faith was given expression through *bhakti* and fellowship.

Meanwhile, for Acharya G., Christian faith was a virtue that could be developed and increased through gaining an awareness and understanding of the biblical accounts of Jesus specifically, and of the Christian scriptures more generally. To Acharya G., faith was a close companion of wisdom and knowledge. For him, the physical healing and the provision of material goods attributed to Jesus were adequate starting points to cause someone to gain an interest in the person of Jesus, but faith did not increase without a deep immersion in the Bible. In this understanding, faith was more directly linked with knowledge of the Lord (*prabhu ka gyan*) than with healing and the subsequent fellowship and *bhakti* that occurred amongst those who had received the healing. The Acharya's phrase 'healing is only healing', is especially revealing of his standpoint that healing in and of itself is not a sufficient expression of, or justification for, one's Christian faith, even though he allows that 'it is important, of course'. In his ultimate analysis, however, Christian faith was to be grounded in an ever-increasing knowledge of God as revealed through the Christian scriptures.

These types of exchanges happened somewhat frequently following SoE students' testimonies. On a different night, after Uncle Pratyush had shared his testimony and given further accounts of how he regularly preached about Jesus in the villages, Acharya G. questioned him directly about the content of his preaching. Uncle Pratyush responded,

P: I tell them that Jesus Christ is the forgiver of sins. I also say that if you have faith in him then the sick will be healed.

AG: But you must tell them that Jesus offers salvation (*mukti*)! Otherwise the person can walk away after hearing you, it can go to waste. The most important thing is to know that Jesus was crucified for our sins. For *my* sins. This is the most important [thing].

P: Yes, of course, but if I tell them that first then I could get beaten up!

AG: I mean to say that the salvific message of Jesus Christ should be delivered to them. This is the purpose of our preaching. And of our lives.

P: Yes, sir, when they have ailments (*pareshani*) they will come to Jesus. And slowly they realise that He is the one healing them.

The fundamental disagreement between Uncle Pratyush and Acharya G. with regards to what was 'the most important' aspect of Christianity to share with others in the context of preaching is an echo of a debate which has long reverberated in theological and missiological circles. The distinction between these two viewpoints has been highlighted by F. Hrangkhuma as one between 'mission from above' and 'mission from below' among Protestant groups in India.[61] Another contrast that emerges from this disagreement between Acharya G. who emphasizes Bible study and Uncle Pratyush who highlights the worldly afflictions of his audiences is the classic distinction between the rational and the affective dimensions of the human person. We can phrase the question in this way: Is devotion to Jesus a thing of the intellect or the emotion? Or, put alternately, is discipleship to Christ the result of first recognizing oneself as a sinner in need of salvation, and then seeing Christ as the God who offers this salvation, or of witnessing first-hand Christ's power and then choosing to devote oneself to Christ? As we have also seen in the student-teacher conversations at the SoE, this theological messiness continues to play out on the ethnographic terrain of STA, fractured by the two disjunctures that we have indicated above.

4.4 Conclusion

The first half of this chapter explored some of the various social, historical and political contexts of the decades leading up to the establishment of the SoE in 1992. Following that, we have seen that there are significant differences between the type of Indianness that E. Stanley Jones envisioned when founding STA in 1930 and the realities of the SoE students in the present day. We also have seen a number of crucial differences between the ways that the SoE students and the

SoE teachers conceptualize and live out their expressions of Christianity. By interweaving some macro transitions across northern India with certain micro shifts at the site of STA, we have highlighted the point that the agential capacities of individuals such as Acharya G., Vihaan and Suhasini are ongoing negotiations which are transacted against this dense backdrop.[62]

In this vein, we might think of this chapter as having explored an 'absence' of what was expected to occur at STA. Among the SoE students there was, after all, an 'absence' of Brahmanical rituals, categories and mentalities that Jones envisioned would have existed amongst STA's visitors. This silent absence, ultimately, became its own form of active presence – in the way that the existentialist philosopher Sartre speaks of absence. Sartre describes an individual in a cafe who expects to see their friend Pierre but, not finding him, instead notices (or *sees*) the absence of Pierre. It is, Sartre argues, our expectation to see something (or someone), and then not seeing it, that causes us to 'experience' and 'discover' the absence as 'a real event'.[63] In other words, when we expect to see something – say, a group of Hindus and Christians all living a Brahmanically inflected lifestyle together at an ashram – its very absence becomes a glaring presence that we cannot help but become aware of and focus our attention on. Across the four ethnographic moments of labour, conversion, music and healing, we consistently noted an 'absence' of Brahmanically structured or flavoured Hinduism. While this 'absence' was most evident when exploring the temporal disjuncture between Jones's envisioned ideals with the actual demographic realities of the SoE students, we also explored a second synchronic disjuncture: the ways that the teachers and the students of the SoE conceptualize, indwell and enact Christianity. Consistently, we saw that the teachers and the students held somewhat differing views regarding which beliefs and actions were the most imperative to their Christian faiths.

Indeed, with varying levels of forthrightness, the teachers often attempted to correct the students' understandings of what it meant to enact Christian faith. Reflecting on our discussion in Chapter 3 regarding Stanley Jones's 'Ashram Ideals' in which he stated his desire for STA to be 'truly Indian', we can here add the question as a subtext: '*Whose* Indianness?' Is the Indianness expressed by the students of the SoE – the sheer mundanity of labour, the sociopolitical anxieties relating to conversion, the passionate-albeit-offbeat worship music and the healing-centred faith – a kind of Indianness which could be accepted (if not encouraged?) as a legitimate form of inculturated Christianity? Would it be 'truly Indian'? And, on the topic of inculturated Christianity, what do we make of the fluidity of religious devotion and passionate proclamations of becoming healed on the part of the SoE students? Are such expressions 'truly Christian'? I do not ask these seemingly rhetorical questions from a standpoint that claims to have arrived at a singular, tidy definition of that which can be 'truly Indian' or 'truly Christian'. Nor am I trying to argue, picking up on our discussion of Bauman and Fox in Chapter 3 (Section 3.2.2), that the SoE forms of Indianness align neatly with orthodox Christian theology – others in the fields of systematic theology and ecclesiology have passionately undertaken this enterprise,[64] but this is not my aim. Rather, I ask these questions with the phenomenological aim of understanding and articulating the sociocultural influences that impact the atmosphere of STA. Indeed, especially through considering some of the ethnographic moments at the SoE organized under four themes, we have seen some of the ways that the ideals held by the teachers have direct pedagogical implications for the students, and for the environment at STA more broadly. We highlighted some of the *embodied* ways that the SoE students expressed their understandings of *Indian* and *Christian* – the foods they ate, the labour they performed (or avoided), the hymns they exuberantly sang, their emphasis on corporeal and holistic healing, and so on – and the ways this often differed from what the SoE teachers expected. As I explored in Chapter 3, Jones emphasized that the Christian faith must centre around a soteriological encounter with the person of Jesus Christ. However, as the spiritual leadership at STA passed through different Acharyas over the years, each Acharya brought along his own ideas and convictions concerning what it meant to live as a Christian. Thus, each in their own way, the Acharyas aimed to impart particular Christian values to the ashramites and to the SoE students. We have seen how these *social transitions* have played out within Christian environments at the SoE and, as Chapter 5 shall explore in more detail, the various Acharyas and their particular convictions concerning Christian doctrinal points have also crucially shaped STA's interactions with individuals from *non*-Christian religions.

5

The negotiations of belonging: Relational dynamics of World Amrita and Sat Tal Christian Ashram

5.1 Introduction

As Chapters 3 and 4 explored, STA facilitates some of its own programmes including the Winter Ashram, Summer Ashram and SoE – but in the remaining months (and sometimes also overlapping with these two–three months of STA programmes), STA frequently rents out its space to various groups who are keen to make use of the tranquil and scenic atmosphere for their own programmes and retreats. Many of these groups are indeed Christian groups who run their own Christian spiritual programs. But there are also various secular groups – such as physical education groups and school leadership camps – who hire the space. Some of these secular groups hail from Christian institutions, but groups from Hindu (or other) institutions are equally present – the religious affiliation of education or athletic-oriented groups is not of particular importance to STA. The staff at STA do not typically interact much with these visiting groups beyond ensuring that their physical needs (lodging, meal times, help with taxi arrangements, etc.) are met.[1] Indeed, the ashram staff seem primarily concerned with how their group members behave on the ashram's grounds – do they place any unreasonable demands on the hostess or servants of STA? Do they clean their dishes properly, and push in their benches after mealtimes, and are they otherwise orderly? Overall, spiritual guidance is kept to a minimum, because either (1) the group, as in the former case, is accompanied by Christian pastors who have formulated their own teaching material and worship practices – both of which are assumed to be compatible with STA's own spiritual teachings – or (2) the group, as in the second case, has not come for an explicitly spiritual purpose.

However, there is one other group who, since 2003, has frequented STA on a near-annual basis. This group, which I will call World Amrita (WA), is the sole group, both present and past, that hires the ashram space in order to run its own spiritual programme *and* which is not *explicitly* Christian. This unique position that WA occupies in the contexts of STA has resulted in ample informal discussions among STA ashramites – along with more formalized discussions at the STA board meetings – on the topic of where precisely WA fits into STA's spiritual landscape, including whether WA should be there at all. These ongoing debates amongst members of the wider STA community, especially recalling one of Jones's original visions for STA to be a place where people from diverse faith backgrounds would all be welcome to share in spiritual community together (Chapter 3, Section 3.5), makes the study of the relational dynamics between STA and WA particularly fruitful for our present exploration. Thus, this chapter explores the social interactions and the relational boundaries between STA and WA from 2003 to the present. My goals are both descriptive and analytical: I present ethnographically based phenomenological descriptions of these aspects of present-day life at STA, but I also explore the prolonged interactions and dense contestations between STA and WA as a case study that can help us understand some of the motivations and challenges of creating an interreligious spiritual community.

5.1.1 World Amrita

WA is a small not-for-profit organization whose founders' expressed goal is to offer spiritual 'awakening' to seekers. The teacher (one of WA's two original founders) with whom I have extensively interacted over the course of my ethnographic research, and whom I will call Dana, draws from her experiences in a diverse range of spiritual and existential styles such as Christianity, Hinduism, Jin Shin Jyutsu, Body-Mind Centering, and her love of poetry and the outdoors. Dana herself is an American who grew up within Christian contexts, but she has lived in India (primarily in Lucknow) for several years both as a student of Hindu gurus and, since being authorized to give spiritual instruction (*dharma*) in 1998, as a spiritual teacher in her own right. The group facilitates silent meditation and 'deep rest' retreats not only in India but also in Israel, Western Europe and North America; they first hosted one of their retreats at STA in 2003 and, barring the years during which they were not able to use the ashram space (I return to this point in Section 5.4.2), they have returned to STA on an annual basis, usually around March–April and for any duration from two weeks to one month. From an Indian perspective, WA's participants are mostly 'foreigners' though some Indians also participate in the group. During the retreat I attended at STA in April 2017, only one of the twenty-five participants was Indian; during the two retreats I attended at STA in April 2018, there were three Indians. (We can contrast this demographic with the WA retreat I attended in England in May 2018, which comprised exclusively of Europeans and North Americans, none of whom had Indian origins.) Because only a handful of foreigners visit STA throughout the year – and an additional few live in STA's estate during the summer months – WA's foreign participants stand out like small speckles of white against an otherwise brown background, and indeed the WA group is often referred to by STA's workers as '*videshi log*' (the foreign people) or, simply using the English word, the 'foreigners'.

The topic of WA's use of STA for their own spiritual retreats frequently arose in conversations during my early months at STA; STA ashramites eagerly provided me with their own varied interpretations of what WA is and what its participants do while on retreat – including their assumed reasons why these foreigners have sought out a spiritual retreat in the first place. On one side of the spectrum were descriptions such as that the people who came with WA were 'lost' foreigners who were searching for some semblance of redemptive spirituality, or even that they were recovering drug addicts who were in need of a rehabilitative haven in which they could recuperate. Concerned by the impact that these 'lost' spiritual seekers might have on the wider atmospheres of the STA, some STA ashramites (albeit a minority) went so far as to write a formal letter of complaint to the STA leadership, requesting them to banish WA once and for all. Other regular ashramites of STA, along with some of the management, were perfectly content to have the group members come to STA, and spoke pleasantly about WA's individual participants, but did wonder whether WA using STA's space for their own meditation retreats was truly the type of ecumenical engagement that Jones himself would have wanted. These ashramites emphasized that the individual participants of WA should indeed be welcomed to the ashram – but as *individuals*, and not as members of WA participating in an institutionalized WA retreat. Rather, the ashramites proposed, WA individuals should join in STA's own programmes, thus intermingling with STA's own ashramites in order to hear about the teachings of Jesus that Jones had deemed to be so crucial to personal transformation. And still other ashramites were happy to have WA come and conduct their own meditation retreats which facilitated their own spiritual practices, but these ashramites lamented that they had always felt a deep sense of estrangement from the WA group. 'And *that* [feeling estranged from others] is not how Ashram should be', Uncle William once told me decisively.

These active contestations and controversies surrounding WA's presence at STA are particularly interesting for me as an ethnographer because one way for anthropologists to understand people – and their values, beliefs and motives – is to pay particular attention to the *inter*personal conflicts and frictions which arise in social settings. In the pages that follow, I present several ethnographic vignettes and then engage with them by using a thematically focused analysis. The ethnographic material is divided into two sections. Broadly, Section 5.4 (encapsulating 2003–11) focuses on some of the processes through which belonging is negotiated – including the significant difficulties experienced by both WA and STA as well as the emotional roller coaster experienced by both parties as WA is first welcomed at STA, then expelled from STA and then invited to return. Based on these processes, I offer five distinct phases of belonging. Noting some belonging-related difficulties that both WA and STA experienced upon WA's return to STA in 2011, Section 5.5 (encapsulating 2011–present) explores some of the effects and the ramifications of the partial belongings that ensued from the point of WA's return.

5.2 Multiple religious belonging

Before delving into the primary ethnographic material, let us first look at some of the theoretical discussions that have informed my analysis. In focusing on the relational dynamics between STA and WA, I have found it especially helpful and thought-provoking to draw upon the emerging literature focused on multiple religious orientation (sometimes called multiple religious belonging or 'dual' or 'double' religious belonging) of individuals who sympathize with or participate in religious milieus other than one's home religious tradition. More broadly, I have also engaged with literature from Theology Without Walls (TWW), established in 2015 by a group of academics, which seeks to promote and cultivate spaces of mutual understanding across religious boundaries. Multiple religious orientation has been a key topic of inquiry for individuals involved in TWW scholarship. One of the most clearly articulated discussions to link dual religious belonging and TWW is offered by Paul Knitter who argues that 'the practice of double religious belonging is a synonym for, or lays the foundation for, the practice of theology without walls'.[2] In the same work as Knitter, scholars such as Mark Heim also suggest a direct correlation between what Heim refers to as 'people who are hybrid in their religious identities and practices' (or even simply individuals who are not firmly embedded in a singular home tradition) and TWW.[3]

Using standard TWW terminology to classify WA, we could understand WA as a group of multiple religious belongers. Indeed, as Dana told me in one of our conversations, the group's original name before it became 'World Amrita' was 'Sangha Without Walls'. This was a name that Dana had selected due to the ways it conveyed the warm note of hospitality to individuals from a myriad of diverse faith backgrounds – including individuals who, like Dana herself, drew upon more than one religious tradition – who could all feel welcomed into their *sangha* (spiritual family). Furthermore, as I mentioned above, Dana herself intentionally incorporates practices and techniques from multiple religious traditions into her meditation classes, resulting in all participants of WA receiving spiritual teachings influenced by, and inspired from, multiple religious traditions. Moreover, a number of WA participants whom I spoke with after the WA retreats in 2017 and 2018 individually conveyed to me that, even outside their time at WA retreats, they themselves drew upon multiple religious traditions in formulating their own spiritual practices. Thus, I find it especially appropriate to use TWW scholarship to frame my analysis of the contested relationships between WA and STA. Nevertheless, as I shall expand upon below, I use, in turn, the case study of WA to reflect upon, and interrogate, some of the ideas commonly held within TWW scholarship. Specifically, I argue that the lived experiences of WA participants at STA challenge a fundamental assumption of TWW scholarship: namely, that belonging naturally occurs to those individuals who desire it.

5.2.1 Two models of multiple religious life

Two TWW scholars, Peter Feldmeier and Jeanine Diller, have classified the multiple religious concept into several stages. Peter Feldmeier identifies four distinct ways of engaging in some form of (what he refers to as) multiple religious belonging (MRB).[4] Using (F) to refer to Feldmeir, the four phases are: (F1) Allowing 'one's own religion to be influenced by the religious imagination of the auxiliary religion' (this form is identified mainly with Francis Clooney); (F2) Engaging in some official practices of a second religion but still identifying solely as a Christian (Feldmeier provides Robert Kennedy, both a Roman Catholic Priest and a Zen Roshi, as an example of this category); (F3) Identifying primarily with Christianity but holding a secondary descriptive identity, such as 'Buddhist-Christian' or 'Hindu-Christian'; and (F4) Holding onto two or more models of potentially contradictory world views and viewing them both as true (Henri le Saux, Raimon Pannikar, Paul Knitter, etc.). One can note that Feldmeier's first two ways of engaging in MRB continue to maintain the exclusive and sole identity of 'Christian', while the latter two allow for some intermingling and even supplanting of a singular primary religious identity.

Jeanine Diller also identifies several categories which are useful to our discussion here – though it is worth noting the fact that she refers to the phenomenon as multiple religious orientation (MRO) – a term I also choose to use, for reasons which will become evident soon.[5] Diller identifies four distinct categories before arriving at comparative theology in a way that resembles the work of Francis Clooney. We can use (D) and numbers to refer to Diller's phases. Diller's first two categories – (D1) conceptual openness and (D2) material contact – do not require the same level of engagement, commitment or even participation as her latter categories. Her third and fourth categories – (D3) interfaith collaboration and (D4) dialogue – require more active participation with and alongside people of other faith commitments, but do not necessitate that one change one's own beliefs/practices as a result of the increased interaction. (Though, as comparative theologians frequently tell us, it is rare to engage in genuine dialogue with others without some changes to one's own perspective/practice.) Reflecting on these first four categories, Diller notes that 'they are all ways of learning about [another religion] from the outside, watching or hearing about or working alongside others who are doing it. The latter categories go progressively deeper because in them one engages in the tradition *oneself*, from the inside. These represent a new level of intensity of participation, different not just in degree but in kind'.[6] Diller's latter five categories are ones which, as she rightly draws our attention to, are higher-risk in that they necessitate individual participation. In fact, Diller outlines four entire phases before reaching engagement with multiple religious traditions by way of comparative theology; her fifth category correlates to Feldmeier's first category. Her latter five categories include (D5) comparative theology; (D6) adopting belief(s); (D7) adopting practice(s), which Diller recognizes to be a multilayered phenomenon where both the stakes and the depth of engagement can vary immensely; (D8) identity; and (D9) belonging (see Table 5.1).

That is to say, while both Feldmeier's and Diller's models sketch a continuum (in that the farther an individual travels along their respective categories, the deeper one is understood to participate in multiple religions), only Diller's model clearly marks a category called 'belonging' as distinct from the other forms of engaging with multiple religious traditions. It seems likely that Feldmeier's exclusion of 'belonging' as a specific category is because Feldmeier's own model is grounded in his discussion of multiple religious *belonging* and therefore belonging is assumed.

Table 5.1 Comparing Feldmeier's and Diller's Models

				F1: Being influenced by	F2: Engaging with		F3: Identifying as	F4: Holding onto contradictions	
D1: Conceptual openness	D2: Material contact	D3: Interfaith collaboration	D4: Dialogue	D5: Comparative theology	D6: Adopting beliefs	D7: Adopting practices		D8: Identity	D9: Belonging

Reflecting on these categories as an ethnographer, it strikes me that it is of the utmost importance to reserve 'belonging' as a separate phase of MRO. Indeed, scholars who reflect on the dynamic processes of multiple religious individuals (and individuals who live out their lives as such!) cannot assume that belonging occurs readily. Crucially, belonging relies upon acceptance by the religious community (or communities) in question rather than strictly the self-identification of the individual. We might pose the question in this way: If an individual says, 'I belong in this church, because I self-identify as a Christian!' is this claim equivalent to, or concurrent with, that same Christian community accepting that individual's self-identification? I contend that it is not just the individual who can decide when to belong to a community; the community has to also invite or allow the individual to belong. As I explored in Chapter 1, in my discussion of Belief-Inclusive Research (BIR), the ways that an anthropologist's own belief is determined, as far as the community is concerned, is on account of how the community perceives the anthropologist, and not simply by how the anthropologist identifies herself. The crucial point to take away from this is that *belonging* in a religious and/or spiritual context seems to require *both* self-identification as a particular brand of religious world view *and* acceptance on the part of a larger religious community. We cannot belong, even if we identify *as* and participate with – and indeed even if we long to belong within – unless a community accepts us as a belonger. Thus, I argue that it is unwarranted to assume that multiple religious *belonging* occurs simply on account of a multiple religious individual wishing for it to occur. Indeed, considering some on-the-ground realities of multiple religious individuals reveals that *belonging* is a complicated (and, at times, messy) process.

5.2.2 Belonging

This leads me to define what I mean by 'belonging'. While multiple religious *existing* could be a suitable term to describe an individual who has actively drawn upon multiple religious influences in forming their own spiritual identity, multiple religious *belonging* additionally entails some degree of, to risk a tautology, belonging. So what exactly does it mean to belong? I understand belonging as twofold: (1) The word 'belong' is rooted in the Old English word *'gelang'*, which the *Oxford English Dictionary* defines as being 'at hand, together with'. From this etymological observation, I draw the notion that *belonging* necessitates some sense of physical connection, in that the sense of belonging emerges out of a proximal togetherness with other individuals. To belong is to be 'together with'. (2) Additionally, I understand belonging to include an emotional and psychological component in the way that leading public figures like Brené Brown have spoken of belonging – feeling that one's entire self is wholly accepted without judgement or conditions. Brown describes this as living vulnerably. It might be a helpful and even crucial clarification point to here think of vulnerability not as weakness nor as someone who is at risk of being attacked; rather, to be vulnerable in this sense is to be unguarded due to a confidence that any form of 'protective armour' is simply not needed.[7] Speaking of vulnerability along similar lines, Jean Vanier, a Catholic philosopher and the founder of l'Arche community projects, describes a community as a place where one must 'come out of one's shell of protection, to become vulnerable in order to love and understand others, to call them forth as special and unique, to share and to give space and nourishment to them ... Community is the place where people grow in love and in peace-making'.[8] By belonging to such communities where individuals can feel fully accepted, Vanier claims, individuals 'are earthed and find their identity'.[9]

So belonging as I am discussing it here refers to both a feeling of 'togetherness' and also the feeling that one can be accepted as their whole identity without feeling a need to hide any part of it. With this twofold understanding of belonging, we might ask: Where do multiple religious individuals belong? Namely, who are the other individuals who form their proximal communities, and who is it alongside whom they can feel wholly accepted, or feel that no part of themselves must be either hidden with a protective armour or strategically placed to the side whenever they are within that community setting, lest they be 'ousted'?

Although there are a number of self-professed dual religious belongers who have written about their experiences of belonging to two or more distinct religious communities,[10] my subsequent analysis takes as its fundamental starting point the observation that there are also a significant number of multiple religious *existers* who struggle to feel that they truly *belong*, since *belonging* to communal systems involves, as we have seen, more full-blooded participative modes than *existing*.[11] That is to say, belonging does not always occur in the ways one might long for. The messiness of this in-between interpersonal reality, I argue, is a direct challenge to a fundamental assumption in much of recent TWW scholarship. The assumption that dual religious *existing* necessarily leads into dual religious *belonging* can be seen quite clearly in the work of Knitter who writes that '[the dual belonger] finds oneself, surprisingly, at home in both [the primary and newfound traditions]'.[12] Dual belonging in the way of Knitter, who self-identifies as belonging to both Buddhism and Christianity, is indeed possible, but it is not an assured fact for all individuals who operate within multiple religious milieus. Thus, rather differently from Knitter, I argue that to unhesitatingly superimpose the thicker category of 'belonging' to the thinner category of multiple religious 'existing' perhaps suggests a feeling of at-home that is not always present in the lived realities of those who have to navigate these somewhat turbulent spiritual waters.

I think, as Jeffery Long's work in the volume *Dual Belonging in Hinduism and Christianity* highlights, there is a crucial distinction between *belonging* to a tradition versus *practising* (parts of) it. As Long writes about Ramakrishna, 'He did not claim that he belonged to many religious traditions. He did not claim to be a Hindu-Christian … He did not claim to *belong* to any single tradition, but rather to have *practiced* many'.[13] While Long invokes the example of Ramakrishna for an argument different from my own (Long highlights the ways in which Ramakrishna found belonging in his own sense of self, rather than looking for it from a community), the lesson learned is applicable to this context. This crucial distinction between personal practice or affiliation and *belonging* should become clearer in our next section, as we consider the on-the-ground realities of STA in which *belonging* proved to be a genuine struggle – both for the spiritual community who strived to be a place where all individuals could *belong* and for the individuals who sought to take part in it. Keeping in mind this kind of belonging without ready-made guarantees, we return to the particular case study of WA and their time at STA.

5.3 The relational dynamics of Sat Tal Ashram and World Amrita in terms of multiple religious belonging

As I have already indicated in Section 5.1.1, and will continue to demonstrate below, both STA and WA are particularly concerned with the extent to which WA participants 'belong' in STA. Certain members of STA actively debate whether or not WA's presence fits within the spiritual ethos envisioned by Jones, while some members of WA are painfully aware that their invitation to use STA can be possibly revoked and, thus, they intentionally act (or refrain from acting) in particular ways to ensure that their welcome at STA continues. Of course, as is evident from some of the scholarship on TWW that I summarized above, multiple religious belonging is often spoken of in reference to one individual who appears to 'belong' (or not) to two or more religious communities; that is not the way, however, that I am exploring multiple religious belonging here. TWW scholars often look at the process of one single individual belonging (or not) to multiple distinct religious communities. In a rather different vein, I am exploring the wider communitarian processes of one guest group (WA) – which both comprises some 'multiple religious' individuals, and which is also guided by spiritual leaders who intentionally draw upon multiple religious traditions – and the ways that WA appear to 'belong' (or not) to the home group (STA) – which, according to the proclamations of Jones, was formed with the intent to be open to people from a number of religious traditions (Chapter 3, Section 3.4). Indeed, just as WA itself consists of a spectrum of multiple religious individuals, so too does STA exist as a theoretically well-suited place for such individuals to feel a sense of belonging and being welcomed. Keeping these individual as well as structural features in mind, when I explore the phenomenon of multiple religious belonging, I am concerned with the occasionally subtle ways that WA has had to negotiate a sense of welcome and belonging, and also navigate hostility and opposition, within STA. By focusing our attention to the matter of 'thick' belonging as I define it above and – following Diller who resolutely reserves the stage of 'belonging' as a separate category which does not automatically permeate the other categories of multiple religious engagement – through examining some of the particular moments where such 'belonging' is either experienced or left wanting, we can speak to the various stages of negotiating belonging in the existential and the institutional spaces between WA and STA. As we shall see in the ethnographic descriptions below, full belonging does not always occur even if one or even both parties wish for it to occur.

5.4 Negotiating belonging: A continuum of phases

Having now outlined some of the key terms and theoretical backdrops that inform my analysis, we can proceed to ethnographic descriptions which demonstrate some of the relational dynamics of hospitality and hostility between WA and STA. In a fashion similar to Feldmeier and Diller who have mapped out some phases of multiple religious life in their respective models of MRB and MRO, I have selected four ethnographic moments which encapsulate the processes of negotiating belonging in the context of the relational dynamics between STA and

WA. I classify these as four stages: invitation and welcome, restrictions, attempts of correction, and re-establishing belonging. Crucially, my presentation of these stages as the first, second, third and fourth phase is not meant to convey that I envision them as having a strictly linear and sequential progression; on the contrary, especially when considering the interplay of phases two and three, we can see how these four phases do not always occur chronologically, nor does entering one phase entail that one has finished entirely with the preceding phase.

5.4.1 Inviting the Other: Initial invitation and welcome

When considering the processes involved in negotiating a sense of belonging, we can begin with the initial welcome. Dana, one of the leaders of WA whom we encountered above (Section 5.1.1), recollects first finding out about STA while in Bodh Gaya (Bihar, India) around 2002. A Catholic sister who attended a retreat in Bodh Gaya at the same time learned that Dana was looking for places to host her own retreats. The sister later informed her own bishop about Dana's search, and shortly thereafter Dana received a letter from Bishop Anthony Fernandes of the Roman Catholic diocese of Bareilly. The bishop offered to show Dana around his diocese and informed her about a handful of different places in Uttar Pradesh and Uttarakhand which might serve as a suitable retreat venue. One of these options included STA and, upon hearing the bishop's description of it, Dana thought that its remote location and tranquil environment would be an ideal spot to host her retreats. In 2003 she arranged to meet with Auntie Eleanor, who was working as STA's hostess at the time, and during their meeting it was agreed that WA could start using STA to host its retreat that coming spring. Dana does not recall having very many interactions with the manager Mr Ram or Acharya (Acharya V., whom we encountered in Chapter 4, Section 4.2), and instead remembers all of her communication with STA leadership going through Auntie Eleanor. Thus, for example, when Dana wondered whether the group could sing sacred songs from a variety of religious traditions in the evenings, she and the WA manager, whom I will call Emilia, first checked this matter with Auntie Eleanor, who told them that their singing was permissible and that they were free to do as they wished so long as they did not become a disruptive presence for any other guests. Rather quickly, Dana explains, she and her group felt comfortable and welcomed at STA – so much so that Dana began to experiment with new meditation techniques and bodily postures during her time at STA. Dana's current meditation practice is characterized by – and in the broadly Western-based spheres of meditation retreats in which she participates, she is renowned for – lying down as a meditation posture and encouraging others to try introducing it to their own meditation practice. Her sensorimotor comfort with this posture, which she claims can be helpful in bringing about 'deep rest', is something she developed at STA, she explains, due to feeling wholeheartedly welcomed there.

5.4.2 Restricting the Other: The barn and the banning

This section looks at the oppositional pinnacle of non-belonging insofar as the straining of relationship between WA and STA is concerned: in 2008, in the middle of their month-long retreat at STA, WA was prohibited from using STA's chapel for their meditation practice. And, in 2010, WA was 'banned' from returning to STA at all. Both these actions are significant due to the fact that, since their first retreat in 2003, WA had been consistently using STA on an annual basis to host their retreats. There are somewhat contradictory stories about precisely what WA did which caused the STA leadership to, first, restrict WA's use of the chapel in 2008 and, then, ban the group entirely from STA in 2010. All that seemed clear was that, whatever it was, it had gone against the STA's unwritten code of conduct which had, in turn, made the STA leadership wary of WA. Were two people from WA holding hands? Did the group worship Hindu gods and goddesses? Was the anonymous artwork (a handful of twigs and greenery, configured to resemble a seated meditation posture) once left on a common-room table for all to see, intended to be a 'statue' of the Buddha? And, then, were the flowers later placed around these twigs indicative of the 'statue' being revered as a sacred shrine? Perhaps it was the chanting and singing of other sacred songs that occurred by candlelight in the evening hours? Were group members secretly doing drugs? (drugs, after all, many STA ashramites reasoned, would explain the way that WA participants sometimes lay down in the tall grass – an action most Indians would never do in the wilderness due to a well-founded fear of scorpions and poisonous snakes). There were several ideas floating around regarding precisely what it was that WA had done to lose the trust of the STA leadership; these numerous possibilities were whispered amongst some STA ashramites and narrated to me in the early months of my stay at STA from August 2016 onwards. And, over a year later, when I became better acquainted with some of the teachers and participants of WA after attending my second annual retreat with WA in April 2017, I realized that many individuals from WA itself also wondered about precisely what had resulted in them being kicked out and – when the topic came up – they speculatively mused upon a number of explanations, some of which were similar to the speculations of the STA ashramites. To concretely demonstrate the multiplicity of viewpoints and speculations about the reasons why WA was kicked out of the chapel in 2008 and, subsequently, banned from STA in 2010, I provide a few different recollections of the relevant events.

First, Dana recounted the scenario to me as follows:

> Each group [which forms the WA retreat each year] has a different feel and this one group [in 2008] had a lot of anger and creativity ... some people made really cool sculptures during the retreat ... but apparently someone made some pile of stones somewhere that looked like an altar or a shrine, and maybe some people saw it and bowed to it, or maybe a person from our retreat was doing something that looked like worshipping at the pile of stones ... I don't know, I think maybe it was the first ... I really don't know. But this was the first thing that happened. And then also someone made a thing out of flower petals and twigs ... it looked like a person meditating. But I guess it also looked like a Buddha. This was the second thing. And, of course, we were lying down in the chapel ... we were not made aware of how shocking that could be to any person in any religion in India. Because we had felt so welcome when we first came to STA, we just felt we could be without reservation. And, for me, over the years, lying down as a meditative posture had begun to feel normal, so I invited people to meditate like that if they wished. And, as you know from being on retreat with me, it's not like *savasana* [corpse pose in yoga] ... it's with pillows and cushions and blankets and it can look more like a nap. So I guess it can be shocking. But I had seen that plaque on the house [the Midlakes building of STA] where it says that people from all or no religions are welcome[14] ... and that felt encouraging to us. I don't know precisely what was a problem and what wasn't, but I know we were banned. And, ever since we were invited back [in 2011], we've done whatever we can imagine to keep that from happening again.

The manager of STA since 2007, Kabir Likhna, in his recollection of the events, offered a similar account:

> Dorothy walked by the chapel one time and saw that the group was lying down in the chapel. That did not sit right with her, and so she told Acharya Biswas about it. He went and saw it too. They wanted to kick the group out [of STA entirely] at that point, but they [WA] still had two weeks left of their retreat. Eventually we agreed that they'd move to a different building [and refrain from using the chapel]. It was either that, or they'd go. It wasn't great, but we did it. And now [World Amrita] uses the New Fellowship hall for their retreats – and only Christian groups use the chapel.

Kabir never forthrightly told me that it was almost entirely due to his personal, persistent advocacy of the good character of WA that the group was allowed to stay at STA at all – the extent of his efforts and his institutional influence on this matter were only shared with me later by members of WA. Amongst the STA leadership, Kabir was undoubtedly the strongest and most vocal supporter of keeping WA at the ashram, and he was also steadfast in declaring that the group had never worshiped Hindu idols while at STA. He was so convinced of this absence of 'idolatry' that he once, unprompted, offered the following reasoning to me:

> They [the participants of WA] are foreigners, Nadya. How could foreigners even begin to create a Hindu statue or a shrine? They were doing some art: one person came and bent this metal into a shape, another person added some flowers around it – it is all art to them. They're on a retreat, in beautiful nature, and they made some art. It was all blown out of proportion!

We can also consider an excerpt from one of my many conversations with Dorothy and Auntie Eleanor who had both been deeply involved with STA at the time when WA first began visiting it. Like Kabir, Auntie Eleanor was also a strong supporter of allowing WA to stay at STA and, as we shall see in the conversation below, from April 2017, she, too, fiercely defended WA against any accusations of their alleged idol worship.

Nadya (N): During Acharya G.'s talk this year [2017], we met at the chapel for the [World Amrita] group but every other time we meet in the New Fellowship Hall. But Dana and Kabir have told me that the group used to have all their meetings in the chapel. Do you know why [World Amrita] doesn't meet in the chapel anymore?

Dorothy (D): Actually, the Board asked them not to come to the ashram. Because they used to put Hindu idols in front of the chapel.

Auntie Eleanor (E): That's a lie!!!! That never happened. They all made it up.

D: I have it seen it!! You never even went out of the kitchen!!

E: Rubbish! That's rubbish, I saw them. No idols, no *pooja*. But the ashram committee did refuse them once, one year, but then later we took them in again. But they never worshipped idols, no. Yes, some foreigner came during the night one time, he had drugs and incense and when the Acharya

	saw all that he asked him to leave. But this was a random foreigner ... he was not from their group!
N:	But why did the Board not want the group to come?
E:	I think they felt that they didn't respect the chapel. They were lying down, meditating ... But they respect the *mandir* (temple) [that is, from stories that WA individuals have told Auntie Eleanor, she understands that they are respectful of Hindu temples and other religious places whenever they visit them], they respect the ashram. It's just, you don't [i.e. one should not] lie down. You can just listen and sit down and meditate. No problem. It's a quiet place, you have more time to meditate. But lying down?! It is not very good.

One element of the story that all parties agree on is that, following Acharya Biswas's and Dorothy's sighting of WA participants lying down in the chapel in 2008, Acharya Biswas declared that the group should leave the ashram entirely. This, Dorothy pointed out to me in the same conversation from above, seemed the natural response to seeing a group use the chapel in that alleged sacrilegious manner – lying down in a sacred space was incomprehensible to many involved in STA's leadership, and the very act suggested a kind of irreverence in a sacred space. In response to the Acharya's decision, Kabir and Emilia scrambled to see if there were any compromises that could be made in order to allow WA to finish their retreat at STA. In the end, Kabir and the servants transformed an unused building (referred to as 'the barn') into a makeshift meditation hall, and Acharya Biswas agreed that WA could remain at STA for the duration of their retreat but they were no longer allowed to enter the chapel. Once the barn was sufficiently tidied, Dana, Emilia and the WA participants moved their meditation mats and cushions out of the chapel and set up their spaces in the new location. Some of the WA participants whom I spoke with in 2016–18 could recall the 2008 shift to the barn, and they described the process as moving from a beautiful, spacious chapel to a stinky, cramped barn with flies and fleas everywhere – not the most inspiring of places for meditation by any means, they lamented. Further, many struggled to make sense of the ways they had been treated, claiming that it felt 'unfair' to be initially accepted to the ashram, with the expectation that they would use the chapel space with its tall ceilings, large windows and beautiful interior designs, only to be abruptly relegated to a smelly, overcrowded barn – especially midway through a retreat.

But, for many of the individuals who regularly came to STA with WA, the group's demotion to the barn was not *just* a physical relocation. Many described it to me in a vivid manner that conveyed it was also a symbolic turning point in the relationship between WA and STA: WA no longer felt that they were free and welcome to conduct their spiritual practice with the exploratory openness that they had originally felt they were encouraged to undertake. 'It says, right there, [that] "people of all different faiths" are welcome', Emilia once told me, emphatically gesturing towards the stone plaque on the main building's verandah which contained Jones's words from the Ashram Ideals. 'So, yes, we were a bit surprised to realize that there were certain spiritual practices [that] we just could not do.'

Let us, however briefly, take one large step back from considering the present-day specifics of the relational dynamics between WA and STA, and recall that, in his Ashram Ideals, Jones explicitly stated that he wished for STA to be a place where all individuals who 'sincerely desire to find God' would be welcomed (see Chapter 3, Section 3.4). Jones deeply desired for all individuals to seek, and find, God – since he had himself been so profoundly transformed by his own encounter with Jesus, but, as we saw extensively in Chapter 3, Jones repeatedly emphasized the unique, transformative power of Christ and Christ alone. Having also noted Jones's unrelenting desire to share his spiritual findings with other individuals, I am prompted to revisit some questions that we entertained towards the end of Chapter 3: What did Jones understand 'sincerely desiring' and 'God' to mean? Must the 'seeking' inevitably involved in the 'finding' follow a specific pattern or protocol? Was 'God' to be used as a synonym for 'Jesus' – that is, the personal Christ whom Jones dearly loved and preached about? Through considering the case of WA, we can see that some of the Acharyas and other members of the STA leadership since the time of Jones believed that spiritual quests for God should indeed take on a rather specific style which has recognizably Christian undertones. Thus, some of the practices of WA – the prolonged silence, the varying postures of meditation, the drawing upon of sacred texts from a number of religious traditions, including those outside of the Christian canon and so on – can seem incomprehensible as modes of spiritual seeking.

STA's dismissive attitude of spiritual practices that are not understood to have clearly Christian undercurrents has resonances with our earlier exploration of STA's navigation of practices which were 'truly Christian and truly Indian' (Chapter 3, Section 3.2); the spiritual practices which were not deemed to directly relate to furthering an individual's soteriological relationship with the person of Jesus were eventually abandoned as spiritual practices. In this same vein, some members of STA leadership wondered whether or not WA could be correctly understood as seeking *God* in their spiritual quests, since, as evidenced by WA's unhesitating adoption of practices and beliefs from religious contexts other than Christianity, WA was clearly not *sincerely desiring to find* the person of *Jesus* in the ways that Jones had desired individuals to encounter him. In Chapter 3, I pointed out that Jones's somewhat ambiguous equivalence between 'Christianity' and 'Christ' is either wonderful or disturbing, depending on one's comfort with ambiguity (Section 3.1.1). Through considering the relational dynamics between STA and WA, we can see that some members of STA leadership took active measures to remove any ambiguity regarding what precisely it meant to 'sincerely desire to find God' in the context of STA: around 2008, Acharya Biswas petitioned to the STA leadership board that STA formally amend Jones's statement which welcomed to STA any and all individuals who 'sincerely desire to find God'. Instead, Acharya Biswas proposed that the stone plaque on the Midlakes building should be changed to read that anyone who desires to find, and thus seeks, *Jesus* should be welcomed at STA. This Christocentric modification of Jones's original vision was clearly prompted by STA's interactions with WA, and exemplifies some of the ways that belonging is negotiated – even in behind-the-scene manners.

The following year, in 2009, WA returned to STA – this time arranging ahead of time to use a section of cabins in a part of the ashram's large estate which was not in the immediate surroundings of the ashram's main buildings. The leaders of WA conducted their usual silent meditation retreat but, Dana and Emilia recount, they were particularly apprehensive about which spiritual practices to include or exclude from their retreat. When the retreat finished that year, WA participants left STA in the ways they had always done – some individuals left immediately to attend another meditation retreat in a different part of India, others lingered on as individuals in the solace of STA's quiet hills and lakes for a few more days and still others returned to their workplaces or other points of interest. Dana took a train to Lucknow to be near one of her own spiritual teachers, and Emilia began the long journey of returning to her home in Auroville (South India). However, though it was unknown to them at the time of their leaving, they were not to be welcomed back the following year. When, later that autumn, the time came for WA to plan the details of their retreats for 2010, Emilia was informed by Kabir that the members of the STA leadership committee had met to discuss the contentious topic of WA's presence at STA, and ultimately decided to discontinue their relationship with WA. The details of the discussion, along with the angles from which the various STA committee members had approached the discussion, were never disclosed to me by anyone at STA – perhaps because these proceedings took place so many years ago and the details were murky. When I asked Dana about the year they were not invited to return to STA, she also confessed that she could not remember many details. 'All I remember', she told me, 'is that I didn't actually speak with anyone other than Kabir about it. It was the same as before [in 2008 when they were moved to the barn]. The decision was made, by someone else surely, and Kabir came as the regretful messenger.' 'Which time do you mean?' I asked, 'the year you did not return back?' Dana barely let me finish my question before emphatically clarifying, 'The year we were *banned*'. Her sense of hurt at being excluded by a once-inviting ashram was palpable.

Both the incidents of being moved from the chapel to the barn in 2008, as well as being disallowed entirely in 2010, are important to narrate due to the ways that these agonistic interactions fundamentally changed the relational dynamics between WA and STA and set the stage for the ways in which WA had to renegotiate their sense of belonging at STA.

5.4.3 Correcting the Other: Acharya Biswas gives a sermon to WA

The third phase that we will consider is that of one party – STA, as host – attempting to correct and realign the spiritual practices and beliefs of the other party – WA, as invitee. In 2009, the year between when WA was moved from the chapel to the barn (2008) and when they were 'banned' entirely from the ashram (2010), Acharya Biswas asked Dana if he could deliver two lessons to the group during their one-hour teaching sessions. Dana agreed, but, after getting a sense from Acharya Biswas about the content of his preaching, she told the WA participants that their attendance was optional and that anyone, especially those who might be particularly sensitive to certain 'exclusivist' teachings within Christian contexts, was allowed to skip the talk if they wished to do so. However, she emphasized to the group that it would be good for WA to be well represented at the talk so as to demonstrate the group's receptivity to the STA leadership and their teachings.

A long-time participant of WA described his recollection of Acharya Biswas's first teaching:

> All I remember is that he was angry; there was a lot of emotional energy coming from him – anger. He was shouting at us in this sermon. It felt

like listening to a television kind of preacher, speaking about fire and hell and brimstone. Obviously, it was assumed we're Christians since we're foreigners.[15] He said we were lost. He told us that we'd go to hell if we don't come back to Christianity … and that, if we meditate, we'll go to hell. On and on. Not just his words but also his energy. I think he felt disappointed that so many foreigners were coming to this ashram, he assumed we were from some Christian backgrounds but had ceased practising. He found it disappointing that he couldn't get through to most of us. He must have been surprised that people coming here don't want to have anything to do with Christianity … but he was angry.

Dana referred to the Acharya's sermon in more succinct terms: 'He told us that meditators go to hell. It was very painful. I don't think he could understand why anyone would be anything other than Christian.' News of Acharya Biswas's now-infamous and somewhat apocalyptic 2009 sermon to WA had also circulated amongst STA ashramites. On one occasion, when I was speaking with Auntie Eleanor and two long-term STA ashramites about whether STA's various Acharyas had ever delivered messages to the WA group, one of the ashramites chuckled, and went straight to the point that I had tried to avoid bringing up so directly myself: 'You mean Biswas's sermon? He was *direct!*' And, another time, Acharya G. referred to Acharya Biswas's sermon with the following turn of phrase: 'good heart but unwise action'.

I was never able to meet Acharya Biswas in person, though we did correspond by phone and email on several occasions. I purposefully never raised the topic of WA with him, but he once brought it up of his own accord:

> 'Sometimes non-Christian groups come to our ashram', he explained. 'There is one such group, WA. Once they invited me to speak. They were gentle and very systematic … but they were seeking an alternative to Christ. I said that it is not possible to find an alternate for Christ, as He is the Ultimate. Some of them agreed [with me] but not all.'

When Dana tried to make sense of Acharya Biswas's actions, she drew upon her own background within evangelical Christianity in America. She told me, 'I can understand why he gave that sermon. It's what he does as a pastor. He was trying to *save* people … people who he probably thinks are lost. Maybe he thought this was his only chance to save them. I get it.' In spite of efforts from both sides to understand the other party, the phenomenon of one party attempting to correct the other had decisive consequences for the relational dynamics between WA and STA.

5.4.4 Circumnavigating the Other: Efforts to re-establish belonging

The fourth phase that we shall look at is the effort of WA to re-establish a sense of being and feeling welcomed at STA. Above, I have already mentioned the lengths that some members of STA, including the STA Manager Kabir, went to in attempting to re-establish a sense of belonging for WA by petitioning for them to be able to continue to use STA as a base to host their retreats. Here, we will look specifically at the various measures that WA undertook in order to try to secure their ongoing welcome at STA. For this discussion, it is important to gain first a basic understanding of the format of WA's retreats.

At the beginning of WA's retreats at STA, all of the WA participants meet in the meditation hall and the WA manager, Emilia, informs the group about the format of the retreat. Emilia tells the participants that, once the retreat commences, all participants are to remain completely silent for the duration of the seven days, other than during (optional) one-on-one interviews with Dana which occur daily from 10 am to 11 am. Body language (eye contact, etc.) is optional, and individuals can choose the extent to which they want to refrain from body language altogether – the workers at STA have been told, Emilia emphasizes, that nobody is being rude if they refrain from eye contact or the smiling gesture of a 'hello' in the mornings. Even when in the privacy of their room, participants are encouraged to stay away from all forms of communication (no checking emails, no texting friends), and reading books and listening to music is also discouraged so as to enable a deep introspection. In addition to providing participants with the daily schedule which includes various styles and forms of meditation, teachings by Dana, individual's daily work tasks, mealtimes, and so on, Emilia also uses this opening meeting to inform the participants about a number of rules which, she explains, are 'part of the reality of being in an Indian Christian ashram' and which must be strictly followed in order for WA to continue to maintain a positive relationship with STA – a relationship which, Emilia tells the group, 'has deepened over the years'.

Some of these rules, most of which had already been iterated to the group via email correspondence leading up to the retreat, include:

1. No use of any non-Christian religious images, including *malas* [beads often worn around the neck, and used in meditation practice], statues or even T-shirts which have Hindu-styled insignia on them and so on. Retreat participants are told that if they do have any of these items they should

keep them inside their bags in their rooms until they depart from the ashram.
2. No physical contact between men and women. WA participants were told in a pre-retreat email, 'we can feel and express connection with new and old friends in ways other than hugging. Please express your warmth to people of the other gender with a look, a namaste or a warm hello!'
3. During the evening time of meditative chanting, no singing of songs that could be thought of as 'too Hindu'.

These rules were not ones that had been externally imposed on WA by STA. Nor were they rules that were standard to WA's retreats – something I learned later while attending WA retreats in other locations, and also by asking Dana if there were any restrictions that WA observed when hosting a retreat at a location other than STA. On the contrary, these were rules that WA had imposed on itself in the context of STA alone. This self-imposition of rules by WA demonstrates the extent to which WA would restrict their actions and styles of behaviour rather than risk forfeiting their welcome at STA a second time. As Dana tersely said to the WA group during the introductory meeting at the retreat in April 2017, 'and please follow them. The threat is real. We've already been kicked out'.

5.4.5 Navigating the processes of belonging

What we see in the case of the contested middle between WA and STA is that, in spite of an initial invitation and a sense of unconditional welcome, the two parties struggled to maintain an ongoing sense of deep belonging. As I mentioned above, the four stages of negotiating a sense of belonging that I have outlined here – inviting the Other, restricting the Other, correcting the Other and circumnavigating the Other – should not be interpreted as if they are linear processes which pass neatly from one discrete phase to another. At the same time, nor are they clearly cyclical. By this, I mean that, even though WA did indeed regain their invitation to STA, we saw that the re-established welcome (Section 5.4.4) had a rather different existential feel to it than the initial welcome (Section 5.4.1), in which a total and unencumbered freedom was felt by WA. Noting the ways that the belonging which was experienced by WA, the second time around, was what we could understand as a 'partial belonging', rather than the deep belonging originally experienced in their initial welcome, Section 5.5 will focus in more detail on this kind of partial belonging.

5.5 Experiencing partial belonging

Using a selection of ethnographic descriptions, this section demonstrates some of the ramifications of partial belonging. I have selected three moments from my fieldwork which highlight some of the ongoing repercussions – they primarily feature the interactions from April 2018 between the WA group and Acharya G., who was the resident Acharya of STA at that time. I present them, first, as thick descriptions without analysis with the aim of drawing the reader into these vignettes without the interruption that sometimes occurs through analysis. Following the three descriptions, I provide some analytic reflections in Section 5.5.4, which effectively show the difficulties that both sides experienced in their processes of navigating belonging.

5.5.1 Acharya G. gives a sermon to World Amrita

WA had not received a sermon from anyone within STA since the time that Acharya Biswas gave a sermon in 2009. So, when I learned in April 2018 that Acharya G. was scheduled to give a talk to WA, I was rather surprised. Over tea, I asked him whether WA had invited him to speak to them.

Acharya G. (AG):	No, I asked them for it. The ashram committee has decided that every group that comes, university groups or any groups, the resident Acharya must give them a talk. But WA are wary [about receiving a sermon from an Acharya], due to Biswas [and the sermon that he gave to them] from one decade ago.
Nadya (N):	Yeah, I've heard that story [of Acharya Biswas's sermon] from a couple of people.
AG (laughing):	Poor fellow, good heart, but [that particular sermon was given] with very little wisdom. … I think many people have had Christian teachings but they have no love. They have no love for God and no love for their fellow men.

With these comments of wisdom and love in mind, I was particularly surprised when listening to the content of Acharya G.'s talk one or two days later. In his talk, he first spent a few minutes summarizing the history of the ashram and the ways that Jones had envisioned it but, following from this historical account, he went on to articulate some ways that Christian truths are superior to those of other spiritual traditions. I quote extensively from the talk that Acharya G. gave.

> The first time [Jones] met Gandhi was in St Stephen's College, Delhi. He posed a straight question to Gandhi – 'How can we naturalize Christianity in India? What can you as a Hindu leader, tell me, a Christian leader about this?' Gandhi responded: 'First, all missionaries and leaders should begin to live like Jesus Christ. Second, practise religion without adulterating or toning it down. Third: Emphasize love and make it your driving force. Fourth: Study the non-Christian religions to have a more sympathetic approach to the people.' He had put his finger on the sore points of Christianity.[16] When he came to India, Jones felt Christianity was very Westernized. His vision was to reach the educated classes while everyone was working with the lower class. He learnt about many religions and then he found out that the best way to reach them was to start his own ashram. Like the ashrams of Gandhi and Rabindranath Tagore. He used to visit their ashrams and he thought he should start the ashram and invite people of all faiths to shape the community in the kingdom of God. A miniature kingdom – that was the purpose of this ashram.
>
> …
>
> He strived to indigenize Christianity and he was successful to a certain extent. But he never forced anyone. His other method was a round-table conference where he used to travel to different cities, invite people of all and no faith with two rules: You share your experience of God and faith but don't condemn or criticize others. Then, in the end, he would share his experience of Christ. He would never apologize or compromise the uniqueness of Christ. He never diluted his faith.
>
> …
>
> Non-Christian religions seem to have no morality. I don't mean to be negative, but we have all this creativity, all these practices … but where is our morality … how do we manage our affairs? Are we protecting it? Caring for it? Or are we destroying it?
>
> …
>
> Nowadays, nobody talks about sin and repentance. They talk about *faith*. But what is faith?[17] Because even the demons have it. Faithfulness in Old Testament is teaching, doctrine and commitment, surrender. Hebrews 11 says, 'Faith is conviction, assurance of things not seen.' The important thing is not how much you believe but in whom you believe. I have a good friend of mine, psychology professor, religious man, practises yoga but he is also curious about Christianity. He was talking about God being impersonal. I said,

'The chair you're sitting on, is it personal or impersonal?' He said impersonal. I asked: 'Are you a person or impersonal?' He said, 'Person'. Then I asked, 'Who is greater? You or the chair?' He said, 'Acharya G., I got your point.' Then another time, he said that one thing he didn't like about Christians and Muslims is that 'you folks are very *exclusive*'. I replied that *truth is exclusive*. If something is true, then something [else] must be false. Everything cannot be right, and everything cannot be wrong.

Acharya G. finished his sermon the way he had opened it – with a prayer to Jesus – and when he stopped speaking the room was silent. He looked around the chapel at the group, 'Any questions? I know you are all a silent bunch', he said, smiling, 'but do you have any questions? Anything at all?' He was met with more silence. 'Does this mean you've understood me perfectly? ... Or have you not understood anything?'

The somewhat uneasy silence that had descended over the room began to feel noticeably heavier. Finally, one British woman raised her hand. When Acharya G. called upon her to speak, she said with a smile, 'I just wanted to say that the ashram is a very beautiful place. Thank you', and then she made a slight bow with her head, hands pressed at her heart. A few more moments of silence passed and then another woman raised her hand, 'I was just wondering ... why is there a fish on the wall of the dining hall?' The Acharya stared at her somewhat incredulously, presumably wondering if anyone at all would ask him a question related to his sermon, before rattling off an explanation of how the fish is a symbol from early Christianity. 'No questions? About what I said?', the Acharya asked, noticeably perplexed. The questions that were posed to him, Acharya G. later told me, were not at all of the kind he had expected or hoped for.

5.5.2 'The silent bunch' speak out

It was only later, out of the earshot of the Acharya, that people gradually started to share their questions or state their reasons for not posing questions to the Acharya. When the topic of the Acharya's talk came up in the daily Q&A that Dana hosted for the group, one man expressed that he felt that the Acharya's tone and face indicated a clear disinterest in dialoguing with others. 'So I thought – why bother?', he explained with a shrug of his shoulders. Others indicated that they had serious philosophical disagreements with the conclusions that the Acharya had reached in his talk – specifically with regards to the way he presumed non-Christian religions to be lacking in morality, the manner in which he quickly dismissed the idea of an impersonal God and the way that he determined that truth must be exclusive. These same topics were then discussed at length within the WA group, and the discussion was so vibrant that the group exceeded the normally allotted time for Q&A. But, importantly, the same individuals who brought up these topics and contributed to the conversation explicitly mentioned that they had consciously refrained from bringing them up with the Acharya even though he had asked them if they had any questions about the content of his talk. They feared that, if they were to clearly articulate why they read Buddhist texts, or practised meditation, rather than discuss themes more traditional to Christianity, they would be judged as people who had intentionally chosen what, in the eyes of the ashram, was an incorrect spiritual path. Still others admitted that they knew very little about Christianity, and did have some questions about Christian doctrine, but they explained that they dreaded being 'found out' as someone who did not know enough about the Bible. Both of these later possibilities, people worried, might reflect poorly on WA, and might damage the relationship that Dana and Emilia had strived to re-establish since being welcomed back to STA in 2011. Later, after the retreat finished, several individuals from WA shared with me that they consciously chose not to speak with the Acharya either then or at other occasions; they instead chose to stay silent.

5.5.3 Making sense of the Other

As a final description, I want to turn to another conversation I had with Acharya G., in which he asked me a number of questions about WA. It was not the first time that he and I had spoken about WA – after I attended WA's retreat in April 2017 he promptly asked me questions about my experiences with the group – but by April 2018 he had himself been in contact with the WA group, and his curiosity had peaked.

AG: All of them are from Christian backgrounds?
N: I don't know.
AG: Which countries do they come from?
N: Well ... countries don't always indicate the faith, you know? But ... they're from all over: lots from Germany, Australia, US, Israel.
AG: Do they come to India only for this programme or do they live in India?

N: Some of them have just come to India for the programme, some of them have lived in India for four months. Some of them live in India year-round, I think.

AG: So what is the teacher's [Dana's] background?

N: You should ask her, from what I know, she is American and she grew up in a Christian context, I don't know from which denomination. I don't know if then she had some time –

AG: Is she married?

N: I am not sure about that; I don't know. I know she did move to India for a number of years where she was receiving teachings from one particular guru, and I think –

AG: Hindu guru?

N: Yes. I forget his name.

AG: I had a chat with Dana yesterday for about fifteen to twenty minutes … but, too short to understand. [i.e. There is not much that you can understand in such a short time about someone.] You need to know a person, and all their background to understand.

N: Yeah, when they say something and you don't know exactly what they –

AG: And what were the lectures that she was giving? What were some of the topics?

N: They are not structured in the same way that the ashram programme is structured. The topics are not so easy to define, for me. It is sometimes led by the group, and the teacher responds. The topics are not usually preselected.

AG: You see, when I was talking, I asked her a few questions, but I was not very satisfied with the answer. She said they do "meditation", I asked her what kind of meditation. She said thinking about our own past lives and present lives, you see but those are very general terms.

N: Yeah, I think her teachings are also very general. I would say there are influences from Hinduism, Christianity, but she is not teaching Christianity or Hinduism per se. She reads a lot of poetry out loud, written by different nature poets, I guess – you know, some Romantic poets have felt very connected to the trees or water or air. She has shared a lot of those poems in her teachings … and this place [STA] is so fitting for it, *hai na* [isn't it]? Maybe you could ask her if you could attend her teaching.

AG: Well I went down [to the teaching time yesterday] and I couldn't understand half the things she said because firstly she spoke very softly.

So I went away, I so wanted to stay. I mean they seem very nice, very decent people. Also they're disciplined and keep to themselves when they're here. But … I mean, so much of silence is peculiar.

N: What is peculiar about it?

AG: So the *entire day* they are silent. But God has given us the gift of speech. Silence is important, I agree. I like being alone for some time in quiet, too. Silence is important, you meditate yes … but for us Christians it's meditating on God's word, God's nature and God's creation. I mean we meditate on God's word, and she said it's not words [that they meditate on] and I said "but words are connected with ideas". There's an old English saying, 'sow a thought, reap an action'. I add to it, 'sow a phrase or a word and reap a thought'. You see, no thoughts will come without words … I think we cannot empty our mind.

N: I don't know that anyone is trying to do that.

AG: The Hindu concept is yoga, you empty your mind, it's just theory, you can't do it in practice.

N: Well, I haven't heard anyone here saying that they're trying to do that, and I haven't been taught to do it by the teacher. I think many people come here to reflect on a life event that has happened to them and they think that having a time of silence will help them get through that … It is different than STA programmes – this week of silence – but I think it's a very –

AG: In the ashram, we [at the SoE, or in the Ashram Programme] have to be silent in the middle of a meditation or the end but very few people actually manage to do that. And there is the silence day … every Sunday.

N: Acharyaji, I have never noticed anyone observing this silence day. Now, a day of sightseeing in Nainital … *that* I have seen!

AG: Well, when you have a big group, it's very difficult and people normally come [to STA] for holidaying. Whether you like it or not, you say it or not, it's a fact. But this [World Amrita], they are different, because they are so disciplined in their conduct. Not holidaying, purely meditating. They are very spiritual. Very focused. They keep quiet and meditate, but the thing is … what are they trying to achieve or what are they heading for? That is the question. And I don't know why they didn't ask me any questions, they all just sat there. Listened politely, sure. Very polite. But no questions, just silence! Always silence. I prefer the groups who engage you.

5.5.4 Analysing the repercussions of partial belonging

When we consider these three ethnographic descriptions, there are a number of features which stand out regarding the relational dynamics between WA and STA. I consider these as expressions and repercussions of partial belonging, and, more specifically, I look at belonging within a broader context of power dynamics.

The intentional withholding of questions and dialogue that followed Acharya G.'s sermon, as well as the ardent decisions of many WA individuals to 'stay silent' in the presence of the STA leaders even after their retreats had finished, clearly show that there are power dynamics at play.[18] At first glance, it might seem straightforward to suggest that STA leaders hold a clear upper hand as far as asymmetrical power is concerned. After all, it is STA which owns the ashram grounds, and the STA leadership could refuse to allow WA to return if they so wished. As we saw in Section 5.4.2, STA leaders have the institutional power to make WA leave the chapel, or to even ban them from STA entirely, thus suggesting that any invitation of welcome and belonging can come along with certain prescriptive terms and institutional conditions. In other words, the one who has been invited to belong is normatively bound by these terms and conditions and cannot always express themselves freely or fully – and, crucially, in this interpretation the 'guest' group is thus in a less powerful position than the 'home' group.

However, I propose an alternate interpretation. If we reflect on this dynamic through the lens of Foucault's critique of the notion of power as a top-down structure in which power is wielded in order to control people's bodies and actions, we can reconsider whether WA's reactions to the institutional structures of STA is indeed an expression of WA being less powerful than STA. Foucault rejects the notion that power acts through repressive mechanisms or filters down from an apex of a pyramidical structure, and instead conceives of power as an impersonal force that permeates a plurality of sites and which is neither unidirectional nor exclusively top-down.[19] This power is present everywhere. Individuals, who simultaneously dominate others and are involved in their own domination by others, move along the threads of networks of both power and resistance – since resistance, too, is intertwined with power. In this Foucauldian understanding of power, then, the binary between ruler and ruled, or powerful and powerless, is dissipated. Following Foucault in this particular respect, I want to highlight the ways that members of WA also exercise some measure of agency in acting (or refraining from acting) from within their own places of power.

This analytical lens can therefore illuminate the ways that WA regulated and censored its own group members (Section 5.4.4) in restrictive ways that the WA leadership do not adopt at other retreat locations, as well as the ways that some members of WA chose to 'stay silent' and to not dialogue openly with the STA leadership (Section 5.5.2). These complexly dynamic interactions between WA and STA echo the observations made by some theorists of the Subaltern Studies group that the two domains of the 'elite' and the 'subaltern' in colonial India were not entirely disconnected from each other but rather existed in a series of oppositional relationships which were historically negotiated through various alliances, strategies and mobilizations.[20]

When we employ this analytical framework in which individuals exercise agency against dense structural backdrops, our discussion of power becomes particularly interesting. Namely, we can consider the dynamic routes along which there are ongoing negotiations of power at play, and we can see close-up the ways that power and resistance are far from unidirectional. That is, WA individuals are themselves exercising a form of power through leveraging their own agency: they consistently choose to be silent, and to not engage in dialogue with the ashram leaders about questions of faith. In the past, some participants have even developed creative means to ensure that the Acharya does not have an opportunity to speak to their group.[21] They choose when (or when not) to act vulnerably, and they use (or avoid using) their freedom to speak about topics – topics about which many *do* hold strong opinions – not solely to respect the ashram, but also to strategically hold onto their welcome at and by STA. Some participants from WA describe STA itself not just as a beautiful place for meditation, but also as being suffused with a certain spiritual atmosphere which makes them feel spiritually at home and which enables and promotes their own spiritual practice. As such, they take calculated measures in order to ensure that they can stay. Thus, we do not see, simply, one group being hegemonically silenced and submissively giving up all power to the authoritative summit of the ashram. Rather, a more nuanced Foucauldian consideration of the microprocesses of the situation reveals that WA is also wielding a 'softer' form of power themselves; one which is crafted out of its self-interested designs, projects and visions. I do not mean to suggest that WA did not genuinely want to respect the ashram – indeed, I think they did. But their goal to remain at the ashram effectively led to an exercise of their own power and agency, and they did not refrain from exercising this power.

I understand both forms of power – the power of STA to regulate and direct WA's actions and the power of WA itself in taking calculated measures with regards to which of their actions or beliefs they would share with STA – to shape the possibilities of open dialogue, and even the very idea of people from different backgrounds being truly welcomed to join in together. Often, when theorizing about interreligious dialogue and ecumenical community, or dual-religious belonging, it is tempting to assume that in a dialogue of existential and institutional transparency we speak and we are understood; we invite the others to speak and then, as we listen, we also understand them. But, as played out on the ethnographic terrain of STA, this ideal-typical scenario is not always realized. Sometimes we do not speak. Sometimes we do not – either directly through our words or indirectly through our relational postures – invite others to speak to us. Sometimes we do not listen. Sometimes we listen but do not understand. And, sometimes, we understand but we do not want to accept or to believe what we hear. There can be a plethora of real-world reasons behind why open dialogue does not occur. We have to ask ourselves, then, what do these potential dynamics mean for our discussions of communities that seek to welcome and integrate – indeed, to *invite* – others to join in their spiritual community? Just as we saw in Chapter 1 in our discussion of BIR, and again here in our discussion of belonging, sometimes the desire and the intention to be a part of something does not automatically result in the materialization of that desire.

We see a slightly different iteration of this intuitional failure to actualize the desire to bring together different individuals and world views into one singular community in the conversation with Acharya G. (Section 5.5.3). In varying ways, the Acharya tried to make sense of WA, but he found it difficult to accept their spiritual practices as worthwhile. Indeed, he had the utmost respect for their discipline and work ethic; he also thought that they pursued their spiritual practice with a fervour that he admitted he did not frequently see amongst STA's own Christian ashramites. And yet, he could not seem to wrap his mind around what precisely WA's spiritual practice *did* for them in real-world terms, or, in turn, why they did the things they did. Why did they keep such long periods of silence? Why, especially if they had already been exposed to Christianity through their cultural backgrounds, did they go out of their home traditions and seek out spirituality in a different tradition? Not only was he not able to comprehend these matters of existential quests and shifting identities but, in many ways, he frankly admitted that he was not interested in trying to do so. His desire to dialogue, or not to dialogue, was inseparable from his Christocentric evaluation of what was an 'interesting' or even 'useful' form of spiritual practice. The result was that he was not interested, seemingly at odds with some of the original visions of Jones, in either pursuing a dialogue with the group or in exploring how both he and them – with their differing views of spirituality – might form a spiritual community together.

5.6 Conclusion

Within the context of ongoing scholarly discussions of multiple religious belonging, this chapter has taken up the question of 'belonging' in multiple religious contexts through considering the relational dynamics between STA and WA. Does the process of belonging change depending on the religion/s in question? Is the kind of belonging that I have described here truly the type and depth of belonging that multiple religious individuals seek to experience?

In this present chapter, by considering Feldmeier's and Diller's respective models for MRB and MRO side by side, we noted, highlighting Diller's work specifically, that belonging does not always occur in the lives of individuals who navigate two or more religious traditions; on the contrary, belonging is an ongoing process involving the decisions and attitudes of all parties involved; belonging necessitates a negotiation of sometimes complicated relational dynamics including the initial invitations, restrictions, corrections and re-establishments of belonging. We also noted that WA, which occupies a unique place in the landscape of STA as far as visiting groups are concerned due to the way in which they are the only visitors who are there for a spiritual purpose which is *not* explicitly Christian, navigates a form of 'partial belonging'. In this partial belonging, the first aspect of belonging, being 'together with' others, is experienced, but the whole-hearted vulnerability correlated with a sense of feeling fully accepted is left wanting. By documenting and exploring some of the ongoing relational dynamics between STA and WA from 2003 to the present, I have provided original ethnographic material which demonstrates an important aspect of present-day life at STA; additionally, the ethnographic material also acts as a case study which provides us with real-life material through which we can reconsider and further nuance our understanding of multiple religious belonging. Through highlighting the relational dynamics between STA and WA, I have offered four phases of belonging (Section 5.4) and have also shown some of the microprocesses involved in negotiating existential belonging, thereby prompting us to reconsider some fundamental assumptions about belonging. Indeed, as this chapter has clearly demonstrated, much of the scholarship on multiple religious belonging takes as its starting point that belonging naturally occurs for those who wish it; our close-up examination of the tensions, negotiations and resolutions between WA and STA have shown that belonging is an ongoing – and, at times, challenging – process for both sides.

Conclusion

In the introduction I suggested that the events and relational dynamics of STA should be understood as both *transitional* and *embodied* social processes. Throughout this book, we have seen some of the many ways that the individuals of STA and, consequently, STA as a microsite itself, experienced near-continual changes. Regarding Jones's own understandings of Christian identity and Christian theology more broadly, we have seen how Jones repeatedly underwent transformations of thought as a result of the social interactions that he had with others – especially the interpersonal interactions he had with non-Christians in India. As a result of these transitions and transformations, at STA we see a number of ever-changing processes: not only are the defining features of identities like 'Christian' and 'Indian' challenged, reconfigured and redefined throughout the decades of history at STA since its establishment in 1930 but so too are the very social dynamics of STA itself. These shifting social dynamics were revealed rather concretely through exploring some of the *embodied* social processes of STA – the postures of meditation, the selections of songs, the embodied gestures such as the three-fingered signal of 'Jesus is Lord', the consumption of (non-)vegetarian food, the chosen styles of Western versus Indian dress and so forth. Further, these embodied social processes also signalled another form of transition that occurred at STA: there were stark changes not only in the social dynamics and interpersonal relations of STA, but there were also changes in the very socio-demographics of the individuals who attended the ashram – these contrasts were shown clearly when considering STA in the 1930s, 1990s and 2000s and noting the respective changes in attendance from upper-class Brahmins, to individuals from low caste and low socio-economic backgrounds, and to 'foreigners' from broadly Western backgrounds.

In addition to highlighting the *transitional* and *embodied* elements of STA, the introduction also noted that STA's relational dynamics needed to be understood *synergistically*. That is, while it is certainly important to focus on some of the intricate and mundane details of daily life at STA – after all, this sort of particular focus and 'thick' description is what gives life to any ethnographic study – I emphasized that we must *also* focus on the broader contexts in which STA exists – and, indeed, within which STA is deeply embedded. In this vein, we summarized not only some of the crucial moments of the historical relationships between Christian and non-Christian communities in India throughout the decades and centuries preceding the establishment of STA but we also highlighted some of the external factors which influenced STA during its formative years – the various social and political landscapes which have surrounded STA in the 1930s, leading up to the 1990s, and the present day.

Through considering our exploration of STA in light of its *transitional* and *embodied* elements, and also, *synergistically*, within the context of its broader frames of reference, this book has demonstrated not only that the negotiations of Hindu and Christian identities have changed over the course of the ashram's life but also that these very changes matched – indeed, they were the product of – surrounding shifts in the social and political landscapes of India. Through focusing on both the microcosm of STA and the macrocosm of the external contexts which have influenced STA, we have been able to formulate, explore and at times redefine a number of important philosophical themes and questions – especially those related to concepts of invitation, belonging, Otherness[1] and interreligious relations. Put alternately, and returning to an image alluded to in the introduction, we have seen how STA can be understood analogously as the mouth of the infant Krishna: wonderous enough to encapsulate the entire cosmos, and yet simultaneously small enough to be seen in one single glance. Our fieldsite of STA – as Krishna's mouth – is filled not with stars, galaxies, planets and oceans, but with deeply interwoven political, historical and social histories. And, of course, it is filled with *people*. It has been through considering these interlaced contexts – meticulously stitched into the fabric of individuals' interpersonal and intrapersonal relationships and life stories – that we, in turn, have been able to pose and explore deeper philosophical questions.

'What is the secret to getting along with those who are different from us?', 'What works and what doesn't?' 'What does it mean truly belong?', 'What does it look like to navigate our genuine differences while also being true to our own beliefs?'

Questions such as these, which, as I mentioned in the earliest pages of this work, were posed to me by family and friends numerous times throughout the course of my PhD, were also questions that I, at times, asked myself while in the field or at my library desk. Although they are not, as I forewarned, questions that I have sought to answer in this work, I trust that my analysis and writing has given the reader helpful tools with which to explore these very questions more deeply. On one level, this work has documented and explored many different manners of *invitation* in each of its chapters – something that Section 6.3 summarizes in more detail. And, in this vein, this work contributes to ongoing scholarly discussions on the topic of invitation – adding to recent works by influential scholars like Joel Robbins and Muthuraj Swamy.[2] But this work is also an invitation in and of itself; it is an *invitation* to allow the personal narratives and the on-the-ground nuances contained in the ethnographic data to *reshape* some of our existing conceptual understandings. Specifically, through coming to terms with the inevitable on-the-ground messiness of the social dynamics at STA, we have been challenged to reconfigure our conceptual understandings of what it means to *invite* an Other into our midst, and what it looks like to *belong*. This book has documented and described many of the tensions, ambiguities, struggles, negotiations and resolutions which collectively comprise the process of inviting and belonging – for it is indeed a *process* with many phases and layers which, somewhat inconveniently, do not always follow a predictable pattern. Our ethnographic exploration of STA has demonstrated that the very concept of *belonging* must thus be understood to not automatically occur despite an individual – or even two parties – wishing for it to occur.

6.1 Summary of contributions

In addition to using ethnographic data to reconfigure certain theoretical concepts, this book has made specific contributions to what could be understood as three different categories of readers:

(1) Scholars within the fields of Hindu-Christian studies, Indian Christianity (or, more broadly, World Christianities) or Anthropology of Christianity will have found that the ethnographic particularities of past and present-day life at STA add an interesting dimension to existing understandings of Hindu-Christian relations, Christian missiology in India and Indian Christianity. Indeed, as demonstrated by Chapters 2 and 3, Jones was both influenced by, but also distinct from, the missionaries who came before him – and even those who came after him with explicit models of inculturation. Through situating STA not only within its varying

political and historical milieus, but also through contextualizing Christian ashrams within other expressions of Indian Christianity – the long-established communities of Syrian Christians and, more recently, the movements of Pentecostal and Charismatic Christianity – this book has bridged the gap between different ways of focusing on Indian Christianity and its relationship with Hindu milieus. Considered alongside recent ethnographic studies of Indian Christianity – those by Chad Bauman, Kerry San Chirico, Darren Todd Duerksen and Nathaniel Roberts – this study of STA addresses a rather particular flavour of Indian Christianity and of Hindu-Christian relations, and thus adds unique ethnographic data to these fields.

(2) The ways that this research has been approached from an interstitial position between the two disciplines of Cultural Anthropology and (Christian) Theology is likely to be of significant interest to those scholars who actively participate in, or are intrigued by, the emergent conversations between these two disciplines. As Chapter 1 explored in substantial detail, the (Protestant) theological emphasis often placed upon religious belief can, in fact, be of central importance to the anthropologist as she formulates and conducts her ethnographic research. This book not only demonstrated the extent to which a researcher's religious beliefs can be formative in shaping her access to ethnographic data but also the extent to which the alleged binaries of *belief* and *doubt* can, in fact, work together to shape the ways that a researcher is understood by her informants whilst in the field. In this vein, through honestly sharing one's beliefs – as well as one's doubts – a researcher can sometimes establish oneself as a co-seeker of spirituality, and thus be *invited* in to observe, or otherwise learn about, certain aspects of their informants' lifeworlds.

(3) Whether or not the reader situates himself or herself within one or more of the particular academic fields of scholarship outlined above, all readers are – to some extent and in some way – embedded in the processes of interacting with Others, and formulating understandings of the Self in relationship to one's own Otherness. Through the detailed, nuanced explorations in this work, we are not only invited to learn more about the dynamics of Self and Other that unravel at our fieldsite of STA, but we can also be prompted to reflect on our own circumstances and narratives, and, in doing so, we can grapple with the ways that *we* experience and navigate belonging.

6.2 Ideals as functional directional markers

Here, in the final pages, I want to return specifically to the ways that, in his 'Ashram Ideals', Jones idealized STA as an inviting locale without any prohibitive boundaries. Perhaps unsurprisingly, when Jones's universalist ideals were implanted into the rough and rocky terrain of the real world, various conceptual and structural borders – related to caste, creeds and individual convictions – gradually emerged, impeding his vision of forming a 'miniature Kingdom of God' in which individuals' religious backgrounds and chosen practices would not impede their efforts to establish a spiritual community with each other. The ethnographic material that I have engaged with throughout this book has vividly depicted some of the difficulties that arose in the midst of these dense negotiations between religious idealization and concrete sociohistorical circumstance, but, I hope, in highlighting and exploring these lived-out realities, the importance of the original ideals themselves has not been overlooked or dismissed. Far from meriting dismissal, ideals – including ideals unrealized in fact or even unrealizable in principle – can function as helpful compass points or directional markers insomuch as they bring us ever closer towards the objective we wish to reach.

I sometimes think of ideals, if I can turn to an analogy, like an individual facing the sun and consciously choosing to walk in its direction. Of course, we will never reach it, and we will sometimes have to turn away from it out of necessity. Of course – to use an image from a Wendell Berry poem – we are sometimes blinded by the very light we seek.[3] And of course, sometimes the sun itself will (or, rather, will *seem to*) set – whether we walk calmly or run frantically towards it. We will not reach it; that's fine – and it would be naive to assume that we could. But, if what we are seeking is illumination and enlightenment, a posture which faces in the direction of the sun is better than one which does not. In other words, perhaps the navigations of existential, structural, and social tensions and difficulties that occur in the real world of STA – compared to the somewhat *idealized* world envisioned by Jones – are themselves worthy endeavours; for they are the ongoing processes and products of a community that has faced the sun and is attempting to walk in its direction.

Our explorations of STA, and the contexts which preceded and continue to influence it, have demonstrated that, in the processes of striving to become (or participate in) a community comprising differently minded individuals, we end up learning not only about the 'Other' but also, and at the same time, more about our own selves. As anthropological literature frequently reminds us, Self-understanding and Other-constitution are dialectically entangled through complex feedback loops. This dialectic seems, to me, to result somewhat naturally from holding a posture of strong conviction in one's own beliefs and world views while at the same time striving to remain conceptually and existentially open to those who believe and act differently – not unlike a comparative theologian who views religious Others as dialogical partners from whom one can learn deeply. Temporarily occupying the interstitial spaces between clearly marked religious traditions, comparative theologians thus allow themselves, and their own religious views, to be addressed, interrupted and surprised by the new insights contained within and offered by contrasting – and even conflicting – religious world views.[4] One's own views are thus loosely, but confidently, held, allowing space for others' religious ideas and insights to enter in and envelope one's own religious lifeworld, sometimes delicately reconfiguring and reshaping one's religious view itself and other times giving new life to religious muscles that may have atrophied. In navigating such Self-Other relationships, we are forced to grapple with 'the relationship between commitment and openness'.[5] In doing so, we can better understand which values we are not willing to compromise on, which types of religious belief or practice we find interesting and worthwhile, and which world views we are either disinterested in or even made uneasy by.

6.3 Self-Other dynamics

Keeping in mind these processes of *inter*personal grappling that occur when navigating the relationships between Self and Other, we can recapitulate the various Self-Other dynamics that this book has explored. We investigated, in Chapter 1, the relational dynamic that I proposed between the disciplines of anthropology and theology, and suggested that the historically secular discipline of anthropology could benefit from actively *inviting* its researchers to intentionally adopt a posture of BIR while conducting their ethnographic research amongst religious communities where 'belief' is particularly important. In doing so, we also considered the Self-Other dynamic that unfolds in the ethnographic encounters of researcher and informant. What would it look like to conceptually open up more disciplinary space for researchers who want to actively reside in the in-between of these two currently distinct disciplines of anthropology and theology; and how might this interstitial location of the researchers affect the relational encounters that occur on the fieldsites? In

Chapter 2, after highlighting the long-standing reputation that Christianity has had in some Indian circles as a religion of 'foreigners', we explored some of the missiological and ecclesiological shifts towards permitting and actively encouraging inculturated forms of Christianity; thus, the previously foreign-looking Christianity began to consciously incorporate Indian cultural idioms, thereby *inviting* the Hindu socioreligious Other into its midst.

Chapter 3 moved away from the macro trends in Indian sociopolitical histories and focused close-up on the particular microcosmic fieldsite of STA: we saw some of the various practical measures that Jones implemented in his attempts to *invite* (Brahmin) Hindus into STA's spiritual environment after establishing the ashram in 1930. This Brahmanical and Advaita-inflected notion of 'Hinduness' that Jones held, however, would be later challenged by the increasing presence of Hindu converts whose lifeworlds did not resonate with those of the Brahmins envisioned by him. Chapter 4 – along with its overview of some key features of Dalit theologies – demonstrated some of the various ways that the presence of the SoE students from 1991 onwards was a significant 'rupture' from what Jones had envisioned. In *inviting* Indianness into its Christian ashram, STA has had to continuously (re)consider questions such as 'Precisely *whose* Indianness would it attempt to weave into the social fabrics of STA?' and 'What are the boundary lines that could demarcate one practice or belief as helpful and desirable for Christian living while signalling other features of Indian identity as spiritually or socially unnecessary?' And, finally, through examining the active contestations and negotiations of belonging that WA has experienced during their times at STA from 2003 onwards, Chapter 5 highlighted some of the challenges that arise when *inviting* a group which is explicitly other-than-Christian. How, then, is belonging negotiated in the midst of different ways of being and believing? Each of these Self-Other relationships involved, at times, intricate and intense navigations and negotiations from all parties involved.

But, we have not yet finished our inventory of Self-Other relationships explored here. There was, as the reader may recall, another *invitation* given in the introduction (Section 0.4.3) which we can reiterate here: one made from me, the writer, to you, the reader. We – you and I – have been navigating this hermeneutic Self-Other relationship since the moment I started writing and, much later, since you started reading my words. For my part, I have tried to anticipate your responses to my words, and I consequently have added or deleted references to analytical theories, anthropological or theological works, thought-provoking tangential information and snippets of ethnographic description. In fact, it was through this process – all the while *me* keeping *you* in mind – that

I have learned anything at all. And, for your part, you have chosen to open this book and patiently read my words; even as I approach the absolute maximum of my word count, you are still reading. (*Thank you, for that.*)

In some ways, I may seem to have held a position of authority and power over you. I have taken you on a tour of specific historical and sociopolitical contexts that *I* deemed important (*Did you enjoy learning about Christianity in colonial India? Or about the developments of 'Hindutva'?*); and also, when confronted with the overabundance of ethnographic material from my fieldwork, I have selectively incorporated particular quotations and vignettes, and I reluctantly tossed others aside (*you never even had the chance to learn about some of my favourite moments of the SoE!*). I could have sent you down several other – I think, fascinating – rabbit holes had it not been for this pesky word limit to which I must adhere. And you, dutifully, would have trudged through the various narratives, subplots and settings, until reaching the point when I would have finally laid down my proverbial pen. However, we can recall, à la Foucault, that power is not unidirectional or one-dimensional: you also hold various powers over me. You can abruptly close the book, or roll your eyes heavenward, or point out the inevitable shortcomings of my arguments, or portray me in a bad light to my colleagues (*'the nerve of some junior scholars these days! She even tried to justify her foolishness by invoking Foucault!'*). But the inescapable reality is that we have already met each other, in some – albeit veiled – form, in this work.

Still, here we are. I wonder, as we navigate our Self-Other relationships through the intrinsic limitations of the page, whether we will both allow ourselves to be seen, addressed, interrupted and pleasantly surprised by what is on offer – perhaps even to mutually change each other in ways that we both deem to be positively transformative; it is often in these dense encounters between reader and writer that meaning arises.

Or maybe we will load our argumentative guns and rapidly fire away. It is a risky business, this inviting the Other.

Appendix 1: Key Hindi terms and their English translations

Ashram	Etymologically 'no-work'. Comparable to a hermitage, a monastic community or a place for spiritual retreat
Bagri	An Indian dialect which draws upon the languages of Rajasthani, Punjabi and Haryanvi; the mother tongue of the students from Rajasthan who participated in the SoE
Bimari	Illness and sickness
Changayi	Healing
Dhyan	Profound meditation
Gyan [Jnana]	Knowledge
Jai Masih ki	An exclamation: 'Victory and praise is due to Jesus the Messiah!'
Mukti	Salvation
Pareshani	Troubles, ailments, diseases, difficulties, disturbances
Parmeshwar	The God of the Universe
Pita Parmeshwar	Heavenly Father
Shanti	Peace
Shramdaan	Work which is freely given in the spirit of generosity
Viswas	Faith

Appendix 2: Social mapping

Overview of leadership at STA

At any given point, STA has several individuals who form its leadership. Even the role of 'Acharya' (spiritual leader) is divided into three different roles: Chief Acharya, Residential Acharya and Deputy Acharya – all of which have slightly different, complementary responsibilities – who work in synchronization to provide STA with spiritual leadership and direction. The Acharyas focus both on the 'big picture' (e.g. by choosing the thematic topics for the ashram's programmes) and on the small details of spiritual life at STA (e.g. they meet individually with ashramites to offer spiritual guidance, and they sometimes make an effort to continue this spiritual mentorship even after the ashramites have left STA).

Leadership at STA also comprises the manager (who runs the logistical operations at STA and approves visiting groups), the hostess (who is the primary contact for visiting ashramites and visiting groups and who ensures that individuals have a smooth experience at STA) and the STA board. The STA board has several individuals on it, generally including the Acharyas and the manager, and there are also secretarial and treasurer roles, along with other positions. For over a decade, the Indian Government has restricted foreign nationals from serving on the board. As such, since that time, STA's board has comprised solely of Indian nationals.

Names and titles/affiliations[1]

Acharya E. Stanley Jones – former Chief Acharya (deceased)
Acharya James Mathews – former Chief Acharya and son-in-law of E. Stanley Jones (deceased)
Acharya T. – former Resident Acharya (deceased)
Acharya V. – former Resident Acharya and founder of the SoE programme
Acharya B. – former Resident Acharya
Acharya G. – Resident Acharya during the time of my fieldwork; former Deputy Acharya

Ms Dorothy Firr ('Dorothy') – former manager of STA (deceased, July 2021)
Mr Ram – former manager of STA (deceased)
Mr Kabir Likhna ('Kabir') – current manager of STA
Ms Eleanor Changay ('Auntie Eleanor') – former hostess of STA
Uncle William – long-time ashramite of STA; participant of the Winter ashram programme
Mr D. – teacher of the SoE
Uncle Pratyush – student participant of the SoE
Uncle Rahul – student participant of the SoE
Suhasini – student participant of the SoE (wife of Anil)
Anil – student participant of the SoE (husband of Suhasini)
Shreya – student participant of the SoE
Vihaan – student participant of the SoE
Dana – one of the founders and spiritual teachers of World Amrita
Emilia – one of the managers of World Amrita

Notes

Introduction

1 Pohran, 'Christ-Centered Bhakti'.
2 Hess, 'An Open-Air Ramayana: Ramlila, the Audience Experience', 116.
3 Braak and Kalsky, 'Introduction to the Topical Issue "Multiple Religious Belonging"'.
4 Goel, *Catholic Ashrams: Sannyasins or Swindlers?*
5 Ricoeur, *Oneself as Another*; Moyaert, *In Response to the Religious Other*; Volf, *Exclusion and Embrace*.
6 As I will clarify in Chapter 5, WA is not technically the only non-Christian group hosted by the ashram. However, they are the sole group I am aware of who are both non-Christian and who used STA for an explicitly spiritual purpose.
7 Jones was denied a visa by the British government in 1939 due to his perceived affiliation with, and support of, India's independence efforts. Thus, unable to enter India in the 1940s, Jones spent most of his time during this decade in the United States. One of his biographers, his granddaughter Anne Mathews-Younes, refers to these decades as 'the transplanting decades', and documents the various ways that Jones began to establish Christian ashrams in the United States during that time period. See Mathews-Younes, *A History of the Christian Ashrams*. See also Haskell Khan, 'The India Mission Field in American History, 1919–1947', 228.
8 FirstPost, India Has 79.8% Hindus, 14.2% Muslims, Says 2011 Census Data on Religion'.
9 San Chirico, 'Khrist Bhaktas: Catholics and the Negotiation of Devotion'; Duerksen and Dyrness, *Ecclesial Identities in a Multi-Faith Context*; Selvanayagam, *Kristu Bhakti and Krishna Bhakti: A Christian-Hindu Dialogue Contributing to Comparative Theology*.
10 During the aforementioned 'transplanting decade' (see note 2) of the 1940s, Jones 'transplanted' Christian ashrams into US soil. Today, there remain several ashrams in the United States and Canada which point back to Jones as their founder; many of these North American Christian ashrams fall under the umbrella organization of the E. Stanley Jones foundation, which is operated by Jones's granddaughter.
11 Ricoeur, *Oneself as Another*; Volf, *Exclusion and Embrace*.
12 Miner, 'Body Ritual among the Nacirema'.
13 Robbins, 'Anthropology and Theology'; Robbins, 'The Anthropology of Christianity: Unity, Diversity, New Directions: An Introduction to Supplement 10'; Robbins,

'Engaged Disbelief: Problematics of Detachment in Christianity and in the Anthropology of Christianity'; Robbins, 'Anthropology and Theology: On Transformative Dialogue and Its Limits'; Wigg-Stevenson, *Ethnographic Theology*; Cannell, *The Anthropology of Christianity*.

14 Geertz, 'Deep Hanging Out'.
15 Nagel, *The View from Nowhere*.
16 Gadamer, *Truth and Method*, xxiii.
17 Nassim Soleimanpour's unique play *White Rabbit, Red Rabbit* has inspired some of the reflections contained in this paragraph. I first saw the thought-provoking production in Delhi, while conducting my fieldwork, and, captivated by its content, I later directed and produced three productions in Canada and the UK.

1 An introduction to belief-inclusive research

1 Out of the four methodological postures indicated in a recent introductory textbook to the anthropology of religion, BIR most closely resembles the fourth posture, called 'Methodological Theism'. However, BIR remains distinct from Methodological Theism due to the ways that an active embracing of informants' truth claims is not a requirement of BIR. See Bielo, *Anthropology of Religion: The Basics*, 33–44.
2 This is one of the visions for STA as articulated by Stanley Jones in 1930. I elaborate upon this in Chapter 3.
3 Heidegger, *Being and Time*; Husserl, *Ideas: General Introduction to Pure Phenomenology*; Berger, *Sacred Canopy*; Berger, 'Some Second Thoughts on Substantive versus Functional Definitions of Religion'; Clifford and Marcus, *Writing Culture*; Blanes, 'The Atheist Anthropologist'; Howell, 'The Repugnant Cultural Other Speaks Back: Christian Identity as Ethnographic "Standpoint"'.
4 Howell, 'The Repugnant Cultural Other Speaks Back: Christian Identity as Ethnographic "Standpoint"'.
5 Meneses et al., 'Engaging the Religious Committed Other: Anthropologists and Theologians in Dialogue', 93–4.
6 Meneses, 'Religiously Engaged Ethnography'.
7 Haynes, *Moving by the Spirit*.
8 Harding, *The Book of Jerry Falwell*; Luhrmann, *When God Talks Back*; Webster, *The Anthropology of Protestantism*.
9 Pouillon, 'Remarks on the Verb "to Believe"', 491–2; Ruel, 'Christians as Believers'; Ritchie, 'Contesting Secularism: Reflexive Methodology, Belief Studies, and Disciplined Knowledge'; Coleman, 'The Obligation to Receive: The Countertransference, the Ethnographer, Protestants, and Proselytization in North India', 118.

10 Meneses, 'Religiously Engaged Ethnography', 3.
11 Asad, *Formations of the Secular*; Warner, VanAntwerpen and Calhoun, *Varieties of Secularism in a Secular Age*.
12 Smart, *The Science of Religion and the Sociology of Knowledge*, 54.
13 Bialecki, 'Does God Exist in Methodological Atheism?', 33.
14 Bowie, *Introduction to German Philosophy: From Kant to Habermas*; Nagel, *The View from Nowhere*; Polanyi, *Personal Knowledge*, 142; Clifford and Marcus, *Writing Culture*; Geertz, *Works and Lives*; Rabinow, *Reflections on Fieldwork in Morocco*; Crapanzano, *Tuhami*; Ruby, *A Crack in the Mirror*; Crapanzano, 'Hermes' Dilemma: The Masking of Subversion in Ethnographic Description'.
15 Northcote, 'Objectivity and the Supernormal'; Porpora, 'Methodological Atheism, Methodological Agnosticism and Religious Experience'; Larsen, *The Slain God*, 8; Merz et al., 'Occupying the Ontological Penumbra'; Howell, 'The Repugnant Cultural Other Speaks Back: Christian Identity as Ethnographic "Standpoint"'; Ewing, 'Dreams from a Saint: Anthropological Atheism and the Temptation to Believe', 572; Hufford, 'The Scholarly Voice and the Personal Voice: Reflexivity in Belief Studies', 61; Cantrell, 'Must a Scholar of Religion Be Methodologically Atheistic or Agnostic?'; Poewe, 'The Nature, Globality, and History of Charismatic Christianity'; Moll, 'Television Is Not Radio: Theologies of Mediation in the Egyptian Islamic Revival'.
16 Bialecki, 'Does God Exist in Methodological Atheism?'.
17 Blanes, 'The Atheist Anthropologist', 228.
18 Guédon, 'Dene Ways and the Ethnographer's Culture', 52.
19 Guédon, 43.
20 Wilson, 'Seeing They See Not', 204.
21 There are further research difficulties when the researcher is obligated to be a participant rather than strictly an observer. Susan Harding (1987) provides an excellent example of the difficulties of conducting participatory research amongst Baptists who practise different Charismatic traditions.
22 I explored this ritual in more detail in my MA thesis: this is a physical enactment of raising someone from the dead so to symbolize their new life in Christ and their freedom from past bondages.
23 While this question is also one that has been asked by proponents of the Ontological Turn (see Holbraad and Pederson 2017 for an overview), the ways in which these scholars sought to take seriously the belief of informants was focused more on the world views of the informants, rather than of the scholars (see Meneses, 'Religiously Engaged Ethnography').
24 Coleman, 'The Obligation to Receive: The Countertransference, the Ethnographer, Protestants, and Proselytization in North India', 116–18.
25 Gordon, 'Getting Close by Staying Distant: Fieldwork with Proselytizing Groups'.

26 Robbins, 'World Christianity and the Reorganization of Disciplines: On the Emerging Dialogue between Anthropology and Theology', 241.
27 Robbins, 'Anthropology and Theology', 293.
28 Robbins, 'The Anthropology of Christianity: Unity, Diversity, New Directions: An Introduction to Supplement 10'; Robbins, 'Anthropology and Theology'.
29 Morse, *Not Every Spirit*.
30 With gratitude to Joel Robbins and my fellow PhD students in our Anthropology of Christianity group who met during my time at the University of Cambridge. This topic came up in our discussion of an earlier draft of this chapter, and I am grateful for the collective thoughts and insights that were shared with me.
31 Turner, 'A Visible Spirit Form in Zambia'.
32 Scholte, 'Toward a Reflexive and Critical Anthropology', 432.

2 Foreignness or Indianness? Indigenizations and representations of Christianity in India

1 In his PhD thesis on Jones's missionary contributions, Paul A. J. Martin also identifies 'naturalization' as the 'nearest equivalent to "indigenisation"'. Martin, 'Missionary of the Indian Road', 126.
2 Goel, *Catholic Ashrams: Sannyasins or Swindlers?*, 118–44.
3 Goel, 167–76.
4 Roberts, 'Is Conversion a Colonization of Consciousness', 272.
5 Rajkumar, *Dalit Theology and Dalit Liberation*; Bauman, *Christian Identity*.
6 Nirmal and Devasahayam, *A Reader in Dalit Theology*.
7 Frykenberg, *Christianity in India: From Beginnings to the Present*.
8 Mundadan, *History of Christianity in India: From the Beginning up to the Middle of the Sixteenth Century (up to 1542)*; Hambye, *History of Christianity in India: Eighteenth Century*; Grafe, *History of Christianity in India: Tamil Nadu in the Nineteenth and Twentieth Centuries*; Downs, *History of Christianity in India: North East India in the Nineteenth and Twentieth Centuries*.
9 Haskell Khan, 'The India Mission Field in American History, 1919–1947'.
10 Mathew and Thomas, *The Indian Churches of Saint Thomas*; Brown, *The Indian Christians of St Thomas*; Zachariah, *The Syrian Christians of Kerala: Demographic and Socio-Economic Transition in the Twentieth Century*; Thekkedath, *History of Christianity in India: From the Middle of the Sixteenth to the End of the Seventeenth Century (1542–1700)*, II: 19–138; Hambye, *History of Christianity in India: Eighteenth Century*, III: 65–90; Neill, *A History of Christianity in India: The Beginnings to AD 1707*, 26–48. Mundadan, *Sixteenth Century Traditions of St. Thomas Christians*.

11 Kuriakose, *History of Christianity in India: Source Materials*, 10.
12 Brown, *The Indian Christians of St Thomas*.
13 Abraham, 'Negotiating Hinduism and Christianity in the History of Kerala'; Brown, *The Indian Christians of St Thomas*.
14 Brown, *The Indian Christians of St Thomas*, 12.
15 Ravenstein, *A Journal of the First Voyage of Vasco Da Gama, 1497–1499*; Mundadan, *History of Christianity in India: From the Beginning up to the Middle of the Sixteenth Century (up to 1542)*, I: 243–54.

  See, also, the diary entry of one of da Gama's men, which describes the scene from a first-hand perspective. Peres, Baiao and Basto, *Diario Da Viagem de V: Da Gama*, 66–8.
16 Robinson, 'Sixteenth Century Conversions to Christianity in Goa', 301.
17 Henn, *Hindu-Catholic Encounters in Goa: Religion, Colonialism, and Modernity*, 39.
18 Henn, 39.
19 Hohwy, *The Predictive Mind*.
20 Mt. 13:13.
21 Henn, *Hindu-Catholic Encounters in Goa: Religion, Colonialism, and Modernity*, 21–7.
22 Some scholars argue that da Gama quickly fixed his error and corrected his perception of the presence of religion as soon as he understood that the men were in fact practising a religion well outside the Abrahamic faiths. But other scholars argue that the Portuguese held a 'tolerant attitude' with regards to religious pluralism and diverse modes of spirituality (Henn, 20–8).
23 Robinson notes that, while there were certainly Muslims in the region when the Portuguese arrived, their presence was 'seriously decimated by the Portuguese' and it was therefore predominantly Hindus whom the Portuguese sought to convert. See Robinson, 'Sixteenth Century Conversions to Christianity in Goa', 292.
24 Mundadan, *History of Christianity in India: From the Beginning up to the Middle of the Sixteenth Century (up to 1542)*, I: 443.
25 Robinson, 'Sixteenth Century Conversions to Christianity in Goa', 303.
26 Robinson, 305.
27 Henn, *Hindu-Catholic Encounters in Goa: Religion, Colonialism, and Modernity*, 40.
28 Mundadan, *History of Christianity in India: From the Beginning up to the Middle of the Sixteenth Century (up to 1542)*, I: 475.
29 O'Malley, *The First Jesuits*, 203.
30 O'Malley, 78.
31 Henn, *Hindu-Catholic Encounters in Goa: Religion, Colonialism, and Modernity*, 47; Badrinath, *Finding Jesus in Dharma*, 14.
32 Robinson, 'Sixteenth Century Conversions to Christianity in Goa', 305.
33 Robinson, 313.

34 Brown, *The Indian Christians of St Thomas*, 36.
35 Brown, 36.
36 Brown, 35; Abraham, 'Negotiating Hinduism and Christianity in the History of Kerala'.
37 Neill, *A History of Christianity in India: The Beginnings to AD 1707*, 230.
38 Neill, 230.
39 Robinson, 'Sixteenth Century Conversions to Christianity in Goa', 309.
40 Brown, *The Indian Christians of St Thomas*.
41 Abraham, 'Negotiating Hinduism and Christianity in the History of Kerala'.
42 Brown, *The Indian Christians of St Thomas*, 104–7.
43 Mathew and Thomas, *The Indian Churches of Saint Thomas*, 29–33.
44 Brown, *The Indian Christians of St Thomas*, 107.
45 Brown, 130.
46 Arthur Mayhew writes: 'When the time came for remodeling the charter accordingly, there was no longer any talk of Government patronage and maintenance. There was not even any explicit reference to missionaries as apart from other philanthropists.'
47 Embree, *Charles Grant and British Rule in India*, 271.
48 Ramusack, 'Cultural Missionaries, Maternal Imperialists, Feminist Allies: British Women Activists in India, 1865–1945'.
49 Hindmarsh, *The Spirit of Early Evangelicalism*; Ward, *The Protestant Evangelical Awakening*; Noll, *The Rise of Evangelicalism: The Age of Edwards, Whitefield and the Wesleys*.
50 Brown, *The Indian Christians of St Thomas*, 132.
51 Brown, 134–8.
52 Brown, 138.
53 Bearce, *British Attitudes towards India, 1784–1858*.
54 Lipner, *Brahmabandhab Upadhyay: The Life and Thought of a Revolutionary*, 5.
55 Quoted in Stein, *A History of India*, 265.
56 Clarke, *Oriental Enlightenment*, 57.
57 Schwab, *The Oriental Renaissance: Europe's Rediscovery of India and the East, 1680–1880*, 33.
58 As quoted in Keay, *India Discovered*, 25, from Governor General Warren Hastings's 'Letter in Preface to Charles Wilkins's translation of the Bhagavadgītā' in 1785.
59 van der Veer, *Imperial Encounters*, 6–7.
60 Lipner, *Brahmabandhab Upadhyay: The Life and Thought of a Revolutionary*, 5.
61 van der Veer, *Imperial Encounters*, 21.
62 Bearce, *British Attitudes towards India, 1784–1858*.
63 King, *Orientalism and Religion*, 87–8.
64 Samuel Stokes changed his name to Satyananda Stokes after he had converted to Hinduism in 1931. His conversion (which came after many years of Stokes

advocating that foreign missionaries must embrace an indigenized Christianity) was pointed to by some more conservative evangelicals as an example of the dangers of embracing indigenization. As Susan Khan highlights, the phrase 'doing a Stokes' was later adopted among missionaries to describe the precarious slippery slope of inculturation (Haskell Khan, 'The India Mission Field in American History, 1919–1947', 58).

65 Haskell Khan, 27–8, 34–6, 51–8.
66 Sadhu Sundar Singh (1889–1929) is also recognized by Jones and STA as a model of Indian Christianity (a letter from him, addressed to Jones in 1927, is proudly displayed in STA's library). For Singh's own writings, see Moore's edited collection *Sadhu Sundar Singh: Essential Writings*.
67 Dobe, *Hindu Christian Faqir: Modern Monks, Global Christianity, and Indian Sainthood*.
68 Collins, *Christian Inculturation in India*, 78.
69 Thomas, 'Indian Christian Approaches to the Knowledge of Christ'.
70 Neill, *A History of Christianity in India: The Beginnings to AD 1707*, 280.
71 Neill, 280.
72 Clooney, *The Future of Hindu–Christian Studies*, 24.
73 Clooney, 25–6.
74 Lipner, *Brahmabandhab Upadhyay: The Life and Thought of a Revolutionary*, xv.
75 Collins, *Christian Inculturation in India*, 78.
76 Duerksen and Dyrness, *Ecclesial Identities in a Multi-Faith Context*, 3–10.
77 Badrinath, *Finding Jesus in Dharma*, 104.
78 Lipner, *Brahmabandhab Upadhyay: The Life and Thought of a Revolutionary*, 188.
79 Lipner, 191.
80 Clooney, *His Hiding Place Is Darkness: A Hindu-Catholic Theopoetics of Divine Absence*.
81 Voss Roberts, *Tastes of the Divine*.
82 Lipner and Gispert-Sauch, *The Writings of Brahmabandhab Upadhyay*, II: 177.
83 Kuriakose, *History of Christianity in India: Source Materials*, 268.
84 Lipner and Gispert-Sauch, *The Writings of Brahmabandhab Upadhyay*, II: 202.
85 Lipner and Gispert-Sauch, II: 206–7.
86 Shah, *The Letters and Correspondence of Pandita Ramabai*.
87 Schouten, *Jesus as Guru*, 67.
88 Rajkumar, *Dalit Theology and Dalit Liberation*, 2010.
89 Ramabai, *A Testimony of Our Inexhaustible Treasure*, 295–324. Reprinted in Kosambi, *Pandita Ramabai*, 307–8.
90 Kosambi, *Pandita Ramabai*, 10–11.
91 Kosambi, 120.
92 Shah, *The Letters and Correspondence of Pandita Ramabai*, 27–8.

93 Schouten, *Jesus as Guru*, 74–6.
94 Kosambi, *Pandita Ramabai*, 11.
95 Kuhlin, 'Hindu-Christian Relations', 41.
96 Schouten, *Jesus as Guru*, 79.
97 Ralston, *Christian Ashrams: A New Religious Movement in Contemporary India*, 113–15.
98 Collins, *Christian Inculturation in India*, 79.
99 Taylor, 'Christian Ashrams', 283.
100 Collins, *Christian Inculturation in India*, 79.
101 Taylor, 'Christian Ashrams', 284.
102 Collins, *Christian Inculturation in India*, 81.
103 Kuttiyanikkal, *Khrist Bhakta Movement*, 95.
104 Vandana, *Gurus, Ashrams and Christians*; Taylor, 'Christian Ashrams'; Collins, *Christian Inculturation in India*, 77–89; Kuttiyanikkal, *Khrist Bhakta Movement*, 94–103; Webb, 'The Christa Seva Sangh Ashram: 1922–1934'.
105 Cornille, *The Guru in Indian Catholicism*, 125.
106 Downs, *History of Christianity in India: North East India in the Nineteenth and Twentieth Centuries*, V: 106–7.
107 Israel, 'Protestant Devotion and the Development of the Tamil Hymn in Colonial South India', 88.
108 Cornille, *The Guru in Indian Catholicism*, 117.
109 McGregor, *Devotional Literature in South Asia*.
110 Schouten, *Jesus as Guru*.
111 Robinson, *Christians Meeting Hindus*.
112 Advaita Vedanta was also transmitted to Western audiences by groups like the Theosophical Society.
113 Clarke, *Oriental Enlightenment*.
114 Quoted in Clarke, 64.
115 Quoted in Clarke, 65.
116 Ranade, *Vedanta: The Culmination of Indian Thought*.
117 Vandana, *Gurus, Ashrams and Christians*, 54.
118 Clooney, *Theology after Vedanta*.

3 The origins of Sat Tal Christian Ashram and E. Stanley Jones's 'Ashram Ideals'

1 Mathews-Younes, *A History of the Christian Ashrams*, 35–6.
2 Mathews-Younes, 46.
3 Jones, *A Song of Ascents*, 87.

4 Mathews-Younes, *A History of the Christian Ashrams*, 39.
5 Mathews-Younes, *Living upon the Way*, 5.
6 Jones, *A Song of Ascents*.
7 Jones, *Indian Road*, 14.
8 Roy was a slightly controversial figure in Christian circles on account of his Unitarian doctrinal views and his rejection of the doctrine of the Trinity. See Zastoupil, 'Defining Christians, Making Britons: Rammohun Roy and the Unitarians', 225.
9 Jones's biographers – as well as his own writings – give the impression that this evangelical focus on lower castes was in keeping with other standard practices of missionaries during his time. We know, however, that a majority of early missionaries in fact focused their evangelical efforts on upper-caste Hindus; certainly, this was the case for the Jesuit missionaries who approached their missionary work with the understanding that upper-caste Hindus were at the top of the social hierarchy and, if converted, there would be a sort of 'trickle down' effect into individuals from lower-caste communities. See, for example, Lourduswamy, 'Catholic Church and Dalit-Tribal Movements in India', 189.
10 Jones, *Indian Road*, 10.
11 Mathews-Younes, *A History of the Christian Ashrams*, 29.
12 This story can also be found in multiple sources of Jones's own writings. See Jones, *Indian Road*, 10; Jones, *A Song of Ascents*, 86.
13 Some of Jones's biographers date the origin of the round-table conferences to 1930. However, oral histories that I collected during my ethnographic fieldwork indicate that Jones held round-table conferences before establishing STA in 1930. Jones's own writings include tangential remarks to do with the origin of the round-table conferences. In one instance, he refers to a note 'written 8 years ago [in 1917]' in which he developed the style and atmosphere that he wanted to create with his round-table conferences (Jones, *Indian Road*, 13). At another point, writing in 1934, Jones claims that he had 'listened in for fourteen years' on the round-table conferences, indicating that they would have commenced in approximately 1920 (Jones, *Christ and Communism*, 218). Thus, I understand the round-table conferences to have predated the establishment of STA by approximately one decade.
14 Of course, Vedanta is itself divided into multiple strands and sects. Scholars are now careful to be specific in their articulations of which of the many diverse strands they refer to; this is not something that Jones specified.
15 Jones, *Mahatma Gandhi*, 13, 74.
16 Jones, *A Song of Ascents*, 140.
17 Haskell Khan, 'The India Mission Field in American History, 1919–1947', 118.
18 Collins, *Christian Inculturation in India*, 77.

19 Jones, *Mahatma Gandhi*, 64.
20 Mathews-Younes, *A History of the Christian Ashrams*, 52.
21 Jones, *Mahatma Gandhi*, 64.
22 It was in 1931 that Gandhi began to voice his opposition regarding missionary activities in India. Accordingly, in 1931 Jones wrote a letter to Gandhi asking him what precisely it was that Gandhi found so troublesome about conversion. Gandhi replied to Jones in an open letter on 23 April 1931, stating that he found modern-day conversion to be too comparable to a business venture. A few years later, in 1935, Gandhi again made a strong statement regarding his disapproval of conversion. These correspondences are outlined in Martin, 'Missionary of the Indian Road'.
23 Jones, *Mahatma Gandhi*, 64.
24 Jones, 65; Jones, *Indian Road*, 102–3.
25 Dorothy Firr (former manager of STA), interviewed by Nadya Pohran, Sat Tal Christian ashram, India, September 2016.
26 Martin, 'Missionary of the Indian Road', 115.
27 This daily rhythm was repeated throughout the week during the Summer and Winter ashram programme, but the schedule was not followed on Sundays when – unless a church service was offered – there was no ashram programme. Instead, individuals were instructed to keep silence for the entire day.
28 Vandana, *Gurus, Ashrams and Christians*, 16–37; Taylor, 'Christian Ashrams'.
29 Jones, *Victory through Surrender*, 70.
30 Jones, *Indian Road*, 83.
31 Jones, 184–5.
32 Mathews-Younes, *A History of the Christian Ashrams*, 78.
33 Jones, 'E. Stanley Jones on the Ashram Ideal (1930)'.
34 Coward, *Hindu-Christian Dialogue*, xvii.
35 See, for example, Webster, *The Anthropology of Protestantism*; Robbins, 'The Anthropology of Christianity: Unity, Diversity, New Directions: An Introduction to Supplement 10'.
36 Jones, *Christ and Communism*, 215.
37 Jones, *A Song of Ascents*, 220–1.
38 Niebuhr, *Christ and Culture*.
39 Sugirtharajah, *Imagining Hinduism: A Postcolonial Perspective*.
40 Haskell Khan, 'The India Mission Field in American History, 1919–1947', v.
41 Jones, *Indian Road*, 22.
42 Jones, 87.
43 Tilak had claimed, 'If Christ could be presented to India in his naked beauty, free from the disguises of western organization, western doctrines and western forms of worship, India would acknowledge Him as the Supreme Guru, and lay the richest

homage at His feet' (quoted by Winslow, *Narayan Vaman Tilak: The Christian Poet of Maharashtra*, 118).
44 Jones, *Indian Road*, 3–6.
45 Bauman and Young, *Constructing Indian Christianities*.
46 Harrison, Humfress and Sandwell, *Being Christian in Late Antiquity*; Boyarin, *Border Lines*; Fredriksen, *When Christians Were Jews*.
47 Pelikan, *Jesus through the Centuries*, 206–19. For a summary and discussion of Pelikan's argument, see Barua, *Debating 'Conversion'*, 159.
48 Jones, *Round Table*, 201.
49 Eph. 4:5.
50 *Rethinking Missions* was a collaborative report published in 1932 and aimed at reforming American Protestant missionaries' approaches to evangelism. It drew heavily on (and spoke favourably of) Jones's writings such as *The Christ of the Indian Road*, which promoted indigenous Christianity, and called to replace the focus of 'church plantation' (and, consequently, conversion) with the teaching of 'Christian values'.
51 Haskell Khan, 'The India Mission Field in American History, 1919–1947', 206–9.
52 Thomas, *Christian Indians and Indian Nationalism 1885–1950: An Interpretation in Historical and Theological Perspectives*, 76.
53 Mathews-Younes, *Living upon the Way*, 113.
54 Jones, *Indian Road*, 13.
55 Martin, 'Missionary of the Indian Road', 62.
56 Martin, 62.
57 Jones, *Conversion*, 64.
58 See Rom. 1:1, Phil. 1:1, Jas 1:1, 2 Pet. 1:1, Jude 1:1 in which each writer begins their respective letters by identifying themselves as a bondservant of Jesus.
59 Schweig, 'The Rasa Lila of Krishna and the Gopis: On the Bhagavata's Vision of Boundless Love'.
60 Jones, *Christ and Human Suffering*, 54.
61 Jones, *Round Table*, 48.
62 Jones, *Victory through Surrender*, 3.
63 Jones, *Round Table*, 22.
64 Jones, *Christ and Communism*, 222.
65 Jones, *Round Table*, 27.
66 Jones, 269.
67 Jones, 57.
68 Jones, 78.
69 Jones, 93.
70 Jones, 128.
71 Martin, 'Missionary of the Indian Road', 109.

72 Quoted in Cornille, *The Guru in Indian Catholicism*, 98.
73 Incidentally, this view of lower religious yearning acting as pedagogical tools and pathways to fuller religious revelation is similarly claimed by some Advaita Vedanta philosophies, but the theological similarities and divergences between these Advaita philosophies and Jones's Christian theology cannot be explored here.
74 Hedges, *Preparation and Fulfillment: A History and Study of Fulfilment Theology in Modern British Thought in the Indian Context*, 40–1.
75 Jones, *Round Table*, 51.
76 Jones, *A Song of Ascents*, 19.
77 Law, 'Kierkegaard's Anti-Ecclesiology: The Attack on "Christendom", 1854–1855'.
78 Jones, *Round Table*, 71.
79 Jones, *Conversion*, 45.
80 See also Bultmann, *History and Eschatology*, 155.
81 Kierkegaard, *The Point of View*, 22.
82 Jones, *Conversion*, 43, 65–82; Jones, *Indian Road*, 83; Jones, *Christ and Communism*, 222.
83 Jones, *Christ and Human Suffering*, 56.
84 Jones, *Indian Road*, 19.
85 Mathews-Younes, *A History of the Christian Ashrams*, 87.
86 Jones, 'E. Stanley Jones on the Ashram Ideal (1930)'.
87 The extent to which forcing Hindus to consume meat was historically practised by Christians in India remains a contested topic. See, for example, Robinson, 'Sixteenth Century Conversions to Christianity in Goa'.
88 Bowie, *The Anthropology of Religion: An Introduction*, 155.
89 Bowie, 155.
90 For case studies of contemporary instances in which this hierarchy is played out, see Razu, 'Towards a Critical Theology of Risk-Taking', 356–62.
91 Turner, 'Symbols in African Ritual', 183.
92 Bowie, *The Anthropology of Religion: An Introduction*, 155–6.
93 Alexander, 'Ritual and Current Studies of Ritual: Overview', 139.
94 Alexander, 154.
95 Three daily meals were served at STA; tea was also served daily at 4 pm.
96 Mk 10:45 and Lk. 22:27.
97 Richards, *Land, Labour, and Diet in Northern Rhodesia: An Economic Study of the Bemba Tribe*.
98 Mintz and Du Bois, 'The Anthropology of Food and Eating'.
99 Singer, 'Conversion through Foodways Enculturation: The Meaning of Eating in an American Hindu Sect', 195–6.
100 Ghassem-Fachandi, 'Hyperbolic Vegetarian', 81.
101 Vandana, *Gurus, Ashrams and Christians*, 11.

102 Ghassem-Fachandi, 'Hyperbolic Vegetarian'; Marriott, 'Caste Ranking and Food Transactions: A Matrix Analysis'; Singer, 'Conversion through Foodways Enculturation: The Meaning of Eating in an American Hindu Sect'.
103 Sathyamala, 'Meat-Eating in India', 1–3.
104 Fay, *Contemporary Philosophy of Social Science: A Multicultural Approach.*
105 A thought-provoking argument concerning gaining an understanding of the self by way of understanding one's relationship with others is articulated by Paul Ricoeur. In a vein somewhat different from what has been suggested in this paragraph, Ricoeur argues that 'the selfhood of oneself implies otherness to such an intimate degree that one cannot be thought of without the other, that instead one passes into the other' (Ricoeur, *Oneself as Another*, 3).
106 Jones, *Indian Road*, 35.
107 Jones, *Christ and Communism*, 222.
108 Jones, 222 (emphases mine).
109 Vos, *The Teaching of Jesus Concerning the Kingdom of God and the Church*, 45–7.
110 Vos, 58.
111 Vos, 76.
112 Farquhar, *The Crown of Hinduism*, 64.
113 Jones, *Indian Road*, 13.
114 Jones, 13.

4 The School of Evangelism and its challenge to the ideal of 'truly Christian and truly Indian'

1 The daily schedule for the SoE was as follows:
   5.30 am – First bell
   6.00 am – Morning *dhyan*
   8.00 am – Breakfast
   9.30 am – Work period
   10.30 am – Morning lesson
   12.30 pm – Lunch
   1.30 pm – Individual time
   4.00 pm – Chai break
   4.30 pm – Afternoon lesson
   6.00 pm – Dinner
   7.30 pm – Evening fellowship hour
2 Lambek, *A Reader in the Anthropology of Religion*; Lessa and Vogt, *Reader in Comparative Religion: An Anthropological Approach*; McGuire, *Lived Religion*; Orsi,

'Everyday Miracles: The Study of Lived Religion'; Stern, *Changing India: Bourgeois Revolution on the Subcontinent*, 37.

3. A group of individuals called the *Khrist Bhaktas*, who express their devotion to Jesus at a Catholic ashram in Varanasi by the name of Matri Dham, share, in a broad sense, many socio-economic demographics with the students of the SoE. Most interestingly, research on the *Khrist Bhaktas* also pinpoints their origins to 'the period between 1992 and 1994' (San Chirico, 'Khrist Bhaktas: Catholics and the Negotiation of Devotion', 28).
4. This social status was especially true of the group of men who came from Rajasthan, many of whom shared one of two surnames, indicating that they belonged to the same caste: 'Meena' (listed as a Scheduled Tribe in Rajasthan and as an Other Backward Caste in most parts of Madhya Pradesh) or 'Kharadi' (literally, a 'turner' who works with wood).
5. Author's interview with former Acharya V, Sat Tal Christian ashram, September 2016.
6. Weber, *The Theory of Social and Economic Organizations*, 358–72.
7. Weber, *Selections in Translation*, 229.
8. This challenging transition affiliated with the loss of an original guru, and the consequent loss of charisma, has also been noted to be a real and pressing issue in Hindu contexts. See Aymard, *When a Goddess Dies: Worshipping Ma Anandamayi after Her Death*, especially chapter 3 and the conclusion.
9. Jenkins, 'Legal Limits on Religious Conversion in India', 114.
10. Bauman, *Christian Identity*, 3–4.
11. Gandhi, *An Autobiography: The Story of My Experiments with Truth*, 234.
12. Gandhi, *The Collected Words of Mahatma Gandhi*, 62: 37.
13. Gandhi, 64: 99.
14. Bauman, *Christian Identity*, 4.
15. Bauman, *Pentecostals*, 4.
16. Metcalf and Metcalf, *A Concise History of India*, 224.
17. Metcalf and Metcalf, 225.
18. Goel, *Catholic Ashrams: Sannyasins or Swindlers?*
19. Maiorano, 'Indian Politics and Society in the 1970s'.
20. Jaffrelot, *Dr. Amdbedkar and Untouchability: Analysing and Fighting Caste*, 145.
21. Maiorano, 'Indian Politics and Society in the 1970s'.
22. Samuel, 'Pentecostal and Charismatic Movements', 259.
23. Bauman, *Pentecostals*, 27.
24. Cornille, writing at more or less the same time that STA began to develop the SoE programme in 1991, documents the steady decrease of attendance at Catholic ashrams between 1960 and 1990. See Cornille, *The Guru in Indian Catholicism*, 141–6.

25 Ralph, Birks and Chapman, 'The Methodological Dynamism of Grounded Theory'.
26 Alexander, 'Ritual and Current Studies of Ritual: Overview', 139.
27 Mt. 10:34.
28 Bauman, 'The Violence of Conversion'; Rambachan, 'Conversion from a Hindu Perspective: Controversies, Challenges, and Opportunities'.
29 Kim, *In Search of Identity: Debates on Religious Conversion in India*, 33.
30 Barua, *Debating Conversion*, 28.
31 Robinson, 'Sixteenth Century Conversions to Christianity in Goa', 303.
32 See, for example, Barua, *Debating Conversion*.
33 See, for example, Swamy, *The Problem with Interreligious Dialogue*.
34 Roberts, *To Be Cared For*.
35 Jones, *Conversion*, 36.
36 Jones, 36.
37 Jones, 38.
38 Jones, *Mahatma Gandhi*, 71.
39 Interestingly, Gandhi himself seems to have defended what Jones terms 'vertical' conversion. Thus, Gandhi wrote to Reverend B. W. Tucker in 1928: 'I do not want you to become a Hindu. But I do want you to become a better Christian by absorbing all that may be good in Hinduism and that you may not find in the same measure or not at all in the Christian teaching' (Gandhi, *The Collected Works of Mahatma Gandhi*, 37: 224).
40 Quoted in Jones, *Mahatma Gandhi*, 75.
41 Jones, 68.
42 See also Martin, 'Missionary of the Indian Road', 150.
43 Bauman, *Pentecostals*.
44 Jaoul, 'Le point de vue'.
45 Soni, 'Political Quotas, NGO Initiatives and Dalits' Human Rights in Rural India'; Massey, *Down Trodden: The Struggle of India's Dalits for Identity, Solidarity and Liberation*.
46 Martin, 'Missionary of the Indian Road', 144.
47 Jaoul, 'Le point de vue'.
48 Mt. 6:33.
49 Epstein, *Ethnos and Identity: Three Studies in Ethnicity*.
50 With gratitude to my father, John Pohran, who listened to some of the audio recordings I collected of the Bagri *bhajans* and used his training as a musician so as to help me understand and articulate their musical qualities.
51 This line then reappears after each of the following lines, acting as a refrain.
52 After receiving this written translation from Uncle Pratyush, I have since gone back and listened carefully to the multiple audio recordings I have of this song – I cannot identify any point at which this particular exhortation 'read the

Bible' is sung. I wonder whether, by including this line in our translation and writing exercise, Uncle Pratyush was trying to assure outsiders that the *bhajans* were indeed pukka (legitimate) Christian ones inasmuch as they encouraged specifically Christian practices, that is, the Christian practices which the SoE taught the students to value.

53 This line too reappears after each of the following lines, acting as a refrain.
54 Elsewhere, I have written about *Christ Bhakti* and *bhajans* which are used to express devotion to Jesus in Indian contexts. Though these particular *bhajans* did not feature in my written work, the broader themes and context that I summarized therein play a key role in my interpretation of these *bhajans*. See Pohran, 'Christ-Centered Bhakti: A Literary and Ethnographic Study of Worship'.
55 Stanislaus, *The Liberative Mission of the Church among Dalit Christians*, 183; Nirmal, 'Towards a Christian Dalit Theology', 227.
56 Mukta, *Upholding the Common Life: The Community of Mirabai*.
57 We see this same trend to declare the power of Jesus in the *bhajans* sung by *Khrist Bhaktas* at *Matri Dham* ashram, who proclaim that salvation and peace are received through Jesus's name. See San Chirico, 'Khrist Bhaktas: Catholics and the Negotiation of Devotion', 24.
58 Yeh geet humare adivasi bhasha – local logon ki bhasha hai. Isme Parmeshwar ki mahima ka bakhaandh kiya gaya hai aur saat me a Prabhu Yeshu Masih ke chamatkari geet gaaya gaya hai. Prabhu Yeshu Masih ne jaise andhon ko aakhein di, behron ko kaan diye langdon ko chalaaya, mare hue ko jilaayaa is prakaar se hum bhajan gaate hai jisse Parmeshwar ki mahima ho. Isme dholak saat me, kisiko harmonium bajane aaye toh harmonium saat me aur guitar bhi saat me us ilaaka me manjira wagerah aur tapli bhi bajate hai. Parmeshwar ke naam ... haat taali wagerah ... usko manjira bolte hai. Parmeshwar ki mahima karte hai. Jab hum gaana gaate hai aur Parmeshwar ki upasthithi ko mehsoos karte hai, aur hume shanti milti hai, changaai milti hai aur gaane ke dwara hume ashish milti hai aur Parmeshwar ki mahima hum is prakaar karte hai.
59 *Prabhu Yeshu Masih ki mahima karneka hai ... naach gaan hai, khel kud hai, reeti rivaj hai, jo bhi sanskrutik karekram hai, rivayak sambhandh hai.*
60 Beck, 'Song: Two Braj Bhāṣā Versions of the Rāsa-Līlā Pancādhyāyī and Their Musical Performance in Vaisnava Worship', 197.
61 For an overview, see Barua, *Debating Conversion*, 92.
62 Giddens, *The Constitution of Society*.
63 Sartre, *Being and Nothingness: An Essay on Phenomenological Ontology*, 9–10.
64 Razu, 'Towards a Critical Theology of Risk-Taking', 354; Boff, 'The Poor, the New Cosmology and Liberation', 121–3.

5 The negotiations of belonging: Relational dynamics of World Amrita and Sat Tal Christian Ashram

1 In 2017, STA started an initiative where the Acharya, or another representative of the ashram, gives a short talk to any visiting group. The talk varies, but is generally about the history of the ashram. I highlight Acharya G.'s talk to WA below.
2 Knitter, 'Without Walls = Multiple Belonging?', 492.
3 Heim, 'Of Two Minds about a Theology without Walls', 486.
4 Feldmeier, 'Perils and Possibilities of Multiple Religions Belonging'.
5 Diller, 'Multiple Religious Orientation'.
6 Diller, 342.
7 Brown, *Braving the Wilderness*.
8 Vanier, *Community and Growth*, 31.
9 Vanier, 12.
10 See, as one example among many, the works of Paul Knitter. Knitter, *Without Buddha I Could Not Be a Christian*; Knitter, 'Without Walls = Multiple Belonging?'
11 See Rory McEntee and Michelle Voss Roberts who both focus on the ways that multiple religious individuals sometimes struggle to belong. See also Peter Feldmeier who raises this concern regarding the difficulty of belonging with direct reference to the TWW project. McEntee, 'Interspiritual Theology as a Radical Potential for New Vistas in Theological Thought'; McEntee, 'The Religious Quest As Transformative Journey'; Roberts, 'Religious Belonging and the Multiple'; Feldmeier, 'Perils and Possibilities of Multiple Religions Belonging'.
12 Knitter, 'Without Walls = Multiple Belonging?', 493.
13 Long, 'Hindu, Christian, Hindu-Christian, and beyond', 153.
14 See Chapter 3, Section 3.4.
15 The reader can recall, from Chapter 2, the extent to which many Indians associated Christianity with foreigners on account of the various interactions that European colonial powers had with the Indian public. Though we did not explore it in Chapter 2, equally, there is often an association between foreigners and Christianity; that is to say, foreigners are often assumed to belong to, and actively participate in, a Christian faith.
16 If we compare this narrative with the accounts I provided in Chapter 3, we can see just how standardized and well known this story is amongst the members of STA.
17 Recalling the conversation between Acharya G. and Vihaan in Chapter 4 (Section 4.3.4), we can see the extent to which this question 'What is faith?' was a rather important motif for Acharya G.
18 Several insights from this section are due to my conversations with Nika Kuchuk.
19 Foucault, *The History of Sexuality*, 93; Foucault, 'Disciplinary Power and Subjection'.

20 Sarkar, 'The Conditions and Nature of Subaltern Militancy: Bengal from Swadeshi to Non-Co-Operation, c. 1905–22'.
21 In 2011, Acharya Biswas requested to give another sermon to the group. The leaders of WA agreed, verbally, but intentionally acted in ways so as to delay his sermon, thus subverting any chance for him to give a sermon to their group.

6 Conclusion

1 For those unfamiliar with this reference, found in the *Bhagavata Purana*, the story goes as such: when Krishna was an infant, he was (perhaps wrongly) accused of eating dirt. His mother Yashoda prodded him to open up his mouth so that she could see if there was any mud remaining in his mouth. When she looked into his mouth, she saw the entire universe: all of the planets, skies, stars, rivers, oceans and everything that could be seen. Indeed, the entire cosmos seemed to be contained in his mouth.
2 Swamy, *Reconciliation: The Archbishop of Canterbury's Lent Book 2019*; Swamy, *The Problem with Interreligious Dialogue*; Robbins, 'Anthropology and Theology: On Transformative Dialogue and Its Limits'.
3 Berry, *Given*, 74.
4 Clooney, 'Francis Xavier, and the World/s We (Don't Quite) Share', 178.
5 Robinson, *Christians Meeting Hindus*, 156.

Appendix 2

1 Names are provided for those individuals whom we encounter multiple times throughout this book, and whose role and affiliation will be useful for the reader to keep in mind. Pseudonyms have been used for all individuals other than E. Stanley Jones and his family members. While this practice may confuse readers who wish to understand (or, even more, whom are already familiar with) the social history of STA, I have done so out of a desire to protect the identities of those involved.

Bibliography

Abraham, Renish Geevarghese. 'Negotiating Hinduism and Christianity in the History of Kerala'. In *The Teape Lectures*. Cambridge: University of Cambridge, 2017.

Alexander, Bobby C. 'Ritual and Current Studies of Ritual: Overview'. In *Anthropology of Religion: A Handbook*, edited by Stephen D. Glazier, 139–60. Westport, CT: Greenwood Press, 1977.

Asad, Talal. *Formations of the Secular: Christianity, Islam, Modernity*. 1st edition. Stanford, CA: Stanford University Press, 2003.

Aymard, Orianne. *When a Goddess Dies: Worshipping Ma Anandamayi after Her Death*. Oxford: Oxford Scholarship Online, 2014.

Badrinath, Chaturvedi. *Finding Jesus in Dharma: Christianity in India*. Delhi: SPCK, 2000.

Barua, Ankur. *Debating 'Conversion' in Hinduism and Christianity*. London: Routledge, 2015.

Bauman, Chad M. *Christian Identity and Dalit Religion in Hindu India, 1868–1947*. Grand Rapids, MI: Eerdmans, 2008.

Bauman, Chad M. *Pentecostals, Proselytization, and Anti-Christian Violence in Contemporary India*. New York: Oxford University Press, 2015.

Bauman, Chad M. 'The Violence of Conversion: Proselytization and Interreligious Controversy in the Work of Swami Dayananda Saraswati'. *Open Theology* 1, no. 1 (2015): 175–88.

Bauman, Chad M., and Richard Fox Young. *Constructing Indian Christianities: Culture, Conversion and Caste*. New Delhi: Routledge, 2014.

Bearce, George Donham. *British Attitudes towards India, 1784–1858*. Oxford: Oxford University Press, 1961.

Beck, G. L. 'Song: Two Braj Bhāṣā Versions of the Rāsa-Līlā Pancādhyāyī and Their Musical Performance in Vaisnava Worship'. In *The Bhāgavata Purāṇa: Sacred Text and Living Tradition*, edited by R. M. Gupta and K. R. Valpey, 181–201. New York: Columbia University Press, 2013.

Berger, Peter L. *Sacred Canopy: Elements of a Sociological Theory of Religion*. New York: Anchor Books, 1969.

Berger, Peter L. 'Some Second Thoughts on Substantive versus Functional Definitions of Religion'. *Journal for the Scientific Study of Religion* 13, no. 2 (1974): 125–33.

Berry, Wendell. *Given: Poems*. 1st edition. Enfield, CT: Counterpoint, 2006.

Bialecki, Jon. 'Does God Exist in Methodological Atheism? On Tanya Lurhmann's *When God Talks Back* and Bruno Latour'. *Anthropology of Consciousness* 25, no. 1 (2014): 32–52.

Bielo, James S. *Anthropology of Religion: The Basics*. New York: Routledge, 2015.
Blanes, Ruy Llera. 'The Atheist Anthropologist: Believers and Non-Believers in Anthropological Fieldwork'. *Social Anthropology* 14 (June 2006): 223–34.
Boff, Leonard. 'The Poor, the New Cosmology and Liberation'. In *Religion, International Relations and Development Cooperation*, edited by Berma Klein Goldewijk, 113–25. The Netherlands: Wageningen Academic, 2007.
Bourdillon, M. F. C. 'Introduction'. In *Sacrifice*, edited by M. F. C. Bourdillon and Meyer Fortes, 1–28. London: Academic Press for the Royal Anthropological Institute of Great Britain and Ireland, 1980.
Bowie, Andrew. *Introduction to German Philosophy: From Kant to Habermas*. Cambridge: Polity, 2003.
Bowie, Fiona. *The Anthropology of Religion: An Introduction*. Malden, MA: Blackwell, 2000.
Boyarin, Daniel. *Border Lines: The Partition of Judaeo-Christianity*. Philadelphia: University of Pennsylvania Press, 2006.
Braak, André van der, and Manuela Kalsky. 'Introduction to the Topical Issue "Multiple Religious Belonging"'. *Open Theology* 3, no. 1 (20 December 2017): 662–4. https://doi.org/10.1515/opth-2017-0051 (accessed 18 September 2018).
Brown, Brené. *Braving the Wilderness: The Quest for True Belonging and the Courage to Stand Alone*. New York: Random House, 2017.
Brown, L. W. *The Indian Christians of St Thomas*. Cambridge: Cambridge University Press, 1982.
Bultmann, Rudolf. *History and Eschatology*. Edinburgh: Edinburgh University Press, 1957.
Cannell, Fenella, ed. *The Anthropology of Christianity*. Durham, NC: Duke University Press, 2006.
Cantrell, Michael. 'Must a Scholar of Religion Be Methodologically Atheistic or Agnostic?' *Journal of the American Academy of Religion* 84, no. 2 (June 2016): 373–400.
Clarke, J. J. *Oriental Enlightenment: The Encounter between Asian and Western Thought*. 1st edition. New York: Routledge, 1997.
Clifford, James, and George E. Marcus, eds. *Writing Culture: The Poetics and Politics of Ethnography*. Los Angeles: University of California Press, 1986.
Clooney, Francis X. 'Francis Xavier, and the World/s We (Don't Quite) Share'. In *Jesuit Postmodern: Scholarship, Vocation, and Identity in 21st Century*, edited by Francis X. Clooney, 157–80. Lanham, MD: Lexington Books, 2006.
Clooney, Francis X. *The Future of Hindu–Christian Studies: A Theological Inquiry*. London: Routledge, 2017.
Clooney, Francis X. *His Hiding Place Is Darkness: A Hindu-Catholic Theopoetics of Divine Absence*. Stanford, CA: Stanford University Press, 2013.
Clooney, Francis X. *Theology after Vedanta: An Experiment in Comparative Theology*. Albany: State University of New York Press, 1993.
Coleman, Leo. 'The Obligation to Receive: The Countertransference, the Ethnographer, Protestants, and Proselytization in North India'. In *Being There: The Fieldwork*

Encounter and the Making of Truth, edited by John Borneman and Abdellah Hammoudi, 113–50. Berkeley: University of California Press, 2009.

Collins, Paul. *Christian Inculturation in India*. Burlington, VT: Ashgate, 2007.

Cornille, Catherine. *The Guru in Indian Catholicism: Ambiguity or Opportunity of Inculturation?* Louvain: Peeters, 1991.

Coward, Harold G. *Hindu-Christian Dialogue: Perspectives and Encounters*. Maryknoll, NY: Orbis Books, 1989.

Crapanzano, Vincent. 'Hermes' Dilemma: The Masking of Subversion in Ethnographic Description'. In *Writing Culture: The Poetics and Politics of Ethnography*, edited by James Clifford and George E. Marcus, 51–76. Berkeley: University of California Press, 1986.

Crapanzano, Vincent. *Tuhami: Portrait of a Moroccan*. New edition. Chicago: University of Chicago Press, 1985.

Day, Abby. *Believing in Belonging: Belief and Social Identity in the Modern World*. Oxford: Oxford University Press, 2011. https://www.oxfordscholarship.com/view/10.1093/acprof:oso/9780199577873.001.0001/acprof-9780199577873 (accessed 25 April 2018).

Diller, Jeanine. 'Multiple Religious Orientation'. *Open Theology* 2, no. 1 (2016): 338–53.

Dobe, Timothy. *Hindu Christian Faqir: Modern Monks, Global Christianity, and Indian Sainthood*. Oxford: Oxford University Press, 2015.

Downs, Frederick. *History of Christianity in India: North East India in the Nineteenth and Twentieth Centuries*. Vol. V. Bangalore: The Church History Association of India, 1992.

Duerksen, Darren Todd, and William A. Dyrness. *Ecclesial Identities in a Multi-Faith Context: Jesus Truth-Gatherings*. Eugene, OR: Pickwick, 2015.

Embree, A. T. *Charles Grant and British Rule in India*. London: George Allen and Unwin, 1962.

Epstein, A. L. *Ethnos and Identity: Three Studies in Ethnicity*. London: Tavistock, 1978.

Evans-Pritchard, E. E. 'Religion and the Anthropologists'. In *Social Anthropology and Other Essays*. New York: Free Press, 1962.

Ewing, Katherine P. 'Dreams from a Saint: Anthropological Atheism and the Temptation to Believe'. *American Anthropologist* 96, no. 3 (1994): 571–83.

Farquhar, J. N. *The Crown of Hinduism*. London: Oxford University Press, 1913.

Fay, Brian. *Contemporary Philosophy of Social Science: A Multicultural Approach*. Oxford: Blackwell, 1996.

Feldmeier, Peter. 'Perils and Possibilities of Multiple Religions Belonging: Test Case in Roman Catholicism'. *Open Theology* 3, no. 1 (2017): 73–89.

Fortes, Meyer. 'Preface'. In *Sacrifice*, edited by M. F. C. Bourdillon and Meyer Fortes, v–xiv. London: Academic Press for the Royal Anthropological Institute of Great Britain, 1980.

Foucault, Michele. 'Disciplinary Power and Subjection'. In *Power*, edited by Steven Lukes, 229–42. Oxford: Basil Blackwell, 1986.

Foucault, Michele. *The History of Sexuality*. Translated by Robert Hurley. London: Penguin Books, 1978.

Fredriksen, Paula. *When Christians Were Jews: The First Generation*. New Haven, CT: Yale University Press, 2018.

Frykenberg, Robert Eric. *Christianity in India: From Beginnings to the Present*. Oxford: Oxford University Press, 2008.

Gadamer, H.-G. *Truth and Method*. London: Sheed and Ward, 1989.

Gandhi, Mohandas K. *An Autobiography: The Story of My Experiments with Truth*. Translated by Mahadev Desai. London: Penguin Books, 2001.

Gandhi, Mohandas K. *The Collected Works of Mahatma Gandhi. Vol. 37*. Ahmedabad: Navajivan Trust, 1970.

Gandhi, Mohandas K. *The Collected Words of Mahatma Gandhi. 100 Vols*. New Delhi: Publications Division of the Government of India, 1958.

Geertz, Clifford. 'Deep Hanging Out'. *New York Review of Books* 45, no. 16 (1998): 69–72.

Geertz, Clifford. *Works and Lives: The Anthropologist as Author*. 1st edition. Stanford, CA: Stanford University Press, 1989.

Ghassem-Fachandi, Parvis. 'The Hyperbolic Vegetarian: Notes on a Fragile Subject in Gujarat'. In *Being There: The Fieldwork Encounter and the Making of Truth*, edited by John Borneman and Abdellah Hammoudi. Berkeley: University of California Press, 2009.

Giddens, Anthony. *The Constitution of Society*. Cambridge: Polity Press, 1984.

Goel, Sita Ram. *Catholic Ashrams: Sannyasins or Swindlers?* Enlarged Edition with New Appendices. New Delhi: Replika Press, 2019.

Gordon, David. 'Getting Close by Staying Distant: Fieldwork with Proselytizing Groups'. *Qualitative Sociology* 10, no. 3 (1987): 267–87.

Grafe, Hugald. *History of Christianity in India: Tamil Nadu in the Nineteenth and Twentieth Centuries. Vol. IV*. Bangalore: Church History Association of India, 1990.

Guédon, Marie-Françoise. 'Dene Ways and the Ethnographer's Culture'. In *Being Changed by Cross-Cultural Encounters: The Anthropology of Extraordinary Experience*, edited by David Earl Young and Jean Guy Goulet, 39–70. Toronto: University of Toronto Press, 1994.

Hambye, E. R. *History of Christianity in India: Eighteenth Century. Vol. III*. Bangalore: The Church History Association of India, 1997.

Harding, Susan Friend. *The Book of Jerry Falwell: Fundamentalist Language and Politics*. New edition. Princeton, NJ: Princeton University Press, 2001.

Harrison, Carol, Caroline Humfress and Isabella Sandwell, eds. *Being Christian in Late Antiquity: A Festschrift for Gillian Clark*. Oxford: Oxford University Press, 2014.

Haskell Khan, Susan. 'The India Mission Field in American History, 1919–1947'. PhD, University of California, 2006.

Haynes, Naomi. *Moving by the Spirit*. Oakland: University of California Press, 2017.

Hedges, Paul. *Preparation and Fulfillment: A History and Study of Fulfilment Theology in Modern British Thought in the Indian Context*. Oxford: Peter Lang, 2001.

Heidegger, Martin. *Being and Time*. New edition. Malden: Wiley-Blackwell, 1978.

Heim, Mark. 'Of Two Minds about a Theology without Walls'. *Journal of Ecumenical Studies* 51, no. 4 (2016): 479–86.

Henn, Alexander. *Hindu-Catholic Encounters in Goa: Religion, Colonialism, and Modernity*. Bloomington: Indiana University Press, 2014.

Hess, Linda. 'An Open-Air Ramayana: Ramlila, the Audience Experience'. In *The Life of Hinduism*, edited by John Stratton Hawley and Vasudha Narayanan, 115–35. California: University of California Press, 2006. https://california.universitypress scholarship.com/view/10.1525/california/9780520249134.001.0001/upso-978052 0249134-chapter-9 (25 April 2018).

Hindmarsh, D. Bruce. *The Spirit of Early Evangelicalism: True Religion in a Modern World*. Oxford: Oxford University Press, 2018.

Hohwy, Jakob. *The Predictive Mind*. Oxford: Oxford University Press, 2014.

Holbraad, Martin, and Morten Axel Pedersen. *The Ontological Turn: An Anthropological Exposition*. New Departures in Anthropology. Cambridge: Cambridge University Press, 2017.

Howell, Brian M. 'The Repugnant Cultural Other Speaks Back: Christian Identity as Ethnographic "Standpoint"'. *Anthropological Theory* 7, no. 4 (2007): 371–91.

Hufford, David L. 'The Scholarly Voice and the Personal Voice: Reflexivity in Belief Studies'. *Western Folklore* 54, no. 1 (1995): 57–76.

Husserl, Edmund. *Ideas: General Introduction to Pure Phenomenology*. Translated by William R. B. Gibson. New York: MacMillan, 1931.

FirstPost. 'India Has 79.8% Hindus, 14.2% Muslims, Says 2011 Census Data on Religion', 26 August 2015. https://www.firstpost.com/india/india-has-79-8-percent-hindus-14-2-percent-muslims-2011-census-data-on-religion-2407708.html (25 April 2018).

Israel, Hephzibah. 'Protestant Devotion and the Development of the Tamil Hymn in Colonial South India'. In *Constructing Indian Christianities: Culture, Conversion and Caste*, edited by Chad M. Bauman and Richard Fox Young, 86–110. London: Routledge, 2014.

Jaffrelot, Christophe. *Dr. Amdbedkar and Untouchability: Analysing and Fighting Caste*. New York: Columbia Press, 2005.

Jaoul, Nicolas. 'Le point de vue des fonctionnaires dalits sur les quotas d'embauche de la fonction publique'. *Droit et cultures: Revue internationale interdisciplinaire* 53, no. 1 (2007): 63–87.

Jenkins, Laura Dudley. 'Legal Limits on Religious Conversion in India'. *Law and Contemporary Problems* 71, no. 2 (2008): 109–27.

Jones, E. Stanley. *Christ and Communism*. Lucknow, India: Lucknow Publishing House, 1934.

Jones, E. Stanley. *Christ and Human Suffering*. Lucknow, India: Lucknow Publishing House, 1933.

Jones, E. Stanley. *Christ at the Round Table*. Lucknow, India: Lucknow Publishing House, 1928.

Jones, E. Stanley. *The Christ of the Indian Road*. Lucknow: Lucknow Publishing House, 1925.

Jones, E. Stanley. *Conversion*. Lucknow, India: Lucknow Publishing House, 1997.

Jones, E. Stanley. 'E. Stanley Jones on the Ashram Ideal (1930)'. In *History of Christianity in India: Source Materials*, edited by M. K. Kuriakose, 4th edition, 347–49. Delhi, India: ISPCK, 2006.

Jones, E. Stanley. *Mahatma Gandhi: An Interpretation*. Nashville, TN: Abingdon-Cokesbury Press, 1948.

Jones, E. Stanley. *A Song of Ascents: A Spiritual Autobiography*. New York: Abingdon Press, 1968.

Jones, E. Stanley. *Victory through Surrender*. Lucknow, India: Lucknow Publishing House, 1966.

Keay, John. *India Discovered: The Recovery of a Lost Civilization*. London: Harper Collins, 1981.

Kierkegaard, Søren. *The Point of View*. Edited by Howard V. Hong and Edna H. Hong. Princeton, NJ: Princeton University Press, 1998.

Kim, Sebastian C. H. *In Search of Identity: Debates on Religious Conversion in India*. Oxford: Oxford University Press, 2015.

King, Richard. *Orientalism and Religion: Post-Colonial Theory, India and the Mystic East*. 1st edition. London: Routledge, 1999.

Knitter, Paul F. *Without Buddha I Could Not Be a Christian*. Reprint edition. Oxford: Oneworld, 2013.

Knitter, Paul F. 'Without Walls = Multiple Belonging?' *Journal of Ecumenical Studies* 51, no. 4 (2016): 487–98.

Kosambi, Meera, ed. *Pandita Ramabai through Her Own Words: Selected Works*. Oxford: Oxford University Press, 2000.

Kuhlin, Julia. 'Hindu-Christian Relations in the Everyday Life of North Indian Pentecostals'. *Journal of Hindu-Christian Studies* 28, no. 1 (2015): 40–54.

Kuriakose, M. K. *History of Christianity in India: Source Materials*. 4th edition. Delhi, India: ISPCK, 2006.

Kuttiyanikkal, Ciril J. *Khrist Bhakta Movement: A Model for an Indian Church?: A Model for an Indian Church?; Inculturation in the Area of Community Building*. Berlin, Germany: LIT Verlag Münster, 2014.

Lambek, Michael, ed. *A Reader in the Anthropology of Religion*. 2nd edition. Malden, MA: Blackwell, 2008.

Larsen, Timothy. *The Slain God: Anthropologists and the Christian Faith*. Oxford: Oxford University Press, 2014.

Law, D. R. 'Kierkegaard's Anti-Ecclesiology: The Attack on "Christendom", 1854–1855'. *International Journal for the Study of the Christian Church* 7, no. 2 (2007): 86–108.

Leeuw, Gerardus Van der. *Religion in Essence and Manifestation*. Princeton, NJ: Princeton University Press, 2014.

Lessa, William A., and Evon Z. Vogt, eds. *Reader in Comparative Religion: An Anthropological Approach*. 3rd edition. New York: Harper & Row, 1972.

Lipner, Julius. *Brahmabandhab Upadhyay: The Life and Thought of a Revolutionary*. Oxford: Oxford University Press, 1999.

Lipner, Julius, and George Gispert-Sauch, eds. *The Writings of Brahmabandhab Upadhyay. Vol. II*. Bangalore: United Theological College, 2002.

Long, Jeffery D. 'Hindu, Christian, Hindu-Christian, and Beyond: Exploring the Relations between Identity and Spirituality. In *Hindu-Christian Dual Belonging*, edited by Daniel Soars and Nadya Pohran, 140–56. Oxon: Routledge, 2022.

Lourduswamy, S. 'Catholic Church and Dalit-Tribal Movements in India'. In *Rethinking Theology in India: Christianity in the Twenty-First Century*, edited by James Massey and T. K. John, 181–218. New Delhi: Manohar, 2013.

Luhrmann, Tanya M. *When God Talks Back: Understanding the American Evangelical Relationship with God*. Reprint edition. New York: Vintage, 2012.

Maiorano, Diego. 'Indian Politics and Society in the 1970s'. In *Autumn of the Matriarch: Indira Gandhi's Final Term in Office*. Oxford: Oxford Scholarship Online, 2015.

Marriott, M. 'Caste Ranking and Food Transactions: A Matrix Analysis'. In *Structure and Change in Indian Society*, edited by M. Singer and B. S. Cohn. Chicago: Aldine, 1968.

Martin, Paul A. J. 'Missionary of the Indian Road: A Study of the Thought and Work of E. Stanley Jones between 1915 and 1948 in the Light of Certain Issues Raised by M.K. Gandhi for Anglo-Saxon Protestant Missionaries in India during the Period'. PhD, University of Cambridge, 1988. Manuscripts Room, University of Cambridge.

Massey, James. *Down Trodden: The Struggle of India's Dalits for Identity, Solidarity and Liberation*. Geneva: WCC, 1997.

Mathew, C. P., and M. M. Thomas. *The Indian Churches of Saint Thomas*. Faridabad, India: Today & Tomorrow's Printers & Publishers, 1967.

Mathews-Younes, Anne. *A History of the Christian Ashrams in North America*. California: Create Space Publishers. The E. Stanley Jones Foundation, 2017.

Mathews-Younes, Anne. *Living upon the Way: Selected Sermons of E. Stanley Jones on Self Surrender*. India: Lucknow Publishing House, 2008.

McCutcheon, Russell T. 'General Introduction'. In *The Insider/Outside Problem in the Study of Religion: A Reader*, edited by Russell T. McCutcheon, 1–22. New York: Cassell, 1999.

McEntee, Rory. 'Interspiritual Theology as a Radical Potential for New Vistas in Theological Thought'. *Open Theology* 2 (2016): 391–9.

McEntee, Rory. 'The Religious Quest as Transformative Journey: Interspiritual Religious Belonging and the Problem of Religious Depth'. *Open Theology* 3, no. 1 (27 November 2017): 613–29. https://doi.org/10.1515/opth-2017-0048 (accessed 19 June 2018).

McGregor, R. S. *Devotional Literature in South Asia: Current Research, 1985–1988*. Cambridge: Cambridge University Press, 1992.

McGuire, Meredith B. *Lived Religion: Faith and Practice in Everyday Life*. New York: Oxford University Press, 2008.

Meneses, Eloise. 'Religiously Engaged Ethnography: Reflections of a Christian Anthropologist Studying Hindus in India and Nepal'. *Ethnos*, 2019. https://doi.org/10.1080/00141844.2019.1641126 (accessed 19 June 2018).

Meneses, Eloise, Lindy Backues, David Bronkema, Eric Flett and Benjamin L. Hartley. 'Engaging the Religious Committed Other: Anthropologists and Theologians in Dialogue'. *Current Anthropology* 55, no. 1 (2014): 82–104.

Merz, Johannes, Sharon Merz. 'Occupying the Ontological Penumbra: Towards a Postsecular and Theologically Minded Anthropology'. *Religions* 8, no. 5 (28 April 2017): 80. https://doi.org/10.3390/rel8050080 (accessed 20 June 2018).

Metcalf, Barbara D., and Thomas R. Metcalf. *A Concise History of India*. Cambridge: Cambridge University Press, 2002.

Miner, Horace. 'Body Ritual among the Nacirema'. *American Anthropologist* 58, no. 3 (1956): 503–7.

Mintz, Sidney W., and Christine M. Du Bois. 'The Anthropology of Food and Eating'. *Annual Review of Anthropology* 31, no. 1 (2002): 99–119.

Moll, Yasmin. 'Television Is Not Radio: Theologies of Mediation in the Egyptian Islamic Revival'. *American Anthropologist Association* 33, no. 2 (2018): 233–65.

Morse, Christopher. *Not Every Spirit: A Dogmatics of Christian Disbelief*. 2nd Revised edition. New York: T & T Clark International, 2009.

Moyaert, Marianne. *In Response to the Religious Other: Ricoeur and the Fragility of Interreligious Encounters*. Lanham, MD: Lexington Books, 2014.

Mukta, Parita. *Upholding the Common Life: The Community of Mirabai*. Delhi: Oxford University Press, 1994.

Mundadan, A. Mathias. *History of Christianity in India: From the Beginning up to the Middle of the Sixteenth Century (up to 1542)*. Vol. I. Bangalore: Theological Publications in India, 1984.

Mundadan, A. Mathias. *Sixteenth Century Traditions of St. Thomas Christians*. Bangalore: Dharmaram, 1970.

Nagel, Thomas. *The View from Nowhere*. Revised edition. New York: Oxford University Press, 2003.

Neill, Stephen. *A History of Christianity in India: The Beginnings to AD 1707*. Cambridge: Cambridge University Press, 1984.

Niebuhr, H. Richard. *Christ and Culture*. New York: Harper Torchbooks, 1951.

Nirmal, A. P. 'Towards a Christian Dalit Theology'. In *Indigenous People: Dalits: Dalit Issues in Today's Theological Debates*, edited by J. Massey, 214–30. Delhi: ISPCK, 1994.

Nirmal, Arvind P., and V. Devasahayam. *A Reader in Dalit Theology*. Chennai: Gurukul Lutheran Theological College & Research Institute, 1990.

Noll, Mark. *The Rise of Evangelicalism: The Age of Edwards, Whitefield and the Wesleys*. Nottingham: IVP Academic, 2010. https://www.ivpress.com/the-rise-of-evangelicalism (accessed 20 June 2018).

Northcote, Jeremy. 'Objectivity and the Supernormal: The Limitations of Bracketing Approaches in Providing Neutral Accounts of Supernormal Claims'. *Journal of Contemporary Religion* 19, no. 1 (2004): 85–98.

O'Malley, John W. *The First Jesuits*. Cambridge, MA: Harvard University Press, 1993.

Orsi, Robert. 'Everyday Miracles: The Study of Lived Religion'. In *Lived Religion in America: Toward a History of Practice*, 3–18. Princeton, NJ: Princeton University Press, 1997.

Pelikan, Jaroslav. *Jesus through the Centuries*. New Haven, CT: Yale University Press, 1985.

Peres, D., A. Baiao and A. Basto, eds. *Diario Da Viagem de V. Da Gama*. 2 vols. Porto, 1945.

Poewe, Karla O. 'The Nature, Globality, and History of Charismatic Christianity'. In *Charismatic Christianity as a Global Culture*, edited by Karla O. Poewe, 1–29. Columbia: University of South Carolina Press, 1994.

Pohran, Nadya. 'Christ-Centered Bhakti: A Literary and Ethnographic Study of Worship'. *Journal of Hindu-Christian Studies* 32, no. 1 (1 January 2019). https://doi.org/10.7825/2164-6279.1731 (accessed 2 January 2019).

Polanyi, Michael. *Personal Knowledge: Towards a Post-Critical Philosophy*. 1st edition. London: Routledge, 1958.

Porpora, Douglas V. 'Methodological Atheism, Methodological Agnosticism and Religious Experience'. *Journal for the Theory of Social Behaviour* 36, no. 1 (2006): 57–75.

Pouillon, Jean. 'Remarks on the Verb "to Believe"'. *HAU: Journal of Ethnographic Theory* 6, no. 3 (2016): 485–92.

Rabinow, Paul. *Reflections on Fieldwork in Morocco*. 2nd edition. London: University of California Press, 2007.

Rajkumar, Peniel. *Dalit Theology and Dalit Liberation: Problems, Paradigms and Possibilities*. Farnham: Ashgate, 2010.

Ralph, Nicholas, Melanie Birks and Ysanne Chapman. 'The Methodological Dynamism of Grounded Theory'. *International Journal of Qualitative Methods* 14, no. 4 (20 November 2015): 1–6.

Ralston, Helen. *Christian Ashrams: A New Religious Movement in Contemporary India*. New York: Edwin Mellen, 1987.

Ramabai, Pandita. *A Testimony of Our Inexhaustible Treasure*. 11th edition. High Bridge, NJ: Pandita Ramabai Mukti Mission, 1992.

Rambachan, Anantanand. 'Conversion from a Hindu Perspective: Controversies, Challenges, and Opportunities'. In *Religious Conversion: Religion Scholars Thinking Together*, edited by Shanta Premawardhana, 98–118. West Sussex: World Council of Churches, 2015.

Ramusack, Barbara. 'Cultural Missionaries, Maternal Imperialists, Feminist Allies: British Women Activists in India, 1865–1945'. *Women's Studies International Forum* 13, no. 4 (1990): 309–21.

Ranade, R. D. *Vedanta: The Culmination of Indian Thought*. Bombay: Bharatiya Vidya Bhavan, 1970.

Ravenstein, E. G., ed. *A Journal of the First Voyage of Vasco Da Gama, 1497–1499*. Cambridge: Cambridge University Press, 2010.

Razu, Indukuri John Mohan. 'Towards a Critical Theology of Risk-Taking'. In *Rethinking Theology in India: Christianity in the Twenty-First Century*, edited by James Massey and T. K. John, 347–74. New Delhi: Manohar, 2013.

Richards, A. F. *Land, Labour, and Diet in Northern Rhodesia: An Economic Study of the Bemba Tribe*. London: Routledge, 1939.

Ricoeur, Paul. *Oneself as Another*. Translated by Kathleen Blamey. 1st edition. Chicago: University of Chicago Press, 1995.

Ritchie, Susan. 'Contesting Secularism: Reflexive Methodology, Belief Studies, and Disciplined Knowledge'. *Journal of American Folklore* 115, no. 455 (2002): 443–56.

Robbins, Joel. 'The Anthropology of Christianity: Unity, Diversity, New Directions: An Introduction to Supplement 10'. *Current Anthropology* 55, no. 10 (December 2014).

Robbins, Joel. 'Anthropology and Theology: An Awkward Relationship?' *Anthropological Quarterly* 79, no. 2 (2006): 285–94.

Robbins, Joel. 'Anthropology and Theology: On Transformative Dialogue and Its Limits'. In *Theology and the Anthropology of Christian Life*. Cambridge: University of Cambridge, Faculty of Divinity, 2018.

Robbins, Joel. 'Engaged Disbelief: Problematics of Detachment in Christianity and in the Anthropology of Christianity'. In *Detachment: Essays on the Limits of Relational Thinking*, edited by Thomas Yarrow, Matei Candea and Catherine Trundle, 115–29. Manchester: Manchester University Press, 2015.

Robbins, Joel. 'World Christianity and the Reorganization of Disciplines: On the Emerging Dialogue between Anthropology and Theology'. In *Theologically Engaged Anthropology*, edited by J. Derrick Lemons. Oxford: Oxford University Press, 2018.

Roberts, Michelle Voss. 'Religious Belonging and the Multiple', 26, no. 1 (2010): 43–62.

Roberts, Nathaniel. 'Is Conversion a Colonization of Consciousness'. *Anthropological Theory* 12, no. 3 (2012). https://doi.org/10.1177/1463499612469583.

Roberts, Nathaniel. *To Be Cared For: The Power of Conversion and Foreignness of Belonging in an Indian Slum*. 1st edition. Oakland: University of California Press, 2016. https://www.jstor.org/stable/10.1525/j.ctt1b9s0cs (accessed 10 November 2021).

Robinson, Bob. *Christians Meeting Hindus: An Analysis and Theological Critique of the Hindu-Christian Encounter in India*. Oxford: Regnum Books International in association with Paternoster Press, 2004.

Robinson, Rowena. 'Sixteenth Century Conversions to Christianity in Goa'. In *Religious Conversion in India: Modes, Motivations, and Meanings*, edited by Rowena Robinson and Sathianathan Clarke, 290–322. Oxford: Oxford University Press, 2003.

Ruby, Jay, ed. *A Crack in the Mirror: Reflexive Perspectives in Anthropology*. Philadelphia: University of Pennsylvania Press, 1982.

Ruel, Malcolm. 'Christians as Believers'. In *Religious Organization and Religious Experience*, edited by J. Davis, Vol. A. S. A. Monograph. London: Academic Press, 1982. http://www.scribd.com/doc/80689743/Malcolm-Ruel-Christians-as-Believers (accessed 21 June 2018).

Samuel, Simon. 'Pentecostal and Charismatic Movements'. In *Rethinking Theology in India: Christianity in the Twenty-First Century*, edited by James Massey and T. K. John, 247–88. New Delhi: Manohar, 2013.

San Chirico, Kerry P. C. 'Khrist Bhaktas: Catholics and the Negotiation of Devotion'. In *Constructing Indian Christianities: Culture, Conversion and Caste*, edited by Chad M. Bauman and Richard Fox Young, 23–44. London: Routledge, 2014.

Sarkar, S. 'The Conditions and Nature of Subaltern Militancy: Bengal from Swadeshi to Non-Co-Operation, c. 1905–22'. In *Subaltern Studies III*, edited by Ranajit Guha, 271–320. Delhi: Oxford University Press, 1984.

Sartre, J. P., and H. E. Barnes. *Being and Nothingness: An Essay on Phenomenological Ontology*. London, 1969.

Sathyamala, C. 'Meat-Eating in India: Whose Food, Whose Politics, and Whose Rights?' *Policy Futures in Education; Special Issue: Eating in the Anthropocene: Learning the Practice and Ethics of Food Politics* 17, no. 7 (2018): 878–91.

Scholte, Bob. 'Toward a Reflexive and Critical Anthropology'. In *Reinventing Anthropology*, edited by Dell Hymes. Ann Arbor: University of Michigan, 1999.

Schouten, Jan Peter. *Jesus as Guru: The Image of Christ among Hindus and Christians in India*. Amsterdam: Rodopi, 2008.

Schwab, Raymond. *The Oriental Renaissance: Europe's Rediscovery of India and the East, 1680–1880*. Translated by Gene Patterson-Black and Victor Reinking. New York: Columbia University Press, 1984.

Schweig, Graham. 'The Rasa Lila of Krishna and the Gopis: On the Bhagavata's Vision of Boundless Love'. In *The Bhagavata Purana: Sacred Text and Living Tradition*. New York: Columbia University Press, 2013.

Selvanayagam, Israel. *Kristu Bhakti and Krishna Bhakti: A Christian-Hindu Dialogue Contributing to Comparative Theology*. New Delhi: Christian World Imprints, 2017.

Shah, A. B., ed. *The Letters and Correspondence of Pandita Ramabai*. Bombay: Maharashtra State Board for Literature and Culture, 1977.

Sharma, Arvind. *To the Things Themselves, Essays on the Discourse and Practice of the Phenomenology of Religion*. Reprint 2015. Berlin: De Gruyter, 2001. https://doi.org/10.1515/9783110888447 (20 June 2018).

Singer, Eliot A. 'Conversion through Foodways Enculturation: The Meaning of Eating in an American Hindu Sect'. In *Ethnic and Regional Foodways in the United States: The Performance of Group Identity*, edited by Linda Keller Brown and Kay Mussell, 195–214. Knoxville: University of Tennessee Press, 1984.

Singh, Sundar. *Sadhu Sundar Singh: Essential Writings*. Edited by Charles E. Moore. Maryknoll, NY: Orbis Books, 2005.

Smart, Ninian. *The Phenomenon of Religion*. Basingstoke: Macmillan, 1973.

Smart, Ninian. *The Science of Religion and the Sociology of Knowledge: Some Methodological Questions*. Princeton, NJ: Princeton University Press, 1973. https://www.jstor.org/stable/j.ctt13x0t5r (accessed 20 June 2018).
Soni, Suparna. 'Political Quotas, NGO Initiatives and Dalits' Human Rights in Rural India'. *Journal of Human Rights Practice* 10, no. 3 (2018): 388–405.
Stanislaus, L. *The Liberative Mission of the Church among Dalit Christians*. Delhi: ISPCK, 1999.
Stein, Burton. *A History of India*. Oxford: Blackwell, 1998.
Stern, Robert, W. *Changing India: Bourgeois Revolution on the Subcontinent*. 2nd edition. Cambridge: Cambridge University Press, 2003.
Strathern, Marilyn. *Property, Substance and Effect: Anthropological Essays on Persons and Things*. London: The Athlone Press, 1999.
Sugirtharajah, Sharada. *Imagining Hinduism: A Postcolonial Perspective*. London: Routledge, 2003.
Swamy, Muthuraj. *The Problem with Interreligious Dialogue*. London: Bloomsbury, 2016.
Swamy, Muthuraj. *Reconciliation: The Archbishop of Canterbury's Lent Book 2019*. London: SPCK, 2018.
Taylor, Richard W.. 'Christian Ashrams as a Style of Mission in India'. *International Review of Mission* 68, no. 271 (July 1979): 281–93.
Thekkedath, Joseph. *History of Christianity in India: From the Middle of the Sixteenth to the End of the Seventeenth Century (1542–1700). Vol. II*. Bangalore: Theological Publications in India, 1982.
Thomas, George. *Christian Indians and Indian Nationalism 1885–1950: An Interpretation in Historical and Theological Perspectives*. Frankfurt: Lang, 1979.
Thomas, V. P. 'Indian Christian Approaches to the Knowledge of Christ'. *Indian Journal of Theology* 18, no. 1 (1969): 88–99.
Turner, Edith. 'A Visible Spirit Form in Zambia'. In *Being Changed by Cross-Cultural Encounters: The Anthropology of Extraordinary Experience*, edited by David Earl Young and Jean Guy Goulet, 71–95. Toronto: University of Toronto Press, 1994.
Turner, Victor. 'Symbols in African Ritual'. In *Symbolic Anthropology: A Reader in the Study of Symbols and Meanings*, edited by J. L. Dolgin, D. M. Schneider and D. S. Kemnitzer, 183–94. New York: Columbia University Press, 1977.
Vallely, Anne. *Guardians of the Transcendent: An Ethnography of a Jain Ascetic Community*. Toronto: University of Toronto Press, 2002.
Vandana. *Gurus, Ashrams and Christians*. London: Anchor Press, 1978.
Vanier, Jean. *Community and Growth*. Revised edition. New York: Paulist Press, 1999.
Veer, Peter van der. *Imperial Encounters: Religion and Modernity in India and Britain*. Princeton, NJ: Princeton University Press, 2001.
Volf, Miroslav. *Exclusion and Embrace: A Theological Exploration of Identity, Otherness, and Reconciliation*. Nashville, TN: Abingdon Press, 1996.
Vos, Geerhardus. *The Teaching of Jesus Concerning the Kingdom of God and the Church*. New York: American Tract Society, 1903.

Voss Roberts, Michelle. *Tastes of the Divine: Hindu and Christian Theologies of Emotion.* New York: Fordham University Press, 2014.

Ward, W. R. *The Protestant Evangelical Awakening.* Cambridge: Cambridge University Press, 2002.

Warner, Michael, Jonathan VanAntwerpen and Craig Calhoun, eds. *Varieties of Secularism in a Secular Age.* Cambridge, MA: Harvard University Press, 2010.

Webb, Andrew. 'The Christa Seva Sangh Ashram: 1922–1934'. *South Asia Research* 1, no. 1 (1 May 1981): 37–52. https://doi.org/10.1177/026272808100100103 (accessed 21 June 2018).

Weber, Max. *Selections in Translation.* Edited by W. G. Runciman. Translated by Eric Matthews. Cambridge: Cambridge University Press, 1978.

Weber, Max. *The Theory of Social and Economic Organizations.* Translated by A. M. Henderson and Talcott Parsons. New York: Free Press, 1947.

Webster, Joseph. *The Anthropology of Protestantism: Faith and Crisis among Scottish Fishermen.* 1st edition. Contemporary Anthropology of Religion. New York: Palgrave Macmillan, 2013.

Wigg-Stevenson, Natalie. *Ethnographic Theology.* New York: AIAA, 2014.

Wildman, Wesley J. 'Theology without Walls: The Future of Transreligious Theology'. *Open Theology* 2, no. 1 (2016): 242–7.

Wilson, C. Roderick. 'Seeing They See Not'. In *Being Changed by Cross-Cultural Encounters: The Anthropology of Extraordinary Experience,* edited by David Earl Young and Jean Guy Goulet, 197–208. Toronto: University of Toronto Press, 1994.

Winslow, Jack. *Narayan Vaman Tilak: The Christian Poet of Maharashtra.* Calcutta: YMCA, 1930.

Zachariah, K. C. *The Syrian Christians of Kerala: Demographic and Socio-Economic Transition in the Twentieth Century.* Delhi: Orient Longman, 2006.

Zastoupil, Lynn. 'Defining Christians, Making Britons: Rammohun Roy and the Unitarians'. *Victorian Studies* 44, no. 2 (2002): 215–43.

Index

Acharya 15–20, 104–5, 142–8, 151–9
  Acharya Biswas 142–8, 151
  Acharya G. 20, 93, 109–10, 114–16, 143, 148–59
  Acharya Mathews 84, 100
  Acharya V. 98, 100–5, 140
  healing 120–7
Advaita Vedanta 56, 62, 69, 99, 114
anthropology 12–14, 20–4, 31–4, 63, 168
  Christianity 165
  cultural Anthropology 12–13, 34, 166
Ashram. *See also* Sat Tal Christian Ashram (STA)
  ashram ideals 71–2, 85, 96, 145, 167
  Christian ashram 41, 60, 64, 74 (*see also* truly Christian *and* truly Indian)
assimilative 74–5

Baptism. *See diksha*
Belief-Inclusive Research (BIR) 20–3, 29–35, 63, 136, 159, 168
  beliefs and doubts 21–5, 29–33
beliefs 12, 60–3, 90, 120–1, 134–5
  actions and beliefs 34, 48, 66, 99, 126, 159
  beliefs and practices 37–9, 42, 52, 81, 120, 146–7
  religious 15, 33, 47–8, 81, 166
belonging 11–12, 132–41, 146–7, 164–6, 169
  acceptance 45–9, 73, 136
  deep belonging 150
  partial belonging 132, 150–1, 157, 160
  self-identification 136
  togetherness 137
bhajans 2, 15, 20, 116–19. *See also* music
Bible 19–20, 30–1, 62, 109, 117, 123–5, 154
  Bible study 59, 72, 125
borders 11–12, 167
boundaries 11–12, 43, 58, 90, 130–2, 167
Brahmabandhab Upadhyay 53–5, 64

British 37–8, 42, 48–53, 63, 75, 102
Buddhism 79, 138

caste 13, 39, 42–3, 46, 54, 91, 98, 108, 167
  Brahmin 57–9, 68–71, 84
  Dalit 10, 41, 58, 113, 118
changayi 105, 120–1, 123. *See also* healing
Christianity
  Baptist 50–2, 75
  Dalit 10, 41, 58, 113, 118
  Evangelist 6, 8, 98, 100, 106
  Methodist 3, 65–6, 98, 100, 116
  Protestant 25–6, 42, 49, 60, 63, 104
  Roman Catholic 37, 42–4, 46–9, 55–7, 60, 63
  Syrian 37–9, 42–3, 46–50, 52, 63, 166
  Western 75, 96
colonial 42–6, 61–3, 75, 103, 158
  British 51–3
  colonial powers 6–7, 38–9, 42, 53
community 12–13, 25–8, 31–4 93–4, 136–8, 152, 159–60
  Christian community 7, 54, 72, 95, 111–12, 136
  Syrian Christian community 38–9, 42, 47–50, 52, 63
conversion 41–2, 46–7, 49, 51, 59, 70, 83, 99, 102–6, 110–14, 126
  'horizontal conversion' 83
  'vertical conversion' 111
culture 41, 46, 51, 52, 55–6, 64, 72, 74, 80, 107

da Gama, Vasco 43–5
deep rest. *See* meditation
de Nobili, Roberto 37, 48, 53–5, 64, 85
devotion 2, 3, 44, 81, 125, 126
dhyan. See meditation
dialogue 7–8, 61, 64, 81, 95, 157–60. *See also* Diller, Jeanine
  interreligious 8, 80, 101, 159
diksha 77, 113, 120, 121

Diller, Jeanine 133-4. *See also* multiple religious belonging
disjunctures 8-9, 99-100, 105, 125
doubts 15, 20-2, 25, 29, 31-5, 166
'dual'/'double' religious belonging 132. *See also* multiple religious belonging

embodied social processes 163
embodiment 64
encounter 14, 16-17, 67, 78, 145-6
ethnography 33-4
Europe 53, 62, 130
European 37-9, 45-6, 51-2, 56-7, 62-3, 76
existential 1, 4, 15-17, 22, 67, 130
　belonging 11, 139, 160
　openness 22, 45, 168
　transparency 15, 20, 159

faith 21, 46, 93, 130, 133-4, 158
　(*see also* assimilative)
　Christian 21, 59, 72-5, 77-8, 80, 112, 121-3, 127
　faithful 16, 32, 152
　healing 26-7, 30, 120-6
　(*see also* inculturation)
　no faith 21, 72, 152
　(*see also* Truly Christian and truly Indian)
Feldmeier, Peter 133-6, 139, 160
fieldsite 1, 2, 10, 12-13, 20
　STA 7, 164, 166, 169
fieldwork 12-16, 86-7, 90-1, 98, 105, 151
　(*see also* Belief-Inclusive Research)
　encounters 22
　ethnographic 3-4, 6, 9-10, 13, 16, 20-1, 26, 85
foreign 52-3, 58, 61, 64-5, 68-70, 131
　Christianity 7
　foreigners 69, 143, 144
　foreignness 40, 42, 53, 57, 64, 75
　powers 37, 52
foreigners 48, 84, 131, 143, 148, 163
　religion of foreigners 38-9, 42, 56-7, 63, 76-7, 92
Foucault 157, 170

Gandhi 67, 69-71, 102-3, 110, 112-14, 152
Goa 43, 46-7, 62, 111

healing 28-30, 87, 99, 105-6, 118-21, 123-7
　prayer 26-7, 33
Henn, Alexander 44-6
Hindu 91, 110-17, 149-50, 164-6, 169
　ashrams 71, 91
　culture 46, 48, 52, 55, 72
　family 84, 98, 105, 110, 113-14, 120-1
　government 68
　(*see* identity: Hindu)
　idols 143
　low-caste 87, 98, 113
　socioreligious 38, 46, 59
　spiritual 44, 47, 62, 71, 84
　philosophy 15, 41, 57, 59, 106
　temple 43, 46, 116, 144
Hindu nationalism 62, 69, 91, 102-4
Hindu-Christian 2, 7, 111, 134, 165-6
Hinduism 43-4, 47, 52-3, 61-3, 103, 113
　Brahmanical Hinduism 43, 64, 83-5, 126
　Christianity and Hinduism 3, 56, 74, 138
　devotional 2, 3
　Indian 7, 40, 64, 69, 80
　vegetarian 85, 90
Hindutva. *See* Hindu nationalism
hymns 2, 71, 115-16, 127

identity 56, 72-3, 79, 92-3, 136-7, 169
　Christian 96, 113-14, 121, 134, 163
　European 39
　Hindu 41, 58, 103, 114, 121, 134
　Indian 39-40, 57, 85, 90, 92-3, 112, 114, 134
　religious 83-4, 134
inculturation 10, 37-41, 53-7, 60-1, 77, 102
Indian 37-41, 48-55, 57-66, 103, 126-7, 131, 149. *See also* truly Indian
Indianness 37-41, 43-53, 69, 83-6
indigenization 37, 39, 53-5. *See also* inculturation
indigenized Christianity 38, 55. *See also* inculturation
Indomania 51
Indophobia 51
interreligious 8, 11-12, 80, 101-2, 130, 159

interstitial 12–14, 166, 168
invitation 1–2, 11, 15, 28, 164–5, 169
  initial invitation (WA) 138, 140, 150, 157, 160
  invitation and welcome 140, 157

Jesus Christ 22, 54–5, 66–72, 92–6, 111–21, 124–7, 145–6
Jones, E. Stanley 3–5, 7–10, 37–40, 42, 53–4, 63–75, 77–90, 92–6, 98–104, 106–9, 111–14, 125–7, 130–1, 138–9, 145–6, 151–2, 160, 163, 165, 167, 169

Kozhikode 43, 45
Krishna 6, 79, 119, 164

labour 83, 86–9, 92–3, 105–9, 126–7

meditation 86, 130–3, 140–6, 149, 154–6, 158, 163
methodological 6–7, 9, 12–14, 20, 33–4
methodological bracketing 6, 23, 34, 63
microcosm 6, 100, 164
microprocesses 1, 158, 160
Miniature Kingdom of God 4, 72, 81, 96, 167
missionary 26, 37, 49, 53–4, 66–8, 74, 95
multiple religious belonging (MRB) 3, 8, 12, 132, 133–4, 139, 160, 161
  categories 134, 136, 139
  ways of engaging 133–4
multiple religious orientation (MRO) 132, 134
Munro, Thomas 50
music 3, 99, 105–6, 115–16, 126, 149

naturalization. *See* inculturation
negotiation 115, 160
Norton, Thomas 49–50

orientalism 52, 56, 74
Other 5, 10–14, 44, 140–41, 147–54, 167–70
Other Backward Class (OBC) 69
Otherness 11–12, 44, 52, 166

Peet, Joseph 50
phases of belonging 132, 160

attempts of correction 140
invitation and welcome 140
re-establishing belonging 140
restrictions 140, 150, 160
philosophy 51, 57, 81, 114, 153
Portuguese 7, 37–8, 42–8, 50, 52–4, 63
power dynamics 13, 56, 157
programme 100–1, 116, 130, 154, 155
  SoE 15, 71, 85, 105, 108
  Summer Ashram 71
  Winter Ashram 71, 87, 129
proselytization. *See* conversion

Rajasthan 98, 100, 105, 108, 114–16, 122
Ramabai, Pandita 53, 57, 64, 114
relational dynamics 3–9, 99, 130–2, 138–9, 145–7, 157, 160–3
religion 38–9, 56–8, 70, 73–7, 80–1, 133–4, 142, 152
Right-wing Hindu. *See* Hindu nationalism
rituals 26–7, 30, 43, 59, 119, 126

Sanskrit 55, 57, 59, 86, 119
Sat Tal Christian Ashram (STA) 65–74, 83–102, 129–33, 138–51
School of Evangelism (SoE) 97–127, 156. *See also* Programme: SoE
self 6–11, 63, 83–4, 88–94, 103, 112–15, 136–8, 150, 158. *See also* Self and Other
Self and Other 166–8
Sermon 15, 147–8, 151, 153, 157
Shramdaan. See labour
social history 4–5, 9–10, 12
social transitions 127
sociocultural 49, 54, 77, 85–90, 98, 103, 127
socio-economic 68, 85–8, 98, 104, 110, 163
sociopolitical 40–1, 47, 62, 100–5, 113, 126
soteriological 32, 62, 67, 112, 127, 145
spiritual 1–17, 20–8, 44–8, 51, 57–62, 66–5

testimony 120–2, 124
theology 12–14, 51, 56–9, 77, 82, 132–5
  Christian 32, 127, 163, 166
  comparative 134–5
  Dalit 41, 58, 118

Theology Without Walls (TWW) 3,
    132–3, 137, 139
theoretical framework 13, 23, 86
transformation 81–3, 112–14, 121, 163
    personal 114, 131
    spiritual 57, 81, 95, 108
transitional social processes 4–5, 163-4
truly Christian 54, 73–8, 86, 93–6, 127,
    145. *See also* truly Indian
truly Indian 3–4, 83, 126

untouchables. *See also* caste
    Dalit 68–9, 104

Vedanta 41, 56, 62–9, 82–4. *See also*
    Advaita Vedanta

vegetarian 5, 85–6, 89–3, 96, 163
Videshi log (foreigners/WA) 131

Western 37–40, 49–53, 60–3, 67–8, 71–5
    expressions 40, 96
Westernization 52, 75, 96
World Amrita (WA) 42, 129–33, 138–51,
    156–61, 169
    banned 46, 141–2, 147
worship 5, 43–5, 115–17, 119,
    126–9, 141–3
    Christian 45
    Christian worship 116

Yeshu bhaktas/bhakti 2, 3, 81
Yesu Masih (Jesus Christ) 121

www.ingramcontent.com/pod-product-compliance
Lightning Source LLC
Chambersburg PA
CBHW062225300426
44115CB00012BA/2218